Management in Practice

Preface

This third edition of *Management in Practice* builds on much of the research and work of the last edition.

It still retains the aims of making management accessible to practitioners; supporting their understanding through real live case studies; seeing management in a context, and providing practical examples and applications of management theory.

The book has been revised in a number of respects. First, it has a new diagnostic framework for analysing each case study. This provides a comparative analysis to increase our understanding of organizations and a tool to apply to readers' organizations.

Secondly, a new introduction plus three new chapters have been introduced: Chapter 2 on understanding organizations, Chapter 8 on managing change and a final chapter on managing into the future. These give guidance on managerial issues into the year 2000 and recognize the extent to which all organizations, large and small, are absorbed with issues of change.

Thirdly, each chapter has been revised with case studies being reinterpreted and key learning points clearly identified for each chapter.

Finally, the overall feel, layout and presentation of the book reflects the new revisions, focus and application of organizational theory to management practice.

Cliff Bowman

Michael Jarrett

Acknowledgements

We wish to first thank our families for putting up with the late nights at the computer or locked away in the study! Clients, students and colleagues have all contributed to our thinking along the way. Finally, thank you to the production team who helped put the book together despite our working methods.

1 Understanding management

Introduction

Glancing back to the past shows that the concept of management is not new. The Ancient Egyptians had captured the principles of management in their magnificent feat of building pyramids in the age of antiquity. They took a large pool of enforced labour, resources from the local River Nile and implemented their plans as part of a long term strategy and task to preserve the nation's sense of identity. Few would argue that they did a good job and achieved the task.

The same can be said of Hannibal, the creative hero who took a herd of elephants and his relatively smaller army over the Alps to surprise his Tuscan enemies and gain victory against all odds. History, myths and legends provide us with countless examples of the application of managerial principles. And yet contemporary business magazines and the media often portray it as a modern and contemporary phenomenon which is only the preserve of the likes of Richard Branson of Virgin, Lord King of British Airways and Anita Roddick of the Body Shop.

While managerial practice has been operating since time began, it is not the preserve of the minority and is seen operating as part of our everyday lives. Parents have the task of running a family: another organization. Its task or strategy may be to provide a reasonable quality of life for its members and to support the life chances and opportunities for their children or relatives. They have to manage the family budget and make decisions about how to pay bills and juggle income. Decisions have to be made about whether to spend money now for current enjoyment or to save and defer gratification for future investment: to buy a new car or keep money for that 'rainy day'.

The choices and ultimate decisions that are made will often be the product of many features, factors and priorities. The personal values of the parents will be important. Whether they think it is more valuable to buy a house or send their children to a fee paying school will be a product of their own past and childhood experiences. The family disposable income and the predictability of this will be a significant factor as will be the existing commitments and other aspects of the lifestyle and culture of the family. In addition, the 'managers' of the family also have maintenance tasks in the form of communicating information, norms, rules and practices. They have to resolve conflict, educate the family system, clothe, feed and support members and negotiate differences. They have to be the boundary managers between the family system and the outside world: act as representatives for the members, protectors and ultimately take care of the well-being and safety of all those involved.

By now this must be sounding familiar. Many of these activities and responsibilities are reflected and replicated in organizational settings. Formal roles are assigned. Finite resources are allocated and prioritized. Conflicts and differences are there to be managed. Tasks and strategies need to be formulated and implemented and these will often be influenced by the organization's leadership, culture and structure.

Thus, management in practice is learned very early on in our experiences in the first organizational system that most people experience and that is in the 'family'. Here we learn about roles, responsibilities, the consequences of our decisions and the value of human relationships.

Secondly, this means that 'management' is within the realms of everybody's experiences and potential. Clearly, some people will be able to apply their experiences to different facets of the management task, to different levels of competence and at different levels of sophistication and complexity. That is a reality of the rich diversity of human nature. Imagine if we were all the same – clones. There would be no fresh ideas and the world would be a stagnant and boring place! We need difference and diversity for innovation, reflection and personal and organizational learning and development.

Thirdly, it follows that the management task is multifaceted. Management is clearly about making the best of the resources one has and maximizing staff potential, equipment, time, money and space. This can be seen in many management techniques that are used to 'maximize' returns in the form of stock control methods, financial models to manage cash-flows or investment appraisal decisions currently aided by the use of new technology.

Management is also about working with ideas. Here we see creativity, innovation and strategy being part of that remit. Understanding the nature and relationship of organizations is also part of the scope of management. Questions might include: 'What new products or service improvements might we be looking at over the next five years?'.

Finally, the managerial task is also concerned with managing people. People are the major resource in carrying out the organizational task and making it what it is: that qualitative difference may be hard to measure but you know it intuitively. It is the way you are greeted, the 'vibes' you get. One can feel it. From teachers in schools, doctors and nurses in hospitals to the Chief Executive in IBM or Microsoft, people make a difference to the quality and nature of the service or product. We need their commitment, enthusiasm or at the very minimum their agreement and cooperation to get the work done.

Thus, the management remit can be described as managing resources, ideas and people.

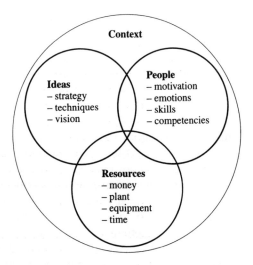

Figure 1.1   *Management is about Ideas, People and Resources.*

2 Understanding organizations

Managers work within a context: an organization. An organization can be seen as a ship that has to be steered. Too fast and it takes time to slow down. Large ones move slower but are more stable than smaller ones. They may need hundreds of people to run them effectively or they can be managed single-handed or by a small crew. The nature of the ship, family or organization forms the context for what constitutes appropriate management.

For example, the creative nature of the design and advertising company Imaginations Design[1] is managed by a Chief Executive, who allows a fair degree of expression of his staff in order to tap their artistic talents, flair and creativity. He regularly has informal meetings and lunches with his staff, and likes to spot talented new recruits from a variety of sources. A clear vision of how he would like the organization to be, along with a friendly management style and organizational culture, is matched by a relatively informal structure. This forms the managerial 'recipe' that is the hallmark of this organization.

In contrast, the stereotype version of the Civil Service is an organization that has tightly defined roles and responsibilities with hierarchical reporting structures. You know your place and operate within defined boundaries. Procedures and systems are valued highly and formality is reflected in the way people address each other and the job titles that people hold. The context here is to manage the organization so that it is efficient; its practices can be publicly scrutinized; and it is operating within the political remit of its powers and accountability.

Thus effective management has to be seen within the context of the task and boundaries of the organization. Thus, a clearer understanding of organizations is required.

Models of organization

When we ask delegates and students at the School of Management to brainstorm their views of an organization we get a list that includes the following: people, structure, task, there to produce a product or provide a service, a group of experts, part of the economy, a system of communication, rules and regulations, a place to meet social needs, a career opportunity.

To be sure, organizations are all of these things. But it is difficult to understand the exact relationships from these ideas. It does not tell us what will happen if we change one part of the organization in an attempt to manage or influence; nor what the consequences might be on the other aspects of the organization. Many writers of organization would agree with the items included in the list. Where they differ is what items to include, which are the most significant and what are the cause and effect relationships between each of the components of the organization, if any.

So what is an organization? A working definition is that: 'An organization is the rational coordination of the activities of a number of people for the achievement of some common explicit purpose or goal, through the division of labour and function, and through a hierarchy of authority and responsibility'.[2]

While this provides a definition it does not provide the rich dynamic and multiple levels of the organization, the irrational and emotional side of organizations, nor the political processes that are enacted in organizations. These elements also need to be incorporated.

How will we know it when we see it?

Most people have a personal view about the world they live in. There is a human need to construct relationships, models and informal frameworks about how the world works to maintain sanity.[3] We like to have some degree of predictability and continuity and manage this by developing cause–effect relationships in our minds. Simple examples are: 'If I ask nicely, I will usually get what I want.' 'Naughty children or deeds, will get punished.' More complex relationships are reflected in the following statement: 'The finance department will aim to block this new initiative therefore I need to rally the troops first and lobby the informal leaders.' It is difficult to imagine having to work out cause and effect relationships for every single situation. It would be both exhausting and mentally impossible. So individuals and those in the role of managers develop personal theories which they apply to familiar and not so familiar situations. These 'well tried and trusted', 'theories in use'[4] inform their decision-making and can often reinforce decisions even when the data are contradictory. In simple situations, such frameworks and models are very valuable. But as the context becomes more complex, assumptions may be erroneous, untested and unhelpful. Thus, any model or framework, be it informal or presented by a management guru, will have its limitations.

Thus, in considering the following frameworks for understanding organization it is important to use them as an initial point of enquiry and to maintain a personal attitude of curiosity.

Many writers agree that various key components be included in our understanding of organizations. Galbraith[5] suggests that for practical purposes our models of organization should include: task, structure, people, rewards systems and information and decision processes. All of these have equal value and all are related to each other. Weisbord[6] identifies: purposes, structure, relationships, helpful mechanisms, rewards, environment and leadership. He sees leadership as the centre-piece of his model. A similar approach was taken by Peters and Waterman[7] in their renowned book *In Search of Excellence*. They used a framework popularly referred to as the 7-S model. This framework includes: Strategy (task), Structure, Staff, Skills, Systems, Style and Shared values. These came together to impact on each other but the centre of the analysis was the organization's 'super ordinate goals' or 'shared values'. They argued that culture was the most dominant feature to manage in order to achieve superior performance. However, while these models suggest links between parts of an organization, they do not identify cause and effect.

Nadler and Tushman[8] (Table 2.1) take a broader view and suggest that organizations form part of an open system with the external environment and internally is a system of key interrelated parts. The relationship with the environment provides a broader economic and social context, a history about the organization, how the organization competes or acquires its resources and how it markets its products or

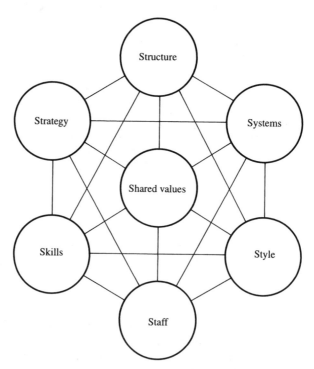

Figure 2.1 *The McKinsey 7-S model.* (Reproduced with permission from *In Search of Excellence: Lessons from America's Best-run Companies* by Thomas J. Peters and Robert H. Waterman, Jr. Copyright © 1982 by Thomas J. Peters and Robert H. Waterman Jr. HarperCollins Publishers, Inc., New York.)

Table 2.1 A summary of the Nadler and Tushman framework

Inputs include:

- *The Environment:* How far it is regulated, its resources, the work and practice of others in the 'Service', and the stability and continuity of the environment.
- *Resources:* These include money, people, physical building space, technology and other intangibles.
- *History:* The patterns of organizational behaviour, key characters and events and their impact on the present.

These all input into the organization's *strategy* – the long term ways of utilizing the resources given the demands and constraints of the environment and historical context.

Transformation processes include:

- *The task* is the work to be done. The complexity of the task, level of skills, inter-dependence and predictability are all relevant.
- *The individual* refers to the skills, abilities, experiences and competence of all staff. It also includes their psychological needs, ego development and expectations.
- *The informal organization* looks at the small group and inter-group dynamics, the power relationships, informal methods, communication patterns and culture.
- *The (formal) organizational arrangement* includes the organizational structure and work design, systems and procedures, measurement and rewards systems and resource and people management.

Outputs include:

- *System functioning:* how well does the overall system perform in relationship to its desired goals, its use of resources, and its ability to adapt to change and learn.
- *Group and inter group behaviour* examines the effectiveness and dynamics of small groups in terms of process and inter groups in terms of communication and relationships.
- *Individual behaviour and affect* looks at the implicit behaviour regarding membership, well-being and designated task performance.

Congruence: As a systems model it is not sufficient to look at the internal elements of task, individual, informal organization and formal organization separately but to consider how 'congruent' they are or how they 'fit' with each other in relationship to the organizational strategy and goals. Thus, managers should be able to see relationships that are relevant for their setting. There is no 'one best way'. Instead, it is contingent upon the most appropriate organizational and systemic arrangements that help to facilitate or reduce hindrances to the organizational goals.

services. Internally, the organization's key elements are the organizational task; the skills, competencies and psychological aspects of the staff; the formal organizational arrangements in the form of structures, procedures and systems; the nature of the informal organization of how small groups operate, network and carry rumours, the organizational culture and the distribution of power and emergent leadership.

This particular understanding of what is an organization is comprehensive, sufficiently inclusive and robust as a test of reality. It covers the rational, emotional and political aspects of organizational life yet provides a base line to explore organizational relationships in a systematic and organized manner, without losing some of the complexity. Thus, in looking at the key element of an organization this framework will be used in examining cases in the later chapters.

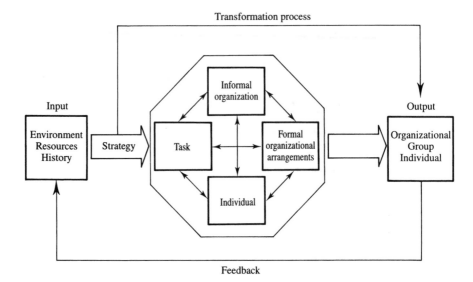

Figure 2.2 *The congruence model diagram for diagnosing organizational behaviour.* (Reproduced with permission from Nadler, D. A. and Tushman, M. L. (1979) A diagnostic model for organizational behaviour. In Kolb, P., Rubin, I. and McIntyre, J. (eds), *Organisational Psychology: A Book of Readings*, 3rd Edition, Prentice Hall: New Jersey.)

The managerial challenge in this model of organization is not just to manage one element or seek partial effectiveness, but to consider the whole and the systemic relationships that exist between the various sub-elements in order to achieve organizational goals. Managers have to manage the degree of 'fit' or congruence between the different

Table 2.2 Organizational fit

How far are the various elements of task, individual, informal and formal organization congruent?

Individual–organization: How far are individual's needs in line with the organization? Were staff committed to the values of the organization?

Individual–task: Do staff have the skills, competence and knowledge to carry out their work to a high standard? Do people experience job satisfaction? Are development needs for the future being catered for?

Individual–informal organization: Do people find the social elements of work rewarding and enjoyable? What are the sub-groups and friendships? Do these links support the organizational goals?

Task–organization: Is the organizational structure supporting or hindering the fulfilment of the task? Do structures motivate behaviour consistent with task demands?

Task–informal organization: How far do informal structures get used to get results and the work done? What networks exist and where are the informal leaders and power brokers in the organization? How do these impact on fulfilling the organization's task?

Organization–informal organization: Are these structures in conflict or in harmony? Do the goals, rewards and structures of the informal system support the formal organization? What are the consequences?

elements as well as for the system as a whole. This means that 'managers need to adequately diagnose the system, determine the location and nature of inconsistent fits, and plan a course of action to change the nature of those fits without bringing about dysfunctional second order effects. The model also implies that different configurations of the key components can lead to effective behaviour. Therefore, the question is not finding the "one best way" of managing, but determining effective combinations of inputs that will lead to congruent fits'.

Summary

The nature of the managerial task is not new. It is something that we are all exposed to in early life. Thus, it is not solely the arena of business tycoons but it is a process that is carried out regularly and daily by men and women in the workplace, at home and in other social settings.

To be able to manage organizations it is useful to make explicit how they are construed in the mind. Thus, formal models and frameworks are a useful handle. Many models of organization suggest a network of inter-related components. However, a systems perspective takes a wider view, is able to put the organization in its context and examine a range of significant internal relationships. The concept of organizational fit provides a basis for examining organizational effectiveness based on a wide number of ways to obtain the desired goals. The rest of this book explores these relationships and the management process in different organizational contexts.

Kurt Lewin (see Chapter 8), one of the most influential contributors to organizational change theory, is reported to have said there is nothing so helpful as a good theory. John Maynard Keynes, the economist, provides another sobering thought that theory illuminates the obvious. It is holding these two positions simultaneously that provide a basis for increasing our understanding of organizations and applying these to the managerial tasks.

The rest of the book considers the management task in context. There are seven settings or 'contexts' that form the framework for the book:

- The small organization.
- The growing organization.
- The large organization.
- The flexible organization.
- The multinational organization.
- The changing and learning organization.
- The future issues for managers.

The model is applied to the case material of these organizational settings, which highlight some issues, approaches and dilemmas that face managers today.

Further reading

Three books provide valuable but different perspectives on management and organization. These are:

Charles Handy's *Understanding Organisation* (Penguin Books).
Gareth Morgan's *Images of Organisation* (Sage, 1986).
A book of readings edited by Derek Pugh called *Organisation Theory* (Penguin Books, 1990).

References

1 Peters, T., *Crazy Ways for Crazy Days*, Video, 1992
2 Schein, E. H., *Organisational Psychology*, Prentice Hall, Englewood Cliffs, NJ, 1970
3 Bannister, D. and Mair, M. M., *The Evaluation of Personal Constructs*, 1968
4 Argyris, C. and Schon, D., *Organisational Learning: A Theory of Action Perspective*, Jossey Bass, San Francisco, 1978
5 Galbraith, J. R., *Organisational Design*, Addison-Wesley, Reading, MA, 1977
6 Weisbord, M., *Organisational Diagnosis; Six Places to Look for Trouble with or without a Theory*, Addison-Wesley, Reading, MA, 1976
7 Peters, T. and Waterman, R. H., *In Search of Excellence*, Harper & Row, New York, 1982
8 Nadler, D. A. and Tushman, M. L., *A Congruence Model for Diagnosing Organisational Behaviour* reprinted in P. Kolb, I. Rubin and J. Mcintyre (eds), *Organisational Psychology: A Book of Readings*, 3rd edition, Prentice Hall, Englewood Cliffs, NJ, 1979

3 The small organization

> The chapter provides an introduction to organizational and management terms that we will use throughout the book. It does so by starting with a case study of a small organization, and examines the organizational issues that the company faces.

1 Case study: Top Gear Driving School

As we explained in Chapter 2, we will start our exploration of the small organization by considering an actual situation by means of a brief case study. The first case consists of abbreviated interviews with a number of people who work for Top Gear Driving School, a firm operating in West Sussex which, in driving school terms, is quite large (twelve instructors). The firm was started by Stan Gordon in 1967.

An interview with Stanley Gordon, Managing Director

I: So how did it all start Stan?

SG: Well, when I left the Army I was still only fifty-five and I couldn't afford to retire, so I looked around to see what jobs were about. The problem was that my job in the Army was basically administration and management. Although I had several interviews for jobs it seemed that my way of doing things didn't suit what the firms were after. So I thought, if no one's going to employ me, I'd better do something where I'm the boss. I took a Ministry course in driving instruction, bought a second-hand Escort, fitted the dual controls myself and that was that: Top Gear Driving School was born!

I: How did you go about getting business?

SG: I put some ads in the local paper, left a few cards in garages, post office windows, that sort of thing. But that really was a waste of time and money. You see, the way you get business in this game is through word of mouth. You get a friend of a friend who wants lessons, she enjoys the lessons and passes her test – so she tells her friends, and so it spreads like that. I still do the odd advert in the paper but more out of force of habit than any belief that it will bring in new business.

I: What about the competition?

SG: As I've proved, I suppose, it doesn't take much to get into this business – so all sorts of cowboys set themselves up, because after all, all you really need is a certificate and a car – I know one bloke who never even fitted dual controls – I don't know what happened to him – I suspect he's dead by now! But most of them don't last, and things settle down after a while. Really I've got three main competitors: the BSM, of course, and two schools who are about as big as us, although oddly enough, we all seem to operate in different parts of the district – so we're not always treading on each other's toes.

I: So what's the secret of your success? How come you grew into a fair sized operation where others fell by the wayside?

SG: That's easy – it's all down to reputation. I've trained all my instructors in the 'Gordon' way of doing things: we have to make sure that every client is getting the best, and the standards I set are very high. I insist on punctuality – if you're supposed to pick the client up at home at 10.00 a.m. you arrive at 9.55 a.m. at the latest, because the customer is paying our wages. Courtesy, fairness coupled with politeness, patience and consideration – in a word 'professionalism' – that's what I demand of my instructors.

I: And what if they don't come up to scratch?

SG: Ah hah! Well, fortunately I've only ever had to sack one man – and interestingly enough I took him on from another school (which I won't name!) so he was the only one I hadn't trained. I started getting phone calls from clients who he'd either not taken out, or he'd turned up half an hour late – but the last straw was when I pulled up at the lights in the high street, alongside his car – he had a client with him at the time and he was smoking! Well it's one of our basic rules – you do not smoke in the car. So that was that, he got his marching orders damned quick. You see, the problem is it only takes a couple of bad apples like him and your reputation goes out the window. Some people think I'm running this place like the bloody army – maybe they're right, but I believe in standards, in doing things right, and my people know what's expected of them. What's so bad about that?

I: Thanks, Stan.

Interview with June Farrow – an instructor, aged forty-four, married, three children

I: How long have you been with TGDS, June?

JF: I suppose I was one of the founder members! I knew Stan socially through the Parents Group at the school, and – I can't remember how it came about exactly – but I knew he had more work than he could cope with, and I was looking to go back to work now the kids were at secondary school, so he suggested becoming an instructor. Obviously I'd never really thought of doing this sort of thing, but Stan offered to train me and we sort of took it from there. I've been an instructor for nine years now and I've enjoyed every minute of it!

I: How do you work out your weekly timetable?

JF: On Saturday lunchtime we all meet in the office for a briefing session. Stan tells us what's happening generally and passes on information about things that have cropped up during the week, but the real point of the meeting is the sorting out of your next week's load. Most of your hours will, of course, be repeats from last week. Clients generally either book a course of ten lessons at one go (so you can pencil them in weeks ahead) while others will arrange it on a week by week basis – depending on when you're free and they're free. But, fortunately, because some of them actually pass their tests, you'll be looking for another client to replace them. Well, at the Saturday briefing we get new customers allocated if we're short – sometimes one of the other instructors has too much on, so we shuffle the clients around the rest of us. Or maybe, someone's off on holiday, but their client's test date has fallen in the middle of the holiday – so we need to allocate another instructor to take them through the test. It all seems a bit haphazard but, because we all get on so well, everything sorts itself out quite nicely.

I: How do you get paid?

JF: By the hour – it's as simple as that! So you can more or less decide how much work you want to do. Some of us are only interested in working ten or fifteen hours a week; others, Darren for instance, will grab anything that's going! I don't know how he does it – he's often up to forty hours in a week – I'm surprised his little daughter knows who her father is! But then, maybe he needs the money more. I mean, you're never going to get rich in this job, but it's a good, steady, enjoyable job where you meet lots of people, and you get a lot of satisfaction when they get that little pink slip which says they've passed. I've had boxes of chocolates, theatre tickets, flowers – all sorts of presents from satisfied clients. But really, you can't beat the thrill you get when a senior citizen who's been plugging away for years finally passes her test. I've had them in tears, overcome with relief!

I: I've heard it said that Stan runs a pretty tight ship, would you agree?

JF: Yes I suppose he does. But I think he's absolutely right to insist on things being done properly. I don't want to be associated with a two-bit cowboy outfit, and I don't think anyone else does.

We're quite proud of our reputation, and if it means biting your tongue when someone's being very rude to you, or keeping your patience when you've explained a manoeuvre for the tenth time, then so be it. Stan drives himself pretty hard, and is a fair boss. You might not agree with everything he does but you've got to respect a man who's built this firm up from nothing in such a short space of time.

Interview with Sarah Simmonds, aged fifty-two, widowed

I: How would you describe your job with TGDS, Sarah?

SS: The problem is where to start? I do the books, take the calls, pass on messages to the instructors, make the tea, pay the wages, you name it – I do it!

I: Stan has referred to you as his 'right arm' – is that how you see it?

SS: I joined TGDS about six years ago and up until then Stan was doing everything. I've gradually taken over most of the admin. side of things, and I suppose I do basically run the show on a day-to-day basis.

I: When you say you 'do the books' what exactly does that involve?

SS: When I took the job everything on the accounts side of the business was, to be frank, a bit of a mess. Stan had devised his own, common-sense approach to the books: you know – one list for outgoings – petrol, car repairs, wages etc., and a week by week total of income. We weren't allowing anything for depreciation on the cars, for instance, which meant that when we needed to replace the older cars we had a major crisis. It's just as well the bank helped us out, otherwise we'd have been out of business. I had picked up quite a bit of knowledge about accounts from my previous job with Jarmons, the fruit wholesalers, so I was able to put things on a more professional basis. Stan, our accountant John and I meet about every quarter to sort out the books, which works very well. If I have a problem I can always get on the phone to John and he'll pop down and help. We get on very well.

I: Do you enjoy your job?

SS: Yes, it's marvellous! Well, you get bad days – everybody gets bad days! – but most of the time it's a lot of fun. I like being busy, and there's always something to be done here – phone calls, instructors popping in with queries, customers asking about fees, all sorts of things. I get on very well with all the instructors – I suppose I do tend to 'mother' the younger lads, but they sometimes need a bit of encouragement if they've had a difficult client. Some of the stories they tell would make your hair curl. I don't suppose half of its true, but never let the facts spoil a good story is what I always say, eh?!

Interview with Darren Watts, aged 26, married, one child

I: Darren, I know you're busy, but can I ask you a few questions?
DW: Sure, no problem – only I've got a lesson in a few minutes.

I: I get the impression from the others that you're working very hard.
DW: Why? Are they moaning that I'm pinching their clients?

I: No, not at all!
DW: Look, sure I work hard – I'd do more if I could. The difference between me and some of the others is that I'm in this job for the money, full stop. I've got a wife and a young kid and bills coming out of my ears. I look at it like this: if I put the hours in here I get a direct pay off. I had a job in a hardware shop before this one. I used to really graft – staying long after closing to rearrange the stock, clean the shelves – I even volunteered to repaint the stock room on my day off. What a mug! I thought that if I worked hard the boss would promote me or something. Not a chance. At least in this job if you're prepared to put the hours in you get the reward.

I: Do you think you'll stay with Top Gear?
DW: I'll stick around until I've got enough put by to set up on my own – not a driving school! I've got other ideas.

I: How do you get on with the other instructors?
DW: All right. Why, what have they been saying?

I: Nothing uncomplementary, I assure you!
DW: Look, I'll admit that we don't see eye to eye on lots of things. I mean, they're a different generation. And they all think Stan's a bloody genius! Christ, I could run this place a damn sight better than he does in half the time he takes. They're all quite happy to swallow this 'discipline and loyalty' garbage. Stan treats me like some dumb idiot, explaining the same thing over and over again. I'm sure he thinks that just because I've got a cockney accent I'm mentally retarded. To be honest, I keep out of everyone's way as far as possible and get on with the job. I can't stand the way they sit around in the office prattling on about nothing. I'd rather be out there earning some cash.

Issues arising from the case

The case interviews give us a feel for this small firm, and they also suggest a number of issues. We can use our list of headings set out in Chapter 2 to group and highlight these issues in a systematic way, starting with the *environment* of this firm.

Environment

1 The organization is working in a market environment where it is easy for people to enter and thus it is potentially highly competitive.
2 Fortunately many potential competitors fall by the wayside leaving the market fairly cut up between BSM, which is the most dominant competitor probably operating across West Sussex, and several smaller towns.
3 The other two 'competitors' operate within different geographical boundaries and thus they stay off each others' toes. There appears to be some degree of collusion by tacit agreement.

History and resources

1 The company was started on limited resources and demands energy and commitment.
2 This start has meant that resources have not been managed as well as possible but that people have 'chipped-in' as they became part of the 'family'.
3 The business has instituted more formal financial controls as it has grown as part of its development.

Task

1 The task of the organization requires high standards in Instruction and Safety. Non-compliance can risk lives for clients, staff and the general public.
2 The core service is supported by performance standards and practice such as punctuality, courtesy and attention to detail.

Organizational structure and management

1 This is a very small organization with only three different types of position: one manager, twelve instructors and an administrative assistant (Sarah Simmonds). Compared to many larger organizations there is a marked lack of specialist jobs. How is this firm able to survive and compete with so few specialist staff?
2 All the instructors, plus the administrator report directly to the owner/manager Stan Gordon. Therefore Stan's 'span of control' is thirteen. Can he adequately supervise this many staff?
3 Knowledge in the accounting area is provided by Sarah on a day-to-day basis, but TGDS goes outside for professional advice to an accountant. Why should this particular skill be required? Why isn't personnel or marketing expertise brought into the firm?
4 We can deduce that no one has a written job description, so how do the staff know what is required of them?

5 Can this organization stay small, or must it grow to survive?

6 Stan Gordon owns and manages the business. Things are done 'the Gordon way'. This means he can hire and fire, set standards of conduct, establish pay rates, and prices, decide on cars and car replacement policies etc. Is this range of responsibilities and powers typical of most management positions?

7 Stan's 'firm but fair' style probably reflects his Army experience and his personality. Is it appropriate to this type of organization? Could he change his style?

8 Why do the staff do as Stan tells them? What is the basis of his power to influence these people?

9 Coordination, sorting out who does what, is largely achieved through the weekly meeting. What other coordination options are open to the organization.

The informal organization

1 Communication between the members of the organization is predominantly verbal and largely informal, except for the weekly scheduled meeting. Why the absence of written communication? Is this informal system adequate?

2 TGDS seems a friendly place to work, with everyone getting on with each other reasonably well, but how closely do they have to *work together*? What is the scope for work related problems and conflicts in this type of organization?

3 High personal standards are essential for a good reputation as a driving school. Are there any ways in which the instructors can exert pressure on the individual to conform to the standards accepted by the group?

4 Sarah seems to enjoy gossiping with the instructors when they visit the office. Should this be discouraged by Stan Gordon? Does it serve any useful purpose for the organization?

5 Darren doesn't seem to fit in, why?

6 Each instructor's performance cannot be *directly* monitored by Stan Gordon, so how can standards be maintained to enable TGDS's good reputation to be preserved?

The individual

1 The members of TGDS seem to have different motives for working there, how might this affect their performance at their jobs?

2 Is there an incentive to perform well built into the system? Will this incentive be effective with all the instructors?

3 Stan's style seems to suit some but not all the people interviewed. Why should this be? How might it affect Stan's ability to manage the staff.

Outputs

The organization:

1 Seems to keep the customers satisfied.
2 Uses resources flexibly through the weekly meetings and internal one-to-ones.
3 As a group report to get on well together, but we know this is not true for everyone.
4 Staff are certainly motivated – albeit for different reasons.

In the rest of this chapter we shall be introducing concepts, and theories which will help us explore the small organization in a generalized way. First, we shall examine the *structure* of the small organization.

Table 3.1   Summary of key factors in the case

Inputs
■ Environment – few barriers to entry – but a settled three horse race
■ Resources – limited
■ History – one man band – business run like a family

Transformation
■ Task – high performance and standards on core task with good support functions
■ Individuals – receive training, collaborative attitude
■ Organizational arrangements – a tight ship, weekly meetings of scheduling and allocation main co-ordinating mechanism
■ Informal – the 'Gordon Way', informal processes

Outputs
■ Goal achievement – successful now and several satisfied customers
■ Resource utilization – short term needs met through weekly meetings
■ Adaptation – long term capability open to question
■ Group performance – 'we get on well': achieve goals but some differences unresolved
■ Individual behaviour target – motivates for different reasons – some staff very satisfied.

---

2   Context

Environment – strategy relationships

Organizations are born when a task that needs doing is too large for an individual to cope with. When two or more people cooperate together to accomplish a task we have a very rudimentary form of organization. So, when Stan Gordon's driving school business started to take off, he found he needed extra people to help him cope with the increased workload. But, as soon as more than one person is involved we have the problem of deciding how to divide up the total task, and how to share it out between the members of the organization. We shall look into the two dimensions of this division of the task in a moment. Before that, we should consider what it is about the task that the organization is carrying out that means it can be done effectively when the organization is small? To understand this we need to consider the environment within which the organization exists.

Most organizations start off small and either grow (some reaching mammoth proportions), or they die. But some start small and stay small. If they are firms they tend to be serving a particular niche in the market, so they themselves may well be very specialized in relation to other, larger organizations which are serving a wider market. This specialization can take a variety of forms. It may be a product-based specialization, for example, a manufacturer of medical equipment components. Here the size of the firm is restricted by the limited extent of the total market for these components – even if the firm had a monopoly, the volume of business is such that the firm would still be a small concern.

Alternatively, the firm may be serving a local market, a form of geographical specialization. This is particularly prevalent in the provision of *services* which cannot feasibly be provided on a large, concentrated scale (e.g. hairdressing). So some industries are necessarily *fragmented*, providing circumstances where small organizations are likely to thrive.

Thus, the firm has developed a niche strategy, with a quality service and high pricing. It sees its competitors as non threatening and has a stable environmental context.

Strategy

Traditionally strategy has been associated with planning: but it's more than that. It is a process or a vehicle for achieving the mission. It is the long term and corporate intention to mobilize resources so as to meet the demands of the environment and a multiplicity of stakeholders both within the business (staff) and externally (shareholders, customers, external financiers, professional associations and government).

Strategy operates at several levels: corporate, business unit level and operational level. In a small business such distinctions are not at all clear and 'strategy' may be something done on the back of an envelope. Furthermore, the strategic intent may not be realized, it may be opportunistic, it may be enforced or it may be even 'emergent' and unplanned. Thus, it is a far cry from the planning models understood in the 1960s and 1970s.[1]

The strategic process has many stages: setting goals, analysing the environment, making choices, implementing and organizing for strategic choices, monitoring and correcting organization to avoid strategic 'drift'.

There are a range of strategic techniques that extend the realms of this book. However, they are listed in Table 3.2 for reference and readers are guided by further reading.[2]

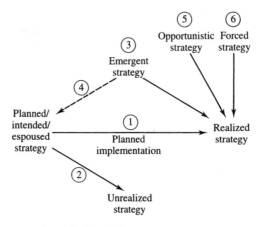

Adapted from: Mintzberg (1987).

Figure 3.1

Table 3.2   Examples of strategic tools and analysis

Level of analysis	Tool	Seeks to
■ Environment – assess and audit environment	– Trend analysis – Scenario setting – PEST	– Identify macrotrends – Examine implications of what ifs – changes in the future – Analysis of political economic, social and technical changes.
■ Structural analysis	– Boston matrix (and those derived from it) – 'Five forces' industry analysis	– Looks at options for product portfolio – assesses cash flow, investment and risk. – Assesses impact of suppliers, buyers, entry barriers, substitutes, and rivalry on strategic positioning.
■ Analysing capability (resources)	– SWOT – Benchmarking	– Weighs and assesses strengths, weaknesses, opportunities and threats. – Comparative and rank analysis of critical success factor against similar companies.
■ Stakeholder analysis	– Political interest – Power and influence	– Assess role of politics – Mapping of power bases.

Adapted from: Johnson and Scholes[2]

The small firm has a distinct advantage over the large bureaucratic organization in the way it can quickly adapt, adjust and respond to changes in the market. Small organizations that are quick to respond therefore thrive in *dynamic environments*.

3 Organizational configuration

This section looks at structure, management, informal processes, groups and individuals.

3.1 Structure

Vertical specialization

When an organization is vertically specialized, most of the planning, controlling and decision making parts of the task are separated out from the 'doing' part of the task. Essentially, the task has been separated into a managerial element, and a subordinate, operative element.

So, in TGDS Stan Gordon's job includes making decisions about pricing, car replacement and taking on new instructors; the instructors just teach people to drive.

Horizontal specialization

In our case example there is very little horizontal specialization, in fact it is difficult to see how the task of driving instruction could be sub-divided into separate specialist areas. Maybe in a much larger driving school there could be instructors who specialize, say, in heavy goods vehicle instruction, but in practice HGV instruction is carried out by a firm specializing in that particular market. Horizontal specialization generally occurs where there are clear benefits to be gained from having people concentrating on a small part of the total task. The argument for this 'division of labour' is that it increases productivity, by enabling workers to improve their performance through repetition of the same task. So this division of labour permits the operative to become master of a small part of the overall task facing the organization.

Small organizations, however, do not tend to adopt horizontal specialization to any great extent. People working in them tend to be flexible, picking up whatever needs to be done, rather than sticking to some notion of a narrow job description. Thus, informal and formal structures and processes often mirror each other. Demarcation disputes about who does what tend to be a luxury afforded only by the larger organization. Partly because of the smallness of the organization, the demands of the task are very obvious and real. It is clear what is required, when it needs to be done and who will have to do it if you don't.

We have a picture emerging, then, of an organization with few specialists. Small organizations cannot afford to employ staff specialists such as, for example, market researchers and work study officers, unless there is sufficient work to justify a full time appointment. So, when some professional expertise is required, the organization buys it in, e.g. the accountant used by TGDS. This has the advantage of flexibility, and of keeping overheads low, but this is achieved at a price. Advice bought in may be very 'generalized', not really tuned in to the particular needs of the organization; expertise may not be there when it is crucially required; the management of the organization cannot 'control' these experts in quite the same way as they can control employees.

Span of control

This refers to the number of people directly supervised by a manager. The 'classical' organization theorists like Graicunas[3] and Urwick[4] suggested that this span should be limited to five or six subordinates reporting to one manager. Clearly, the consequences of applying this 'rule' to an organization are considerable. Every additional five operatives would generate one more supervisor, five more supervisors necessitates another manager, and so on. This limit to the span of control means that the larger the organization, the taller the hierarchy (or number of management layers).

Few modern writers adhere to this limited span of control concept. The basis for the limit is sound enough if we assume that the manager needs to *closely* monitor and control the subordinates, but in many organizations this close supervision isn't necessary on a day-to-day basis. Take TGDS for example: the only way Stan Gordon could directly supervise each instructor would be for him to sit in the back of every car. We shall see in Chapter 5 on the large organization, firms with 'spans of control' of fifty plus which work quite satisfactorily.

The key to this issue is the nature of the task being supervised. Some tasks do require close control from the manager, especially where novel problems are being tackled, or frequent reference to the manager is required for other reasons. Tasks that are straightforward, routine and invariable (like many mass production jobs) require little supervision, and for different reasons, tasks which can be carried out by trained and skilled personnel which may well *not* be routine (e.g. driving instruction, surgery) may similarly require little interference from management.

Depicting the structure

To summarize, the small organization tends to exhibit the following structural features:

■ A fairly *responsive* structure which can cope with the changing demands of a dynamic environment.
■ A degree of *vertical specialization*, with the emergence of management and supervisory positions.

- A very *limited degree of horizontal specialization*, with most jobs being fairly broadly defined, and with *hardly any permanent staff specialists*.
- Quite large *spans of control* depending on the nature of the task.

This structure can be depicted diagrammatically. Figure 3.2 describes the small organization in the typical 'family tree' format of the organization. The example used is Top Gear Driving School, with two alternative ways of representing the 'office administrator' role. The advantage of Chart B is that this staff position is clearly distinguished from the main work of the organization, driving instruction. It is a *support to* the central activity. The charts in Figure 3.2 show quite clearly who is the boss, but it is important to note that they describe relationships between *positions* in the organization; we have not included the names of those who happen to occupy these positions at a given moment. This distinction is important because it begins to indicate a key feature of organizations, the ability they have to survive changes in personnel. However, this tendency for the organization to persist is weakest in small organizations which are likely to be dependent on the founder, or on one or two talented members.

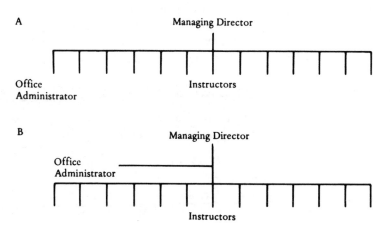

Figure 3.2 *The structure of TGDS*

Figure 3.3 represents the small organization in a generalized way. This diagrammatic form comes from Mintzberg,[5] and we shall use it to depict different types of organization in later chapters.

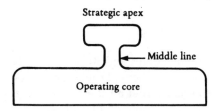

Figure 3.3 *The small organization*

Mintzberg identifies five parts of the organization, three of them are found in the small organization: the operating core, the strategic apex, and the middle line. These three parts are described below.

The operating core   The operating core consists of those members who perform the basic work of the organization, that which is related directly to the production of products/services. It carries our four prime functions:

- Securing inputs.
- Transforming inputs into outputs.
- Distributing outputs.
- Providing *direct* support to the production process (e.g. maintenance).

The strategic apex   These are the people charged with overall responsibility for the organization. They are required to manage the organization so as to achieve the aims of those who control it. Their prime functions are:

- Direct supervision (resource allocation, design of structure, decision making, resolving conflict etc.).
- Managing the organization's relations with the environment.
- Developing the organization's strategy.

The middle line   This comprises a chain of middle managers with formal authority. It connects the apex with the operating core. It is needed because the apex cannot *directly* supervise all the operators (except in a very small organization). In addition, the middle line:

- Provides feedback up the hierarchy about performance in the operating core.
- Makes some decisions and allocates some resources.
- Manages the section's relations with its environment.

As we have said earlier, the middle line is likely to be quite shallow in a small organization, especially if the tasks being supervised do not require close involvement from the management.

3.2   Organizational arrangements

Coordination

The challenge of organization is not only to divide up the task between the various members of the organization, but once having split up the task, to ensure that all the parts fit together, and are coordinated in such a way that the total task is achieved. There are five mechanisms that organizations employ to achieve coordination:

(a) *Mutual adjustment*   Work is coordinated through direct informal communication between the people doing the job.
(b) *Direct supervision*   One individual takes responsibility for the work of others, issuing instructions and monitoring their actions.
(c) *Standardization of work processes*   The *contents* of the work are specified or programmed (e.g. through detailed job instructions).
(d) *Standardization of outputs*   The *results* of the work are specified (e.g. its dimensions, its performance).
(e) *Standardization of skills*   This is accomplished through specifying the *training* required to do a particular job.

The case interviews with the staff of TGDS refer to the Saturday meeting where the instructors, together with Stan, allocate any new clients between themselves. The process is essentially an informal sharing of information – about current workloads, about each instructor's views about taking on more clients – with Stan having the final say in the event of a disagreement. So, through a combination of informal, face-to-face communication, and through Stan exercising his management prerogative, the work gets coordinated. This is a combination of two mechanisms, the processes of mutual adjustment, and direct supervision.

There are, in addition, other forms of coordination taking place:

(a) The standard and style of instruction is coordinated across TGDS by a combination of employing trained and qualified instructors, and by Stan imposing certain codes of behaviour on the staff (e.g. the no smoking rule). An example of coordination through the standardization of skills.
(b) Prices charged are standardized regardless of the instructor, or the client. Standardized timetable sheets, expenses claims, and client record cards have been developed to ease the administration. These are types of work process standardization.

This case example illustrates the point that a number of mechanisms are employed by organizations to achieve coordination. However, Mintzberg suggests that in the very simplest of structures the primary coordinating mechanism is direct supervision. In these, usually small, structures power over all the important decisions is invariably in the hands of the managing director. Small organizations tend to operate in environments that are essentially *simple* to understand, so that one person *can* make all the decisions. This basically simple task, coupled with an often dynamic environment, means that the small organization can adapt to demands for change through the manager issuing new instructions to the fairly flexible staff in the operating core.

In the very smallest of organizations, mutual adjustment can be the primary coordinating mechanism, especially where no hierarchy has been established (e.g. in a partnership or a small cooperative).

Communication

Communication in the small organization tends to be predominantly verbal, and informal. Meetings will usually be loosely structured affairs, often arising spontaneously as a reaction to an immediate problem. Information can flow fairly freely in a small organization, without the encumbrances of tall chains of command and rigid departmental divisions. These organizations are characterized by an often dangerously small volume of written records and stored data.

One important consequence of this relative absence of minutes of meetings, files on particular customers, sales and cost records etc. is that the organization can become overly dependent on particular individuals who have stored the information in their heads, not in files which are accessible to others. Another possible disadvantage with ad hoc meetings is that staff who were not around at the time may not know what was decided, or even what the problem was. Staff who are physically distant from where the action is (usually centred around the managing director) are at an information disadvantage.

Some managers of small organizations may well actively discourage the dissemination of information to other members of the organization; information is a source of power, and if it is feasible that the person at the apex of the organization *can* make all the decisions (due to the relative simplicity of the task) they may well reason that there would be little point in involving others in their decisions.

The 'culture' of the organization is closely bound up with the style of communication. Many small organizations retain a pioneering spirit with everyone 'mucking in' together, generating a family-type atmosphere. Here we would expect information to be freely shared. In stark contrast, some small firms are akin to personal fiefdoms ruled over by an autocratic owner/manager. Suspicion and hostility are endemic, information is hoarded and carefully controlled, and the informal grapevine system emerges to counteract this close control of 'official' information.

Generally however, small organizations possess unsophisticated systems, and most can manage quite happily despite this because their small size permits a free flow of information in informal, overwhelmingly verbal exchanges between staff who work closely together.

3.3 Management

Managerial work

People who write about management can be broadly classified into two groups:

(a) Those who are concerned with what managers *should* do (the 'prescriptive' writers).

(b) Those who are interested in finding out and categorizing what managers *actually* do (the 'descriptive' writers).

If we take the first group, the prescriptive writers, we can find a fair degree of unanimity about what managers should be doing. We would include Fayol, Brech[6] and Drucker[7] in this group, who all have similar views about the tasks of management:

Table 3.3   Earlier theorists on management.

Fayol	Brech	Drucker
■ Planning (and forecasting) ■ Organizing ■ Command (getting the optimun return from all employees) ■ Coordination (unifying and harmonizing all activities) ■ Control (ensuring that things go according to plans and commands)	■ Planning (including determining work methods and setting performance levels) ■ Control (checking actual performance against standards) ■ Coordination (dividing the work and ensuring harmony of effort) ■ Motivation (inspiring loyalty, engendering high morale, exercising leadership)	■ Setting objectives ■ Organizing (including designing organization structures and selecting staff) ■ Motivating and communicating (creating a team) ■ Measuring (setting performance measures) ■ Developing people (directing, encouraging and training them)

'Good' managers should be carrying out all these worthy tasks, and, presumably, if managers did all these things our organizations would be efficient, and harmonious places in which to work. However, the reality of organizational life is somewhat at odds with this picture. This could be because too few managers have been trained sufficiently well in how to plan, motivate people, design organizations etc. It could also be the case that effective management requires certain personal qualities (like fairness, coolness under pressure, 'leadership' ability) that are not found in abundance in our organizations.

One can view this prescriptive approach to management as an attempt to drag imperfect and inadequate managers and potential managers up to an ideal which is probably wildly unrealistic. To many of us, management in practice feels and looks very different from this calm and efficient scenario conjured up by prescriptive theorists. There are, of course, some managers who do appear very competent and in control of events, but all too many managers appear to be reacting to events, not controlling them, fire-fighting rather than planning for the future, trying to sort out disputes and embarrassing errors rather than positively promoting harmony and improving productivity.

The researchers into what managers actually spend their days doing (the descriptive writers) come to somewhat different conclusions to the prescriptive writers. Most prominent in this group are Sune Carlson,[8] Rosemary Stewart[9] and Henry Mintzberg.[10] These researchers used a variety of techniques (interviewing, getting the managers to keep hour by hour diaries of their activities, and direct observation of their work) to derive some very useful insights into the nature of management work. Mintzberg's research, for example, throws up a number of propositions about managerial work which seems to have a definite ring of authenticity about them:

- Management work is open-ended, and consequently some managers feel compelled to perform a great quantity of work at an unrelenting pace, including extensive hours in the office and at home. It is difficult for managers to say they have 'finished managing' for the day.
- Management work is characterized by brevity, variety and fragmentation. Frequent interruptions prevent managers from settling to work on a particular problem for any length of time.
- Managers prefer current, specific and non-routine activities. Very current information (gossip, hearsay, speculation) is favoured, routine reports are not. They make extensive use of verbal media – telephones, unscheduled and scheduled meetings, and tours of the plant.

One key extract from Mintzberg neatly encapsulates the nature of managerial work:

> The pressure of the job does not encourage the development of a planner, but of an adaptive information manipulator who works in a stimulus–response environment and who favours live action.

His own research into the work of five chief executives, coupled with an extensive review of the 'work activity' literature led Mintzberg to draw up a set of ten *roles* which encompass the breadth of managerial work. The ten roles are organized into three major groups: the interpersonal roles, the informational roles and the decisional roles. A breakdown of these roles is shown in Table 3.4.

Mintzberg suggests that these ten roles form a 'whole' picture of managerial work, but in any given management position particular roles will be emphasized.

We can use our case study information to analyse a particular management position using this role set.

Because Stan Gordon is the senior manager (and the owner) of TGDS we would expect the *figurehead* and *leader* roles to be to the fore in a description of his position. In a sense, Stan *is* TGDS – he set up

Table 3.4 Mintzberg's managerial roles.

Interpersonal roles

(a) *Figurehead:* symbolic head; obliged to perform a number of duties of a legal or social nature.

(b) *Leader:* responsible for the motivation and activation of subordinates; responsible for staffing, training, and associated duties.

(c) *Liaison:* maintains a self-developed network of outside contacts and informers who provide favours and information.

Informational roles

(d) *Monitor:* seeks and receives a wide variety of special information to develop a thorough understanding of the organization and its environment; emerges as the nerve centre of internal and external information of the organization.

(e) *Disseminator:* transmits information received to members of the organization – both 'hard' factual information and vague qualitative impressions.

(f) *Spokesman:* transmits information to outsiders about all aspects of the organization (plans, results etc.).

Decisional roles

(g) *Entrepreneur:* searches the organization and its environment for opportunities and initiates improvement projects to bring about change.

(h) *Disturbance handler:* responsible for corrective action when the organization faces important, unexpected disturbances.

(i) *Resource allocator:* responsible for the allocation of resources of all kinds – the making or approval of all significant organizational decisions.

(j) *Negotiator:* responsible for representing the organization at major negotiations.

---

the firm, he lays down the style and policies of the firm. We also know that he has trained most of his instructors, and that he exerts a strong, positive type of leadership with the imposition and maintenance of high standards of professional conduct. We have references to 'the Gordon way of doing things', to the importance of 'courtesy, firmness coupled with politeness, patience and consideration', to 'professionalism'.

We could speculate that Stan has developed a network of outside contacts (e.g. with other driving schools, with staff at the Ministry's Driving Test Centre, with the local garage). Maybe Stan also has contacts through membership of various outside groups which can be a source of future clients, e.g. the Parent Teachers Association, the Rotary Club.

With regard to the second group, the informational roles, we can suggest that, to some extent, all three are carried out by Stan (although it may be stretching a point to describe Stan as the 'nerve centre of internal and external information'). But, no doubt he does pick up snippets of interesting information by keeping his ear to the ground, and by maintaining outside contacts (*monitor*), and he passes some of it on to the instructors at the Saturday meetings (*disseminator*). And, we can assume that any information about TGDS that the local paper might want would be delivered by Stan (*spokesman*).

We would expect Stan to be involved in all the big decisions made in TGDS. He is most certainly an *entrepreneur*, he spotted the possibilities for the business in the first instance, and has responded to growing demand by expanding and adapting his organization. If an instructor was ill, it would be up to Stan to sort out the problem and find cover for his or her lessons (*disturbance handler*). We also know that all decisions about taking on new instructors, replacing cars, pricing and the advertising budget would be taken by Stan (*resource allocator*). The only one of the ten roles that does not obviously fit Stan is the *negotiator* role.

Before we leave this categorization of management work we must emphasize the point that Mintzberg sees this 'role set' as part of a wider, contingency view of managerial work. One manager's work will depend upon a number of different variables:

- *Environmental variables:*   the characteristics of the firm, the industry, the particular part of the organization the manager is in.
- *Job variables:*   the level of the job in the organization's hierarchy, and the nature of the function supervised (e.g. sales, accounts, production).
- *Person variables:*   the personality and style characteristics of the manager.
- *Situational variables:*   the circumstances affecting the manager's job at a particular time, e.g. pressures to complete a large order ahead of time.

In order to reinforce the contingency nature of this role set, we will use it to look at the work of a different type of manager. Wolf[11] has used Mintzberg's model to analyse the work of the audit manager in an accounting firm. He used a research technique based around the identification of critical incidents in the work of the audit manager. These incidents were identified by the managers themselves, the partners to whom they reported, and the field staff who reported to the audit managers themselves. The incidents were then classified into the ten roles, the overall percentages are listed in Table 3.5. This gives us some idea of the relative importance of the different roles in the audit manager's work.

According to the information in Table 3.5 the entrepreneur, resource allocator, leader and liaison roles are to the fore in the work of the audit manager. The informational roles are collectively the least important parts of the job.

Table 3.5   The role set of the audit manager

Managerial role	Percentage of critical incidents	
Figurehead – develops community profile	7.7	
Leader – creates vision and learning opportunities	11.7	
Liaison – builds rapport and relationships	10.5	
All interpersonal roles		29.9
Monitor – checks for competitiveness	4.4	
Disseminator – provides feedback to subordinates	2.1	
Spokesman – communicates well to superiors	8.6	
All informational roles		15.1
Entrepreneur – seizes business opportunities	28.5	
Disturbance handler – proposes solutions to identified problems	2.1	
Resource allocator – plans requirements and delegates	21.3	
Negotiator – reconciles differences with client	3.1	
All decisional roles		55.0
All roles		100.0

Management power

In many respects, the situation of the owner/manager of a small organization provides us with a fairly simple and uncluttered opportunity to explore the issue of management power.

For example, why do the instructors do what Stan tells them? Let us take his rule that no one should smoke in the cars and examine the reasons why instructors may comply with it.

(a) Simply that the instructors see the rule as perfectly sensible, and would not dream of smoking in front of the client anyway.
(b) The instructors comply with the rule because they are afraid they would be sacked if they did not.
(c) The instructors accept that their boss has the right to issue this kind of order, even if they personally do not agree with it.
(d) The instructors respect Stan as a man who has high standards and other admirable qualities.
(e) The instructors wish to be liked and trusted by Stan.
(f) The instructors do not smoke.

Of course, the reason why the instructors stick to the rule may well be due to a combination of these reasons, or indeed, for reasons not listed here. And in any given situation where people comply with an instruction we might not be able to tease out the *real* reasons why they complied. Even with this simple example we have begun to expose the complexities of management power. We have identified five reasons for compliance:

1 *Self-control:*   The instructor's codes of behaviour and values are the same as the manager's (reason (a) above).
2 *Fear of sanctions:*   (reason (b)).
3 *Authority, or legitimate power:*   The instructor sees it as legitimate, or right, that his or her boss should give this kind of order (reason (c)).
4 *Respect for the individual:*   Whereas 3 concerns respect for the *position* of the manager, here we are acknowledging the instructor's respect for the personal qualities of Stan (reason (d)).
5 *Expectation of reward:*   The instructor hopes that compliance will bring forth the reward of Stan's good opinion and trust (reason (e)).

Different managers tend to rely on different bases for compliance. As we have pointed out, if you are a manager and you issue an instruction, you do not know whether your subordinates have complied because they fear you, respect you as a person, or your role as a manager, or whether they merely take a perverse pleasure in taking orders! Organizations, even small ones like TGDS, are complicated social systems and we must guard against oversimplistic interpretations of events and processes in them.

One way of testing out the extent of Stan's authority might be to assume that he had the idea of putting all the instructors in uniform. Darren, for example, may well argue that what he wears on the job is his business, and as long as he is clean and smart Stan should not criticize him. So the right of the manager to give orders, a right in a sense which is *granted to* the manager by the subordinate, is far from being all embracing. Some subordinates will concede to their bosses the right to control large areas of their working life, extending to their dress, manners, hairstyle, and even to the conduct of their spouse. Other subordinates will resent any attempts by management to direct and control anything more than obviously work related activities.

Authority, then, is the formal power vested in the *position* a person holds. In order for it to work as a way of influencing and controlling the behaviour of employees, it requires subordinates to recognize the *right* of managers to give instructions and orders.

We need to look to our society and its processes of socialization to establish the roots of authority. From a very early age children in western society are taught to respect and obey elders, parents, teachers and just about anybody in uniform! So when they come to join a work organization they are usually well prepared to accept the authority of their managers.

Authority, although it is probably the most important source of management 'power', is not the only one, as we speculated earlier in considering why the instructors complied with the 'no smoking' rule. The most widely used categorization of types of power is French and Raven's:[12]

■ *Reward power* is based on the ability to offer a reward which is attractive to the recipient.

- *Coercive power* is the perceived ability to punish.
- *Legitimate power* is based on the acknowledgement by the recipient of the authority of the power holder.
- *Referent power* is based upon the admiration the recipient has for the power holder.
- *Expert power* is based on specialized knowledge or expertise.

We will use this typology of power in our exploration of the concept of leadership.

Leadership

Many people see 'leadership' and 'management' as being more or less the same thing. We do not, and we think it is work taking up a part of this chapter to explain the differences between the two terms. In order to explain leadership it is helpful if we can shrug off the complications introduced by the presence of a formal hierarchical relationship between the leader and the led. To do this we will recall a group situation where no one has formal authority, but where, nevertheless, leadership is being exercised. We will define leadership as a relationship through which one person influences the behaviour of other people.[13]

Most of us have been members of groups or 'gangs' of some sort at school, and if we can think that far back, we should be able to remember who were the influential individuals, the leaders, of those groups. Their leadership manifested itself in a variety of ways – deciding what the group would do, what style of clothes to wear, and generally determining what is acceptable behaviour.

The French and Raven power typology might help us establish the bases of the group's power to influence the other members of this informal group. Physical strength might be the leader's power base of one gang. Yet, it is interesting to note how the leadership role can shift from one member to another as the group's needs and the situation change. Remember the lad who was the kingpin because of his abilities as a footballer, but as soon as discos were discovered he was nowhere because he could not dance (expert power)?

This is leadership in its purest form, no one has put stripes on the leader's arm, or given him or her powers to reward and discipline other people. Leadership can be exercised where there are people looking to be led, and where there is an individual with the qualities to exercise leadership in that particular situation. These qualities, although they are personal, are not necessarily transferable from one group situation to another. The expert on computer aided design systems will be very influential in a group of people who are looking to select a system. He is not necessarily going to carry much weight if the same group found themselves on Dartmoor as part of an outward bound team building exercise.

Figures 3.4(a) and 3.4(b) describe two types of relationship between

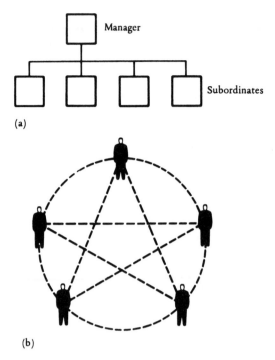

(a)

(b)

Figure 3.4 *Relationship between people in a small organization*

people in a small organization. Figure 3.4(a) depicts the formal relationship between the *positions* in this hierarchy; in Figure 3.4(b) the relationships between the *people* are depicted.

It is the addition of the hierarchy which complicates the relationships between the people in Figure 3.4(b). It is possible that without the hierarchical relationship managers would not be able to influence the subordinates at all – they would have no formal leadership ability in this particular situation. Therefore, in order to get the subordinates behaving in the way they wish, managers must rely on non-personal power bases: formal authority, plus the coercive and reward powers that might come with the position of manager (e.g. to fire staff, to determine pay levels). We can sense that, if that is all that managers having going for them they are not likely to enjoy particularly cordial and trusting relations with their subordinates, and subordinates are not likely to offer managers much respect.

Organizations can be managed using just these positional bases of influence, but these are expensive power systems. Managing people through threats and punishments, or through the offer of financial and promotional carrots, requires that the punishments and rewards be delivered, otherwise they will cease to be effective. And, as we have already discovered, authority is to a certain extent a right granted by the subordinate to the manager, based upon a socialized respect for people in management positions. This willingness to comply with authority will be severely weakened if those put in management positions are seen to be incompetent and not worthy of respect.

Ideally a manager should possess the leadership qualities which would enable him or her to exert influence over subordinates without the need to resort to the formal powers of the position, or with appeals to the authority of management (as in 'do this, because I'm the manager and I say so').

Perhaps the soundest basis upon which to build a leadership relationship with subordinates is respect for the manager's abilities, his knowledge and his personal qualities. This is likely to be more enduring than a relationship based on fear of sanctions and punishments, or on the other hand, a relationship based primarily on friendship. Friendship-based relationships can cause a manager severe problems, especially when unpopular decisions have to be made. The worst case is where the subordinate 'friend' refuses to comply with, or challenges the manager's instructions.

Respect for the manager's qualities is an amalgam of French and Raven's referent and expert power bases. But how can the manager earn this respect? Basically, the manager has two routes to gaining respect, which relate to the two broad aspects of the manager's job. The differences between operative level jobs and supervisory and management jobs are represented in Figure 3.5. As can be seen from this figure the operative's work is 100 per cent 'technical'; this refers to the particular activity the organization is primarily engaged in (driving instruction, nursing, component assembly, auditing). Position B, the first line management position, still retains a fair proportion

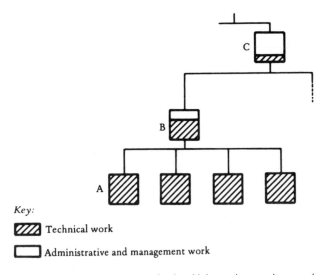

Key:

▨▨▨ Technical work

☐ Administrative and management work

Figure 3.5 *Differences between operative level jobs and supervisory and management jobs*

of technical work. Here the manager or supervisor may well be doing technical work him or herself, in addition to supervising and providing help and guidance on the technical aspects of the operatives' work. As we move further away from the 'shop floor' the technical component reduces, and the job becomes almost entirely managerial (position C); the chief executive would be spending all his or her time carrying out the managerial roles identified by Mintzberg.

Given this dual nature of the lower tier management positions, the new manager has two chances to gain the respect of his subordinates. Most obvious as a source of respect would be the manager's technical abilities. Most people get promoted, at least in part, on the strength of their performance in the operative position. So we would expect new managers to be able to earn some respect for their technical expertise. However, once in post, managers should be able to enhance their positions by performing the management role well: being seen to be fair, being thoughtful but decisive decision makers, defending their teams against outside criticism, setting high personal standards of behaviour etc. Of course, what is seen as 'good' management behaviour which is worthy of respect will reside essentially in the eyes of the subordinate.

It is a pity, however, that we give so little assistance to managers in helping them earn respect through their performance as managers. Whereas it is quite acceptable to invest a large amount of resources to train nurses, engineers, accountants and teachers, it apparently is not acceptable to invest time and money in developing people who *manage* these expensively trained staff.

So far we have not mentioned *styles* of leadership other than to make some passing comments about Stan Gordon's way of managing people. This important aspect of management will be picked up in the next chapter on the growing organization.

3.4 Groups

Formal and informal groups

The structure of an organization places people into formal groupings – into, for instance, sections or departments. The organization chart will indicate how particular staff are grouped together, and it will usually show who is in charge of each group. Most formal groups are established on the basis of some sort of logic. In particular, groupings help coordination, primarily through the processes of direct supervision and mutual adjustment.

Staff can be grouped together for a number of reasons, for example:

■ They are all working on the same products, or projects.
■ They all have the same skills (e.g. draughtsmen, driving instructors), even though they are working on separate products or with

different clients. The advantages here are that they can share the same resources, have a common supervisor and they can exchange information and expertise.

- They serve the same region (e.g. area salesmen).
- They are all working at the same *time* (shift work).

However, within these formal groupings there are *informal* groups which emerge for very different reasons than those listed above. Informal groups provide their members with important benefits like companionship, emotional support, assistance and even a form of protection. The tendency for informal groups to emerge within a formal structure is strong, but highly cohesive groups are more likely to develop where the following conditions exist:

- *Homogeneity:* The members share the same outlook and goals, are of similar ages, the same sex, level of education, etc.
- *Stability.*
- *Freedom to communicate:* Groups cannot form unless the potential members are able to communicate with each other.
- *Small size:* Tends to encourage cohesion.
- *Isolation and outside pressures:* Unite the group members, often against a common 'enemy'.

In the very small organization the formal group may well constitute a cohesive *informal* group. Some of the conditions promoting cohesion are likely to exist in the small firm which is struggling to establish itself (e.g. shared goals, isolation and outside pressures, freedom to communicate). Also new organizations often display a pioneering spirit which encourages the members to put in extraordinary efforts. They may be led by a strong and charismatic entrepreneur to which the individuals, encouraged by a group feeling, owe tremendous loyalty. In these circumstances, new entrants to the organization, who have not experienced the heady days of struggle and sacrifice, and who do not share the same view of the boss as the incumbent members, may find it difficult to fit in. They are likely to be unused to the extra efforts required, and may resent the demands made upon them, and could well be puzzled by the willingness with which the pioneers comply with the manager's requests.

In TGDS, Stan Gordon seems to run a happy ship, with everyone seeming to get on quite well with each other. The only sour note is struck by Darren Watts who does not appear to be integrated into the 'team'. This could be due to his age and outlook being different from the majority of the other instructors.

A task/process model

In this section we will introduce a simple model of groups which can be used to analyse the features of a group situation in a systematic way. The model is presented in diagrammatic form in Figure 3.6. The model makes a distinction between *task* elements and *process* aspects of the group. These distinctions will become clearer as we consider the three lines labelled *content, method* and *interaction*.

Content This is the subject matter of the group's work. 'Raw materials' in the form of skills, ideas, information and physical resources are fed in, and 'finished products' or outputs emerge – these could be completed jobs, or agreed decisions (if the group was a committee, for example). The content of the group's work may be essentially fragmented, as in the case of the driving school, with each instructor tackling his part of the workload almost independently; or it could be highly integrated, a good accessible example here being the football team. The workload can be high or low, or it may exhibit marked peaks and troughs.

Method Having established the content of the group's work, the second element of the model shifts attention to 'how' the group operates. Do we have specialists within the group? Are the working methods clearly defined, or left open? Does the group regularly review its progress? Do we appoint a formal leader? Is the group free to move around from job to job?

The combination of content and method determines the *task* of the group. Most work groups are highly task orientated. That is not to imply that they are necessarily desperately keen on achieving the task, but rather that their thinking about the group concentrates almost exclusively on task related issues.

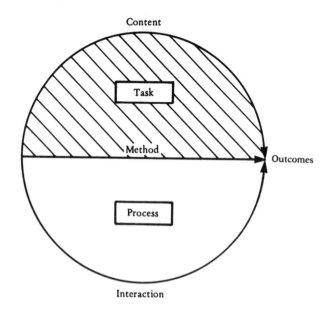

Figure 3.6 *A task/process model of group activity*

This focus on the task can be a problem as the third element of the group's activity could be ignored.

Interaction All groups experience interaction between the people involved. We have already explored one particular form of interaction within groups – the nature of leadership within the group. There are a host of other forms of interaction between group members. For example, who always comes up with the bright ideas which everyone ignores? Who are the comedians? Who stays silent? Who never listens? Why don't X and Y get on with each other?

The interplay between method and interaction constitutes the *process* of the group. This is a rich source of problems which are frequently ignored, or considered irrelevant. Process issues are often more important in explaining poor (or good) group performance, than task elements. Morale, cohesion, and informal group leadership can play a critical part in determining the group's success.

3.5 *The individual*

Why work?

So far we have tended to ignore the individual's basic relationship with the organization which must centre around his or her reasons for joining the organization in the first place. As the major focus of this text is the employing organization (as opposed to, for example, voluntary organizations, like clubs), we shall explore the individual's motives for going to work.

Everyone who goes to work expects to gain something from doing so. The obvious reward is money, and in our society money is essential for acquiring a basic level of existence and the comforts and conveniences expected in an advanced western society. Money can help you to acquire social esteem through your purchases of desirable products, it can be a source of power and independence, and just earning more money can give a sense of achievement. So money is a very flexible reward, it can be deployed in the ways in which it will confer most satisfaction to the individual.

However, this is a very one-dimensional view of work, because work itself can directly satisfy important needs that money can only satisfy indirectly. If we refer back to the case interviews we can identify some very different views about working for TGDS. Darren Watts sees work as a means to an end; as a way of getting the money he feels he needs, whereas June Farrow seems to stress the satisfaction in the job itself, the challenge of the new learner, the shared feeling of achievement when her clients pass their tests. She feels proud to be part of a 'professional' team with a good reputation. Sarah Simmonds, Stan's 'right arm', sees the interruptions and varied demands made upon her as positive features of the job. She also enjoys playing an informal role as 'mother' to the younger instructors.

Attitudes to work

For some people work is by far and away the most important thing in their lives. Let us assume that Sarah lives alone and has few social contacts outside of TGDS. We could represent her 'life space' as in Figure 3.7.

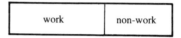

Figure 3.7

Figure 3.7 represents the relative importance of life at work and life outside of work for Sarah. One implication of this imbalance is that when a problem or an upset occurs at work it is likely to hit Sarah pretty hard. She probably will not have much support, or diversion out of work to help her put the problem in a healthier perspective.

On the other hand, June Farrow may well have a different profile altogether, as in Figure 3.8.

```
┌───────┬──────────────┐
│ work  │   non-work   │
└───────┴──────────────┘
```

Figure 3.8

She has a husband and two children, a large circle of friends and hobbies and holidays to fit in as well. Should she be upset by a rude client she can fall back on a lot of support, and with such a busy life she is unlikely to have time to brood on the situation.

The way two people see the same job can differ due to a variety of reasons. We have listed a number of factors which affect the individual's perceptions of the job in Figure 3.9.

Motivation at work

Employers are not just interested in people turning up for work, it is *performance* at work that the employer pays the wages for. The effort that employees put in at work will obviously affect the level of performance they attain, and effort is related to the motivation of employees. As a result of this link between performance and employee motivation, a good deal of research has been undertaken to establish what motivates people to give of their best at work.

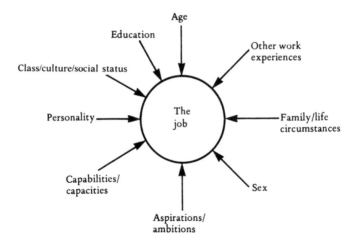

Figure 3.9 *Some factors affecting perception of the job*

Motivation theories can be divided into two groups.

(a) *Content theories:* These try to explain people's needs, and the goals they pursue in order to satisfy these needs. They are concerned with establishing *what* motivates people. Maslow's[14] 'hierarchy of needs' has gained a wide currency in management textbooks, as has Herzberg's[15] 'motivation-hygiene' theory. Two other less popularized content theories are McClelland's[16] achievement theory, and Alderfer's[17] existence, relatedness, growth model. We do not propose to spend a great deal of time on explaining these four theories (in fact there are clear similarities between three of them: Maslow, Alderfer and McClelland). This is for two reasons, the first being the space needed to do the theories justice, and secondly, because we have already suggested that people's motives for working are many and varied, we are not convinced that generalized theories of people's needs are particularly useful. We are all individuals, with individual needs.

(b) *Process theories:* These motivation theories concentrate not upon *what* motivates, but how the motivation process itself works. Given that the individual is striving for some reward, how does this follow through into his or her performance and satisfaction? This group of theories includes Vroom's[18] expectancy theory, and its development by Porter and Lawler,[19] and Adams'[20] equity theory of motivation. We shall be concentrating upon the Porter and Lawler model here, because, despite it being, at first sight, rather complex, it is very powerful in exploring issues in motivation, performance, and satisfaction. We believe it is more worthwhile to fully explore this theory than to skim unsatisfactorily through all the theories mentioned above.

Porter and Lawler's Process Model This model of the processes of motivation treats effort, performance and satisfaction as separate but related variables (see Figure 3.10). We shall work through the model, box by box, starting on the left-hand side of the diagram.

1. *Value of reward:* These are the various rewards that people hope to get from work, the value of the reward depending upon how strongly the individual desires it. The various *content* theories have suggestions to make about how to fill this box. Maslow proposes that needs are arranged in a hierarchy with lower order needs (for food, sleep, warmth, safety and belongingness) at the bottom and higher needs for esteem and self-fulfilment at the top. He suggests that as lower order needs become more satisfied, the higher order needs become more significant for the individual. McClelland identifies socially based needs for affiliation, power and achievement, and suggests that the strength of these needs will vary between individuals. His research shows a higher need for achievement is found amongst managers than in other occupational groups.

For practical purposes, however, the soundest way to view this first box is *not* to assume that people are all basically pursuing the same things, but rather that the manager should try to find out what each individual's major concerns are. It is too easy to make inappropriate assumptions about people's aspirations; for example managers often assume, either that subordinates all want to be managers, or that none of them are interested in progressing up the hierarchy.

2. *Expectancies:* This box is an important and interesting feature of this model, and it is based upon Vroom's expectancy theory. We have separated expectancy into two parts:

(a) *Effort → performance:* This is the individual's perception of the probability that increased effort will lead to improved performance. This probability could be low if he or she sees that no amount of additional effort will help him or her up his or her level of performance because of situational factors beyond his or her control, or because he or she lacks the ability to do the job well.

(b) *Performance → reward:* This is the expectation that good performance will lead to rewards valued by the individual. This, too, could be a very low probability, if, for instance, the individual believes that promotion is based on who you know rather than how good you are. Or, as some teachers believe, that because no one sees how you perform in the classroom, there is little prospect of good performance leading to promotion.

3. *Effort:* This is how hard the individual tries to perform well, and it is determined by the values of boxes 1 and 2. For example, a high value in box 1 (the rewards are strongly desired), coupled with strong expectations that effort will lead first to good performance, and that good performance will bring forth the desired result, will provoke a

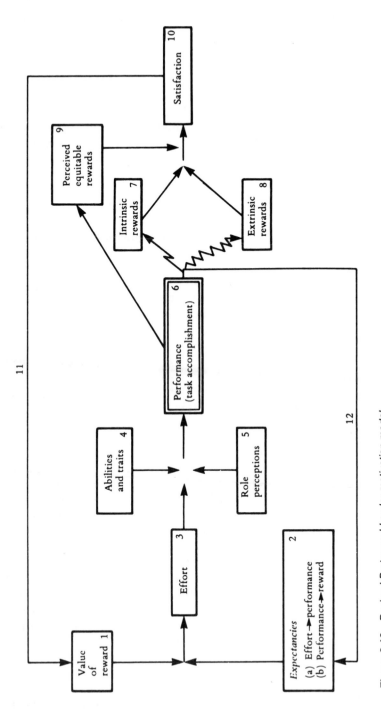

Figure 3.10 *Revised Porter and Lawler motivation model*

great effort. However, the individual with a low box 1 value (maybe he is interested in being a rock star but has got a job as a meat porter), is not likely to try hard as he will not perceive any connections between his desires, and the rewards on offer at work.

4. *Abilities and traits:* Effort does not lead directly to performance. If you have not got the required skills, personality or intelligence to do the job well, you will perform poorly no matter how hard you try. This is of key importance in establishing reasons for poor performance. We are saying here that the individual's *motivation* to work well may be very high, what he needs if more *training*, not exhortations to work harder.

5. *Role perceptions:* This box, and box 4 are mediating influences between the effort put in, and the performance that results. Perceptions of a particular job can differ markedly, the job holder thinking he or she is supposed to be doing X, his or her boss expecting him or her to do Y.

6. *Performance:* This is what the manager is interested in, and low performance will result if the subordinate is trying hard to do the wrong job, or has not got the abilities to do the task well.

7. *Intrinsic rewards:* These are rewards which are, in a sense, given to the individual by him or herself. These include feelings of achievement, of accomplishing something worthwhile, and they are likely to be closely connected with performance. The less jagged line in the diagram represents this more direct link between intrinsic rewards and performance.

8. *Extrinsic rewards:* In contrast to intrinsic rewards, extrinsic rewards are controlled by the organization, and include pay, promotion, status and security. Apart from a straightforward payment-by-results system in which performance and pay are directly related, the connection between performance and these rewards is likely to be indirect, or even very weak. Hence the very jagged line linking performance to extrinsic rewards.

9. *Perceived equitable reward:* This is another mediating box, interfering between the reward boxes, and 'satisfaction'. Most people have some feelings about what constitutes a fair level of rewards for their accomplishments, and if the actual rewards received do not match these perceptions, satisfaction will not result. The important point to note here, is that it is the individual's perception that counts, not the manager's.

10. *Satisfaction:* This is an internal state of mind, which will be achieved if the rewards match or exceed the levels perceived as equitable by the individual. So, in this model, satisfaction primarily

depends on performance. Satisfaction only affects performance through the feedback loop (11) to the value of reward. When the reward that was valued does actually lead to satisfaction, the valuation of that reward may be increased. However, it might be the case that the individual has valued promotion to a managerial position very highly, and this has contributed to a sustained effort over a number of years. On receiving the promotion, the individual discovers that being a manager is not the job he hoped it would be – the reward has been granted, but feelings of satisfaction are low.

Feedback loop 12 provides an opportunity for the individual to revise his expectations of effort leading to performance.

This model has been subjected to some ingenious empirical testing, and, by and large, it has stood up well as a realistic representation of the dynamics of the motivation process. It can be used as a guide, or checklist for diagnosing problems of motivation. It is a complex model, but people *are* complex; we simplify these issues at our peril.

We could usefully test out this model by looking at the situation of two of the instructors working for TGDS, June Farrow and Darren Watts.

June Farrow:　On the brief evidence of the case we can only surmise that June values things like achievement, a sense of doing something worthwhile, meeting people, belonging to a group, and friendship (box 1 in the Porter and Lawler model). Because she sees her job in TGDS as a clear opportunity to achieve these things she values (2) she is likely to put in a high degree of effort (3). It seems that she is capable of doing the job (4), and Stan Gordon's training has ensured that her perception of the job is more or less in line with his (5). The high degree of effort, bolstered by her abilities and training mean that June performs well at the job (6). Her rewards are largely intrinsic (7), although praise from clients, and Stan, are effective extrinsic rewards (8). Moreover, the sense of achievement, of a job well done, is quite tangible and immediate (i.e. a client passing his or her driving test). June feels she gets a fair reward for her efforts (9) and hence achieves feelings of satisfaction (10). As she so enjoys her job, the chances are that the values we attributed to her in box 1 are more than likely to be reinforced by her job experiences and rewards (11).

Darren Watts:　Darren seems to be interested almost exclusively in money. This may reflect his family circumstances, rather than being a permanent feature of his personality. However, he also suggests that advancement and independence are important to him (box 1). Does Darren expect that by putting in a great amount of effort in his job he will earn the rewards he values? Clearly, we can only make educated guesses here. We do know that he sees his job (and perhaps most other jobs) as a *means* of earning much needed cash, rather than as a source of satisfaction in itself. Because of this 'instrumental' approach to the job, and because there is a direct relationship between the number of lessons he gives and the amount of money he earns, we would expect a good deal of effort from him in respect of the hours he puts in (3). We must assume he is competent at the job, although he probably doesn't see the job in quite the same way as Stan (5). We might therefore deduce that although his performance could not be faulted in terms of quantity, it may well fall short of Stan's standards in terms of the quality of the service Darren supplies (6). Extrinsic rewards (cash) appear to be most significant here (8), but it is likely that Darren thinks he is worth more than Stan is paying him (9), so feelings of satisfaction are not likely to be great (10).

Before we leave this section on the individual in the small organization we shall look briefly at the motivation of the small business owner/manager.

Profiles of owner/managers of small businesses

The small firm owner/manager has been the subject of a considerable amount of research in recent years and political interest in the 1980s and 1990s.

Small entrepreneurs tend to be people who do not fit easily into the highly structured large organization. The notion of 'social marginality' is used to describe the circumstances of particular individuals who may be driven to correct the imbalance between their perception of their work and status, and the position in society that they have been 'forced' into. Examples here might be the position of Jews in the past who were socially, and often legally prevented from attaining high status roles. More recently, some black and ethnic minorities in Britain have been placed in similar situations, where these groups do appear to demonstrate a marked degree of entrepreneurial activity despite social discrimination and status.

A large scale European study of small businesses (over 1100 small business managers were interviewed across eight countries) explored, among other things, the objectives of the owner-manager.[21] Highly rated were job satisfaction, making good products and product quality, survival and liquidity. Personal and financial independence were also seen as important. Low importance was attached to high levels of income, social status, life style and playing a role in the local society. When asked about the objectives of the *business*, product quality and survival rated highest, and interestingly, growth was ranked thirteenth out of fifteen suggested objectives.

These findings seem to fit the first of the three entrepreneurial types identified by Boot *et al.*[22] Their 'Artisan Identity' applies particularly to the new entrepreneur. Artisans pursue the intrinsic rewards of autonomy, self-sufficiency and satisfaction from producing quality products, which in turn have particular consequences for the style of organization they establish. They will be reluctant to use advice and expertise offered to them, and their 'go it alone' approach usually results in a very unsophisticated approach to the business. They recruit people they like, which usually means employees share their concerns for quality, as a result the team tends to be harmonious. Recruitment is critical in preserving the 'atmosphere' of the firm.

The artisan's drive for independence can lead him to be autocratic and paternalistic which can result in underutilized subordinates, and resentment from some quarters. The artisan will pay lip service to the importance of growth – in fact he or she may well be against growth as it is likely to threaten his autonomy and independence.

4   Using models

In this chapter we have introduced a further three models which can be used to explore actual situations familiar to the reader. The three models being Mintzberg's ten role-set describing managerial work, the task/process model of group behaviour, and the Porter and Lawler motivation model. We would encourage the reader to use these devices to analyse their own circumstances. If you are a manager, which roles particularly apply to your circumstances? How does your management job differ from a colleague's or your boss's? If you are not a manager, use the role set to examine your manager's job.

The task/process model can be used to identify important differences between groups of which you are a member. The motivation model may shed some light on your attitudes to work and the satisfactions, or lack of them that you experience through your job.

These models are not likely to throw up any particularly startling conclusions. What they can do, if they are applied sensibly, is to ensure a broader view is taken in analysing a given situation, and the process of applying them will enhance your sensitivity to, and perceptions of, organizational life.

Further reading

Two classic texts on management and organization are Mintzberg's *Nature of Managerial Work*[10] and *Structure in Fives*[5]. Chapter 3 of *The Nature of Managerial Work* highlights the distinguishing characteristics of managerial work, and Chapter 4 sets out in detail the ten working roles. Mintzberg's *Structure in Fives* is an abbreviated version of his *Structure of Organisations* (Prentice Hall, 1979), which provides the basis of the contingency approach to structure adopted in this book.

References

1 Mintzberg, H., *Five Ps for Strategy*, California Management, 1987
2 Johnson, G. and Scholes, R., *Exploring Corporate Strategy*, Prentice Hall, London, 1993
3 Graicunas, V. A., 'Relationship in Organization', *Papers in the Science of Administration*, University of Columbia, 1937
4 Urwick, L., *The Elements of Administration*, Pitman, 1947
5 Mintzberg, H., *Structure in Fives*, Prentice Hall International, 1983
6 Brech, E. F. L., *Principles and Practice of Management*, Third Edition, Longman, 1975
7 Drucker, P. F., *People and Performance*, Heinemann, 1978
8 Carlson, S., *Executive Behaviour: A study of the work load and the Working Methods of Managing Directors*, Strömbergs
9 Stewart, R., *Managers and Their Jobs*, Macmillan, 1967 and *Choices for the Manager*, McGraw Hill, 1982
10 Mintzberg, H., *The Nature of Managerial Work*, Harper & Row, 1973
11 Wolf, F. M., 'The Nature of Managerial Work: An Investigation of the work of the Audit Manager', *The Accounting Review*, Vol. LVI, No. 4, October 1981
12 French, J. R. P. and Raven, B., 'The Bases of Social Power' in Cartwright, D. and Zander, A. (eds.) *Group Dynamics*, Third Edition, Harper & Row, 1968
13 Mullins, L. J., *Management and Organisational Behaviour*, Pitman, 1985
14 Maslow, A. H., 'A Theory of Human Motivation', *Psychological Review*, 50, July 1943, pp. 370–96
15 Herzberg, F., *Work and the Nature of Man*, Granada Publishing Ltd, 1974
16 McClelland, D. C., *The Achieving Society*. Van Nostrand Reinhold, 1961
17 Alderfer, C. P., *Existence, Relatedness and Growth*, Collier Macmillan, 1974
18 Vroom, V. H., *Work and Motivation*, Wiley, 1964
19 Porter, L. W. and Lawler, E. E., *Managerial Attitudes and Performance*, Irwin, 1968 and Lawler, E. E., *Motivation in Work Organisations*, Brooks/Cole, 1973
20 Adams, J. S., 'Injustice in Social Exchange', abridged in Steers, R. M. and Porter, L. W., *Motivation and Work Behaviour*, Second Edition, McGraw Hill, 1979
21 'Stratos' Research Project Working Papers
22 Boot, R. L., Cowling, A. G. and Stanworth, M. J. K., *Behavioural Science for Managers*, Arnold, 1977

4 The growing organization

> This chapter develops our understanding of organizations by looking at the issues of growth.

1 Case study: Easton College

In 1975 Easton College was a small commercial college serving a local demand for professional, business and secretarial courses. The college operated in a predictable environment and income from grants and fees was fairly secure. There were thirty-four lecturers divided about equally between two departments, Professional Studies and Business and Secretarial Studies. The heads of these two departments reported directly to the College Principal. The Bursar, who also reported to the Principal ran a small department which dealt with routine administration and reprographics.

A variety of courses was offered, most of them on a part time basis, and the highest level qualification offered was the HND in Business Studies.

Since 1975, Easton College has experienced a period of considerable growth during which the number of lecturing staff has more than doubled, and the range of courses offered has expanded. Growth has also meant a relocation of the college into much larger premises. But, interesting though these material changes are, it is the less tangible aspects of this period of growth that we shall concentrate upon in this case study.

The 'spirit of '75'

Staff who have been with the college throughout this growth period needed little persuasion to reminisce about the 'good old days' when life seemed so much simpler. They describe an organization which was run more along the lines of a school than a university. Staff were expected to be in college from 9 a.m. until 5 p.m., unless they had evening classes, or were given permission to leave the site. Timetables were drawn up by the head of department and were not negotiable. Staff were located in three large rooms, the largest housing twenty-one people, some of whom had to share desks. There was one telephone which could only take incoming calls. All correspondence was routed through the head of department, and carried his signature.

Staff were expected to teach a variety of subjects to a wide range of abilities. The guiding principle seemed to be 'have textbook will teach'.

But the overriding impression of the old days is that they were fun, despite these problems. Drunken students are recalled with affection. The nit-picking and authoritarian head of department nevertheless had his good points, and was a terrific all round performer in the annual staff–student cricket and football matches. Staff tended to socialize a lot together outside of college hours, and seemed to be united against a common enemy, whether it be the students, the externally set examinations, or the Principal.

Easton College today

The college now runs six degree courses which compete with other polytechnics across the country for students. Postgraduate management courses and specialist short courses have been developed to meet the requirements of large, locally based companies. The college has earned a national reputation in the development of the automated office, and several research groups have been set up to investigate a variety of issues ranging from cultural differences in strategic decision making, to goal programming for multi-product operations. It thus has a wider and more complex range of financial arrangements. Furthermore, as a leader in its field the college began to attract both new money and good quality staff.

There are over ninety full time lecturers split into four 'schools', although this is the result of a very recent reorganization, the fifth since 1975. As well as being allocated to one of the four schools, staff are also members of other more or less permanent groupings: 'discipline units', course development teams, research groups and any number of school and college committees.

Lecturers are expected to specialize in one particular discipline. So, whereas in 1975 you might have been a business studies lecturer, picking up a bit of marketing, basic statistics and some 'principles of management' teaching, now you are expected not just to be a marketing lecturer, but a marketing strategy lecturer. The demand for specialization stems from the significant qualitative changes to the college's portfolio of courses. In order to get these degree courses approved by the CNAA, it was necessary to demonstrate a high level of competence amongst the lecturing staff, which cannot convincingly be developed without specialization. Clearly, some of the original group of lecturers have retired or left, and the staff group as a whole has been considerably augmented by an influx of highly qualified academics. Whereas in 1975 a lecturer with a masters degree was the exception, now it is the norm, with a strong expectation that all staff should be engaging in research.

Problems along the way

We have taken snapshots of the same organization at two points in time. What we have not reflected is the painful process that links these two situations. Some staff found the transition period very stressful. Those who were comfortable with the stability and predictability of the small organization found the changes particularly hard to come to terms with.

- Some staff expected to be told what to do, and were not able to respond to a situation of greater staff autonomy.
- Others were intimidated by the demands of the higher level courses.
- The hierarchy of the old days was based primarily on seniority, now promotion is earned more through ability, which has meant that some older members of staff are now reporting to their 'juniors'.

The rapid growth of the college owed a lot to the leadership of the new Principal who was appointed in October 1975. It was his vision and drive which spurred the 'Young Turks' of the college into the development of new degree courses. He was also quite ruthless in 'encouraging' staff who did not fit his plans to leave. He instigated a fundamental change in the organization's culture soon after his appointment by scrapping the nine to five attendance requirement. The demands for teaching, consultancy, course development and research were to be met not by ensuring that staff were physically present on the campus, but through the strong expectation that they would respond professionally to these new freedoms. Most staff did respond positively, some did not, and have continually exploited the increased autonomy to benefit themselves, rather than the college.

The shift in the status system from seniority and position-based authority, towards more of a meritocracy has helped to create a lively and challenging organization culture. It has also exposed deficiencies in some lecturers who are no longer able to hide behind their formal authority.

Developments in the administrative side of the college have not kept pace, however, with the increased number of courses, staff and students. The goodwill of too many lecturers has been relied upon to pick up administrative loose ends. Professionalism and commitment to the courses and the students have resulted in certain lecturers being overwhelmed with responsibilities. Frequent changes in personnel responsible for running courses have led to staff continually re-inventing administrative systems. Record keeping is haphazard, with duplicate copies of some information being stored in separate parts of the college, and with other important information being stored by no one.

Although staff accommodation is of a much higher standard, with nearly all lecturers having their own offices, and access to a telephone, the chumminess, the cooperation and cohesion of 1975 seem to have gone. Staff are more isolated, they no longer socialize together and increasing specialization has forced lecturers into smaller and smaller informal groupings. Newly appointed staff show little interest in tales of the old days, and they often have little regard for people who teach the few lower level courses that remain from 1975.

Increased staff autonomy, and other changes to the management of the college have resulted in a marked erosion of the formal authority system. Now it is quite likely that staff would not only question a request from a course leader, or the head of school (or even the Principal), they may well refuse to comply outright. This has led to staff responsible for running courses, units and committees to rely almost entirely on goodwill, and a system of personal favours to get things done. Challenges to the tattered remains of the formal authority system serve simply to weaken it further. The ultimate powers of discipline and dismissal are so rarely invoked as to render them irrelevant. Lecturers who take advantage of the lack of formal power of those in senior positions not only contribute very little to the college, they also engender resentment in the rest of the staff, who get paid just the same but work twice as hard.

Finally, the continual reorganizations, the seemingly incessant demands for change, for updating, for new courses to be developed, and the shifting priorities set by the management have resulted in an increasing proportion of the staff 'opting out'. They are exhausted by the demands of change, their reservoir of goodwill has run dry, and they are no longer young enough to cope with new challenges. In short, they are hankering after stability, a chance to catch their breath, to take stock, to consolidate. Under the present leadership of Easton College they are likely to be disappointed as the drive for growth is still paramount. So maybe the college is ready for a change at the top?

Issues arising from the case

Environment

1 The college continued to remain in a relatively stable environment, in the field of education.
2 The development of 'new technology' in an industrial and commercial environment provided a new market, and specialism for the college.
3 The college was among the leaders in its field with a national reputation for its work and therefore did not really have to compete for strategic position or resources. But how long could this situation continue?

History and resources

1 The change in leadership from 'authoritarian headmaster' to entrepreneur was difficult for the old staff to manage, what might they have needed to manage the transition?
2 Resources were never a problem but how were they being managed and what does the horizon hold?

Task

1 The teaching task was augmented by other tasks – research, short courses and consultancy, managing and prioritizing these was becoming difficult.
2 The task moved from broadly spread 'have textbook and teach' to specialization and high quality.
3 The tasks generated new demands on the role. How were staff to cope?

Organizational structure and management

1 Adapting the college's structure to the growing and changing tasks facing it appears to be anything but a smooth process. Why is adaptation so difficult?
2 The structure displays more specialization, at both the departmental and individual level. What determines the nature and extent of specialization?
3 Which administrative tasks can be provided centrally, and which must be carried out at department level?
4 Why is it that some staff are overloaded whilst others have an easy time?

Management

5 How crucial is the role of the Principal in promoting growth?
6 How should someone in a management position respond to a direct challenge to his or her authority?
7 As the size of the organization increases (e.g. doubling numbers of staff, students and courses) managers cannot cope with the concomitant increases in workload. How can managers effectively delegate tasks to relieve their workload?

Informal organization

1 In 1975 the Head of Department determined each lecturer's timetable. Is this still feasible given the present size and complexity of the college?
2 Does the shift from the authority based power system to one based more on expertise match the changing nature of the college?

3 Has the increased size, complexity and pace of change caused coordination problems? How are these being tackled?
4 The college does not seem to have sorted out its systems for handling routine information. Why has the development of this aspect of the college's work lagged behind advances made in teaching and course development?

Groups

5 Why were the lecturers a more cohesive group in 1975 than they are today?
6 How important is physical location in explaining the formation of informal groups?
7 Why might we expect there to be tension between the 'old hands' and the staff that have only recently joined the college?

The individual

1 What demands does the growing organization place on the individual?
2 What opportunities does growth open up for the individual?
3 Why is it that willing and competent staff become overloaded with work?

Outputs

1 What was the level of goal achievement after the changes? Were all staff happy with the results?
2 The utilization of resources seemed to change after 1975. What are the key factors that might explain the differences?
3 Adaptation was managed well by some but not others. Who were the losers and winners and why?
4 The 'bonhomie' of the organization changed. How might it now be described and did this support or undermine the college's tasks? (See Table 4.1.)

2 Context

Environment – strategy relationship and impact on task

There is considerable research evidence that suggests that there is a relationship between strategy, structure, leadership and culture.[1-4] In the case of Easton College we see that an opportunistic strategy has been seized by the new principal and through his entrepreneur style the task has increased both in its complexity, range and quality.

The environment was relatively stable or at least changing at a manageable pace. New technology investment and tying the college

Table 4.1 Summary of key factors in the case

	Old	Now
Inputs		
■ Environment	Stable	Relatively stable, change in new tech, CNNA validation.
■ Resources	Fees and grants stable but simple.	Increasing and complex sources of income and contracts.
■ History	'School'	'New Tech College'.
Transformation		
■ Task	Mainly teaching and broadly spread.	Multiple tasks e.g. plus research and consultancy but specialized.
■ Individual	Generalist – low level competence.	Specialist – high level competence, expertise.
■ Organization	Hierarchy, timetables, formidable 'headmaster'.	Entrepreneurial, 'professional', poor admin.
■ Informal	'Social group', chumminess, seniority ≡ length of service.	Autonomy, isolation, more informal groups, conflict.
Output		
■ Goal achievement	Met as stated	In some quarters but not balanced.
■ Resource utilization	Over managed	Scope for abuse, chaotic in places, not corporate.
■ Adaptation	Not necessary	Some better than others but overall difficult.
■ Individual behaviour and effect	Good	Poor–medium

into automated systems was both visionary and seeking to change the image and culture of the college from a 'traditional' school to a commercially related business school. The niche market position, with high added value, quality and professional expertise in the faculty was a strategic and proactive response that gave the college its competitive advantage.[5] The implications of the environment on the college's structure is discussed below. However, a brief look at the environment is useful here.

Four types of environment

A study by Lawrence and Lorsch[6] suggested that the environment will impact on the organization. They identified different ones.

Lawrence and Lorsch pointed out that the *dynamism* of the environment is a significant influence on organizational design. A dynamic environment would exhibit some of these characteristics:

■ Unpredictable shifts in demand.
■ Unexpected changes in sources of supply.

■ Continual customer demands for creativity or novelty.
■ Rapid technological changes.

Dynamic environments are, then, *unpredictable* environments. In contrast, a *stable* environment would display the opposite characteristics: predictable demand, unchanging technology etc.

In our consideration of the Lawrence and Lorsch research we hinted at another environmental dimension, *complexity*. Some firms *are* able to send all the problems up the hierarchy to be resolved, because they are basically tackling a simple task. Making and selling tins of beans is a fundamentally simple process; it can be broken down into lots of easily understood activities which do not necessarily require large numbers of highly trained or knowledgeable staff. Treating heart disease is, by way of a contrast, a complex task, so too is the education of business students. These tasks cannot be broken down into many simple activities that can be performed by unskilled people, or by machines. Another example, a management consultancy, is not only facing a complex task (because the problems encountered are fairly unique), it is also likely to be in a comparatively dynamic environment with a degree of unpredictability involved as well.

We have, then, two environmental dimensions: dynamism, and complexity. These two dimensions generate four possible types of environment as in Figure 4.1. each of these four cells describes the environment faced by different organizations.

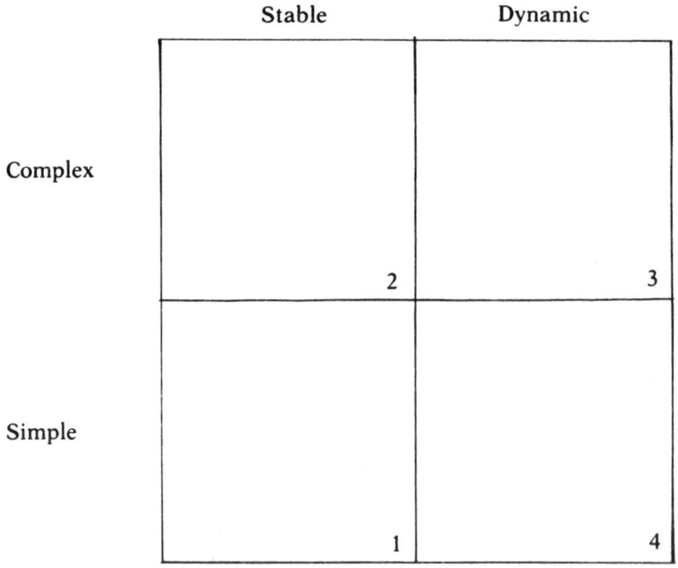

	Stable	Dynamic
Complex	2	3
Simple	1	4

Figure 4.1 *Four types of environment*

Cell 1: Simple and stable Most mass production firms fall into this category. Making cardboard boxes, fish fingers and even cars are all basically simple tasks. High volume, and stable demand is an essential prerequisite for mass production – it is not worth investing £20 million in a new production plant if you are not fairly sure that there will be customers for the product into the foreseeable future.

Mass production firms have particular structural features, the most significant being a high degree of standardization of work processes, products, and procedures. These firms are subject to an extensive exploration in the following chapter.

Cell 2: Complex and stable This is the environment facing Easton College. Complex, because the work is difficult to simplify and routinize, and stable because, for the foreseeable future, there will be a demand for business education.

Cell 3: Complex and dynamic Organizations facing complex *and* dynamic environments would include the management consultancy already mentioned, an advertising agency, and a computer software company. These types of organization need to be flexible to cope with the unpredictable shifts in the environment, whether it be new technologies, or changing fashions. Flexible organizations are the subject of Chapter 6.

Cell 4: Simple and dynamic These organizations also need to be flexible, but because the task is basically simple, changes can be brought about by the boss issuing new instructions to the staff (direct supervision). Dynamism in the environment will tend to preclude the development of mass production techniques, therefore Cell 4 firms are likely to be small, maybe owner/managed and need to be quick to respond to shifts in the marketplace.

3 Organizational configuration

3.1 Growth and structure

In Figure 4.2 we have tried to depict the relationship between the increasing size of the task facing the organization as it grows, and the structural changes introduced to cope with the enlarged workload. Structure 2 looks rather a mess, suggesting that adapting to growth is not a straightforward process. Few organizations are able to smoothly adjust and reorganize their structures so as to maintain a perfect 'fit' between the task and the structure. Structural changes are usually forced on to the management by pressure of circumstances, rather than being carefully planned and implemented. Changes usually take place in a piecemeal fashion, which can lead to problems.

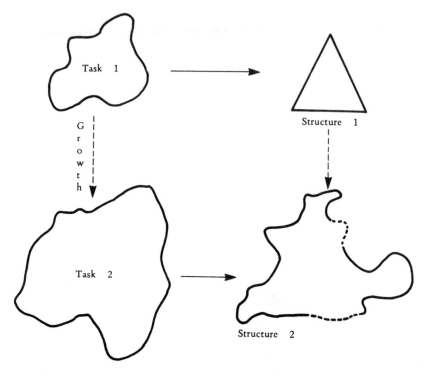

Figure 4.2   *Growth and structure*

- Some departments become chronically short of staff, others may be overstaffed as the work has shifted to a new area.
- The size of some departments may be too large for one manager to cope with.
- Promotion opportunities may not be spread evenly, thereby causing some resentment.
- Shortage of office space can lead to stress on staff.
- Anomalies in pay may result from uncoordinated recruitment activities.
- Frequent reorganizations can exhaust the goodwill of staff and engender cynicism.

Structural change is painful, and will often be resisted by managers until a deterioration in performance convinces them that the nettle of reorganization must be grasped. If the appropriate adaptations are not made in the structure, the organization may well die. A model of growth in organizations will help us explore this issue in more depth.

A model of organizational growth

Greiner[7] identifies five dimensions of organizational growth:

- The age of the organization.

- The size of the organization.
- Stages of evolution.
- Stages of revolution.
- The growth rate of the industry.

The older the organization, the more likely it is that attitudes will be deep rooted and difficult to change. Size causes problems of coordination and communication, especially if increasing size means increasing the number of management levels in the hierarchy.

Stages of evolution are periods of time where patterns of management remain stable, where only small organization changes are required. Stages of revolution are, in contrast, periods of substantial turbulence where serious upheaval of management practices is experienced. In these periods practices that were appropriate for a smaller sized operation are put under pressure. This can lead to frustration and disillusionment. If the organization copes successfully through the stage of revolution, it should then move through to another evolutionary stage of steady growth.

The growth rate of the industry and environment affects the pace at which changes are required in the firm. In a fast growing industry, a firm can, however, delay making the required organizational changes if it is earning profits easily.

Each evolutionary period is characterized by a dominant *management style* which is used to achieve growth. Each revolutionary period is characterized by the dominant *management problem* that must be solved before growth can continue.

We shall concentrate on the first two phases of growth in Greiner's model, the first phase being growth through creativity. Table 4.2 summarizes all five phases of growth.

Table 4.2 Organization practices during evolution in the five phases of growth (Greiner)

Category	Phase 1	Phase 2	Phase 3	Phase 4	Phase 5
Management focus	Make and sell	Efficiency of operations	Expansion of market	Consolidation of organization	Problem solving and innovation
Organization structure	Informal	Centralized and functional	Decentralized and geographical	Line staff and product groups	Matrix of teams
Top management style	Individualistic and entrepreneurial	Directive	Delegative	Watchdog	Participative
Control system	Market results	Standards and cost centres	Reports and profit centres	Plans and investment centres	Mutual goal setting
Management reward emphasis	Ownership	Salary and merit increases	Individual bonus	Profit sharing and stock options	Team bonus

Phase 1: Creativity   The founders of the organization are usually technically or entrepreneurially orientated. They disdain 'management' activities, their energies being directed towards product development and selling. We see this in Top Gear Driving School in Chapter 3. Organizational features of this first phase of growth are:

- Communication is frequent and informal.
- Staff work long hours and rewarded by small salaries and the possibility of 'ownership benefits'.
- Control comes from immediate marketplace feedback – the management react to the customers' actions.

As the size of the business increases various new demands emerge:

(a)   Larger production runs require knowledge about efficient manufacturing.
(b)   Increased numbers of employees cannot be managed exclusively through informal communication.
(c)   New employees are not motivated by an intense dedication to the product or the organization.
(d)   New capital is required, and new accounting systems are needed for financial control.

These demands put the founding managers under a great deal of stress; they are required to take on additional management responsibilities, and they tend to long for a return to the 'good old days' when things were not quite so complicated. What is required is a strong manager, conversant with new business techniques who can lead the firm out of their mess. But the founders may be unwilling to step aside, which may well lead to the stagnation and eventual death of the organization. A successful transition, however, will lead the firm on to a new phase of growth.

Phase 2: Direction   The new 'business manager' introduces the following changes to the organization:

(a)   A functional organization structure is introduced to separate manufacturing from marketing activities, and jobs tend to become more specialized.
(b)   Accounting systems for inventory and purchasing are introduced.
(c)   Incentive systems, budgets and work standards are adopted.
(d)   Communication becomes more formal and impersonal as a hierarchy of titles and positions builds.
(e)   New managers and their key supervisors take most of the responsibility and the decisions, leaving the lower level supervisors to concentrate on specialist functional matters.

These changes to the structure should enable the organization to pass through the crisis of leadership to a stage of evolutionary growth. This is by no means the end of the story, however. This new phase of growth in turn exposes weaknesses in the functional structure which need to be resolved before the firm can continue through to Phase 3, growth through delegation (see Table 4.2).

It is not too difficult to see parallels between Greiner's early phases of growth and the experiences of Easton College. The pioneering ethos in the early years of the college, where everyone mucked in because there were so few specialists, administrators and managers, has given way to a much more formalized, specialized and hierarchical organization. The frequent restructuring of the college, stemming from the growth in student and staff numbers, has not been achieved smoothly and painlessly. Indeed, some staff have clearly not recovered from the pace and scale of the changes visited upon them.

So that we can delve a little deeper into these processes of adaptation we shall pick up on two particular structural developments that emerge in the transition from the small, simple organization in Phase 1, to the increasingly elaborate structure of Phase 2. These are the complications in the structure that are brought about by an increase in specialization. In particular the development of the *functional structure* and secondly, the emergence of staff specialists who are introducing various systems into the organization like budgeting, production planning and quality control.

Functional specialization

One of the features of Greiner's Phase 2 is the reorganization of people into separate functions like for example production, sales, and administration. The advantages of grouping staff by function are as follows:

- *Common supervision:* A manager is named for each function, and is held responsible for it. The manager is able to coordinate the work of the function through giving direct orders, and by monitoring the performance of the staff.
- *Common resources:* Budgets can be established for each department. Economies in equipment utilization can be gained by grouping together staff doing similar work.
- *Mutual adjustment:* Grouping people together physically increases the opportunities for informal communication to assist in coordinating their work.

However, the benefits resulting from the improvements in coordination *within* each function are to a certain extent mitigated by the increasing problems of coordination *between* functions. We now start to see a fragmentation of the once united small organization into a number of increasingly inward-looking sub-units. Functional structures encourage specialization which, although it increases the efficiency with which particular tasks are done, also has the effect of narrowing people's outlooks.

At Easton College separate schools have been established specializing in different aspects of business. Almost inevitably, 'us' and 'them' attitudes are emerging between staff in different schools; the sense of a shared task and a united community has been supplanted by tension, scapegoating and frequent arguments and disagreements. Staff in the School of Accounting tend to consider all other non-accounting staff as rather low level and almost superfluous, and mutterings about 'going it alone' and withdrawing cooperation are growing louder. There is a running battle between academic staff and the now centralized reprographics unit. This revolves around the lecturers' demands for a 'same day photocopying service'. The reprographics unit consider this requirement to be ludicrously unrealistic, and have instituted a procedure which requires staff to submit items for copying a minimum of two weeks before they are needed.

These problems and conflicts never seemed to arise when the college was smaller and, on the face of it, far less 'organized'.

If we shift our sights away from the college situation, and consider functional relations within the typical manufacturing company we can consider how production staff and sales staff might have conflicting views about product policy.

Sales staff	*Production staff*
'Wide product range to satisfy all possible customer groups.'	'Limited product range eases production problems and permits long production runs.'
'Top quality coupled with a competitive price.'	'Low cost coupled with high quality is unrealistic, you can have one or the other.'
'Immediate response to customers requests.'	'Steady demands on production so that we can schedule efficiently.'

So differences of outlook will inevitably emerge, because what makes the salesperson's life easier means additional work for the production supervisor. If we include a third function, finance, we see that they are likely to fall out with everyone! Accounting staff are concerned, amongst other things, with keeping control of working capital, so finished goods, stock, work in progress and inventories should all be kept to a minimum. However, salespeople like to promise delivery today from a stock of all the items the customer would possibly want. They would also like to offer generous credit terms to the customer to make the sale easier. Elsewhere in the structure the production manager is trying to keep utilization of the machinery as high as possible as well as attempting to meet the production targets set for him or her. So what must never happen is a 'stock-out' of components, or a machine breakdown that cannot be repaired immediately with spares kept on site. And one way to increase capacity utilization is to make sure the work is stocked up at the end of the bench waiting to be done. Moreover, when it comes to materials budgets, staff budgets and capital equipment purchases, sales and production managers will all be pitching in with bids for 'essential' resources.

One way of looking at this inter-functional conflict is to view it as a healthy situation of dynamic tension, and whilst everyone is batting for their own department's interests, the interests of the organization as a whole are best served, as long as no one function gets the upper hand and providing each function has been given clear targets to fulfil. Another, less positive view would be of different groups pulling the organization apart, where no one seems to be looking after the interests of the customer.

Where differences occur between the functions, or where a problem arises which cannot be resolved within one function (e.g. the launch of a new product), some form of coordination must be effected *between* the functions. The obvious system is for the manager in charge of the two (or more) functions to get involved – a form of coordination through direct supervision. The chart in Figure 4.3 illustrates the hierarchy of the functional structure, and in this structure any differences between sales and production would need to be passed up to the Managing Director.

These problems arising from functional specialization were considered in an important piece of empirical research carried out by Lawrence and Lorsch. They called the tendency for firms to divide into specialist departments 'differentiation'. Aspects of differentiation include the goals of each department, the time scales they are working to, the style of management, and the formality of the departmental structure. They observed, through studying firms in three different industries (plastics, food and containers), that the environment that the firms were facing influenced the degree of differentiation within the firms. Plastics firms were facing a dynamic environment with a continually changing body of scientific knowledge. Consequently firms required specialist research departments in order to keep abreast

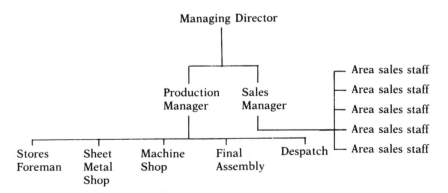

Figure 4.3 *A functional structure*

with changing plastics technology. Presumably, firms who had not bothered to get into research and development in a big way were not likely to thrive as they would always be following the leaders.

To illustrate the degree of differentiation in the successful plastics firms consider the differences in orientation between the production department and the fundamental research unit.

Production	*Fundamental research*
■ Very formal structure	■ Informal organization
■ Short time horizons (days/weeks)	■ Long time horizons (ten years or more)
■ Production goals clearly defined and performance easily measurable.	■ Vague goal; performance measurement difficult.

Lawrence and Lorsch found that those organizations that had achieved a degree of differentiation *consistent* with the requirements of the environment were also the most successful organizations. But, they also found that the most successful organizations were not only highly differentiated, they achieved high levels of *integration* or coordination as well. They defined integration as being:

> 'the quality of the state of collaboration that exists among departments that are required to achieve unity of effort by the demands of the environment.'

For instance, there would be little point in the research and development department coming up with a sensational product breakthrough if either the production people said it was impossible to manufacture the product in sufficiently large quantities, or if the marketing people estimated that the potential market for the new product was too small. Clearly the successful firm requires these functions not only to develop their various specialisms commensurate with the demands of the market-place, but also that they should effectively communicate with each other.

We have suggested that the most straightforward coordination mechanism in this circumstance is the hierarchy; liaison is effected by the instructions delivered by the common boss of the functions concerned. However, Lawrence and Lorsch's research suggested that, whereas this integrating mechanism was successful for firms facing relatively simple and stable environments, it was inappropriate for the firms facing complex, dynamic environments. The managers in the latter firms just do not have the knowledge or the expertise to solve these problems, nor have they the time to spend on them, as dynamic environments suggest that problems will be cropping up thick and fast. The firms facing dynamic environments needed to look for other ways of coordinating and liaising between the functions.

We shall now try to pull together the links between environment and structure.

Stability and standardization

Stability in the environment permits standardization. Depending on the complexity of the task, the organization standardizes in different ways. If the task is a simple one the organization can invest time and effort in finding out the most efficient way of doing it. The task can be broken down into a series of simple steps, furthermore each step can be analysed to produce the most efficient working methods. In some cases the task can be so simplified that manual work can be replaced by machine work. So, where an organization is growing up facing a simple and stable environment it will be looking to take advantage of these circumstances, so as to reap the benefits of standardization.

Complex tasks, however, do not lend themselves to this type of standardization. But, complexity coupled with stability makes it workwhile to invest in the development of skilled specialists who can use their particular expertise to solve these complex problems. It is worth spending seven years training doctors, because we can be certain that their expertise will be needed in the future. We can standardize the skills of these professional people, and they can then use their knowledge to help solve complex problems.

In this chapter, we have selected a college as an example of a growing organization. This organization is facing a complex but relatively stable environment. We would therefore expect to see standardization of skills operating as a primary coordinating mechanism.

We shall now examine how the structure of a growing organization evolves when it is facing a stable environment, using the Mintzberg structure diagram introduced in Chapter 3.

Two forms of bureaucracy

Our small organization was represented by the simple structure of Figure 4.4. The three parts of the structure being the strategic apex, the operating core, and the middle line which links the two together.

The organization growing up facing a stable and simple environment can take advantage of the standardization of work processes, and of standardized outputs. Different groups of staff are involved with these types of standardization.

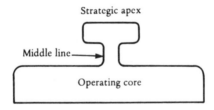

Figure 4.4 *The simple structure*

Work study officers are the people who analyse the working methods, and redesign the production systems to improve efficiency both in manufacturing and in the information processing and redesigned forms in the service sector, e.g. the Department of Social Security. Again it is the simplicity and the stability of the task which makes it possible to devise these improved methods of working.

Planning, quality control and budgeting staff are all attempting to standardize different aspects of the organization's activities so that plans, outputs, control mechanisms and costs are linked.

In the early stages of the organization's life most of these standardizing activities would be carried out by the managers and supervisors in the middle line, and the operatives themselves. But, as the organization grows, these tasks are increasingly shifted away from the line management, to specialist staff. So we have an emerging group of staff who do not fit the three parts of the organization that have been identified so far. This group of analysts Mintzberg has called the *technostructure*, and they are represented as a separate part of the organization (see Figure 4.5).

The powers to plan the way the work should be done, to decide on quality standards, and to order materials, have now been shifted away from the line managers. These things are now decided by staff people who are not held directly responsible for the achievement of production targets and the like. This shift of decision making power away from the middle line can often be a source of resentment, and a perennial area for conflict. The line managers may resent the unrealistic standards and budgets set for them, and they are likely to criticize the lack of direct production experience they perceive in the technostructure. Above all, the ability to make decisions about who does what, when and how was a source of influence that the line managers once had, which has now been taken away from them.

In the developing organization another group of staff-type activities emerges which provides support to the main work of the organization. These *support staff* are not concerned with effecting standardization like the analysts in the technostructure, they provide a range of services which generally could be bought in from outside suppliers. Activities like building maintenance, the works canteen, market research, public

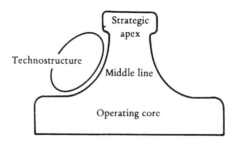

Figure 4.5

relations, the sports club, and the office cleaners could all be subcontracted to outside firms. Large organizations prefer, however, to provide many of these services 'in-house', primarily as a means of exerting more control over them. So, in a developing organization two distinct types of 'staff' activity emerge:

- *The technostructure*, who are very closely tied in to the main work of the organization, and are likely, therefore, to have a fair amount of influence over events and decisions.
- *The support staff*, who by their very nature are fairly peripheral to the main thrust of the organization. Consequently they are likely to be relatively uninfluential, because, in the last resort, they could be replaced by outside contractors.

In the large, mass production organization both of these staff groups are likely to be substantial features of the structure. This structure has been called a *'machine bureaucracy'* by Mintzberg,[8] and the diagram depicting it can be found in Figure 4.6.

The machine bureaucratic form, then, emerges where the organization is living in a simple and stable environment.

The structure that emerges in a *complex* and stable environment, the structure of the college for example, is also bureaucratic, but although the work is predictable (i.e. teaching) it is also complex, and hence the people doing the work must be allowed a degree of discretion. No two teachers approach the topic in the same way, and the same would apply to the work of doctors, chartered accountants, lawyers and social workers. So although the work is stable and predictable, the ways of tackling it are not, except in the general sense. The predictability, coupled with complexity means that *standardized skills* can be brought to the problems. In these *professional bureaucracies* individual workers in the operating core work, to a large degree, independently of their colleagues. Therefore coordination of the activities of all these independent professionals could be a problem. Most of the coordination that is necessary is achieved through training and appointing staff with predictable, 'standardized' sets of skills.

When the lecturers at Easton College come to teach the final year of

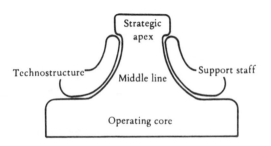

Figure 4.6 *The machine bureaucracy*

a business degree course they can assume that the students will already know something about the financing of a firm, the rudiments of marketing, and personnel management etc. This is because the lecturers know what to expect of their colleagues teaching on the earlier years of the degree. So, through the design of the course and the appointment of a number of different experts, a coordinated and integrated output is assured, i.e. a student with a rounded knowledge of business.

Because so few of the work processes of the professional bureaucracy can be standardized, and standardizing outputs is similarly difficult ('processed clients' in a law practice, 'cured patients', 'taught students' all are difficult areas in which to set agreed, measurable standards), the size of the technostructure in the professional bureaucracy is very small. The only significant technostructure role is played by training and recruiting specialists who are helping in the standardization of skills. Although, in most professional bureaucracies the expensive training necessary is carried on outside of the organization (in universities, for example).

However, the support staff can be quite a sizeable part of the organization; the logic being that it is a waste of money having expensive professionals spending time doing jobs which could be done by cheaper support staff. So, in the college example, we see the emergence of centralized reprographics, 'faculty office' which carries out much of the routine administration formerly done by lecturers (like the examination arrangements, and admissions). Support staff activities would also include data processing, gardening and publicity.

Because the professionals can and do operate with a great degree of independence, they require little supervision. Hence spans of control can be quite large (e.g. the Head of School of Business at Easton College has a span of thirty-three staff). Consequently, even though there are often large numbers of professionals in the operating core, there is no great need for an extensive hierarchy of middle managers. These features of the structure of the professional bureaucracy are depicted in Figure 4.7.[9]

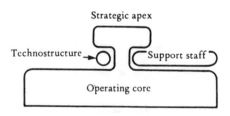

Figure 4.7 *The professional bureaucracy*

3.2 *Organizational arrangements*

Centralization and decentralization

We have seen that a good deal of decision making discretion is located in the operating core of the professional bureaucracy. On the other hand, in most large machine bureaucracies decisions are centralized as far as possible at the apex of the structure. In this section we consider centralization and decentralization as being two ends of a continuum, in between these extremes we can identify two limited forms of decentralization.

In so doing we shall briefly examine four types of decision making structures: a highly centralized structure; a structure with limited vertical decentralization; one with limited horizontal decentralization; and, finally, a horizontally and vertically decentralized structure.

The motives for decentralizing decision making power:

■ All decisions cannot be understood at one point, the apex, of the organization. This may result from the complexities of the decision issues, which are beyond the scope of the individual decision maker. Or it could be because the information required to make good decisions cannot easily be transferred from other parts of the structure to the apex.

■ Decentralization allows a quick response to local conditions. Staff lower down the hierarchy who are in touch with the day-to-day changes in their area of operations can be allowed to react to them without needing to get approval from above.

■ Decentralization can be a stimulus to motivation. Staff who feel they can take on more responsibilities may respond positively to being given more decision making discretion.

Two forms of decentralization will concern us here:

(a) *Vertical decentralization:* This is where formal power to make decisions is passed down the *line* to lower level managers and supervisors.

(b) *Horizontal decentralization:* Here decision making power is dispersed away from the line to staff groups, notably to analysts in the technostructure.

A centralized structure (Figure 4.8) Here all significant decisions are made at the apex of the organization, usually by one person, the chief executive. This implies that the environment facing the organization is simple, otherwise one person would not be able to take all the decisions. As there is no horizontal decentralization to the technostructure, we can deduce that standardization is not a primary means of coordinating the work. So, direct supervision is the likely coordinating mechanism, having taken the decision the chief executive issues new instructions to the subordinates.

Some structures which would normally display a degree of decentralization, can, when faced by a crisis temporarily become extremely centralized. This is because direct supervision is the tightest form of coordination as only one brain is involved; decisions can be made rapidly, and communicated immediately to the staff.

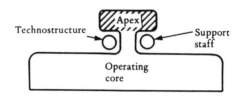

Figure 4.8 *The centralized structure (shaded area indicates the location of the most important decisions)*

Limited vertical decentralization (Figure 4.9) When the size of the task facing the centralized structure becomes too large (either through continued expansion in one market, or maybe because of entering new markets, and developing new products), some form of vertical decentralization must take place. Note that this is not because the tasks of the organization have become more *complex*, it is merely that they have grown too large for one man to keep tabs on. So, in a vertically decentralized structure some formal decision making power is passed down the line to middle managers. This is part of the process of *delegation* (the mechanics of delegation and some problems associated with it, are considered in the following management section). Clearly, in the growing organization the delegation process is one way of coping with an overload of decision making at the apex of the structure.

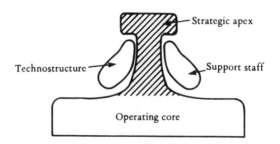

Figure 4.9 *Limited vertical decentralization (shaded area indicates location of the most important decisions)*

Limited horizontal decentralization (Figure 4.10) Here power to make some decisions has shifted away from the line to the staff analysts in the technostructure. Where the organization is making extensive use of standardization of work processes (the machine bureaucracy), decision making powers which used to be with the line managers have been removed. Decisions about work methods, scheduling, quality, and the power to appoint and to discipline operatives may be shifted to specialist staff. However, as we have seen, organizations which adopt extensive standardization of work processes are invariably operating in simple and stable environments. Hence formal power over the big decisions is still likely to be highly centralized at the apex. The technostructure has acquired a limited amount of *informal* power to influence events, through the systems it develops, and through the advice it gives to the line management.

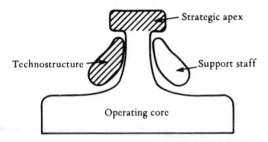

Figure 4.10 *Limited horizontal decentralization (shaded area indicates location of the most important decisions)*

Vertical and horizontal decentralization (Figure 4.11) We have already established that, due to the complexity of the task the professional bureaucracy (the college, the hospital etc.) is a decentralized structure. Decision making power resides with the expert professionals in the operating core, as depicted in Figure 4.11.

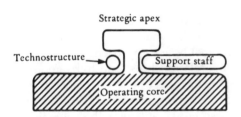

Figure 4.11 *Vertical and horizontal decentralization (shaded area indicates location of the most important decisions)*

Developing an organization's culture

The culture of an organization can be defined as a set of values, norms and beliefs which are shared by the members of the organization.[10] Other words often used to describe this phenomenon include the 'atmosphere', 'norms', 'character', or 'style' of the organization. If you have worked in different organizations, or in different parts of a large organization, you can probably reflect on how differently these organizations 'felt' to be in. In some organizations the atmosphere seems to be quite relaxed and informal, in others people seem to be wary and suspicious. We need to consider whether these differences are inevitable features of particular types of organization, or whether there are a range of options open to all organizations, regardless of the tasks facing them.

We might look first of all at how a culture can come to be established in an organization. In Chapter 3 we explored the workings of a small organization, one established by a strong, entrepreneurial individual. Because a fledgling organization starts almost with a blank sheet, the personalities, attitudes and prejudices of the founding members, particularly the owner/manager, can play a very substantial part in laying down the culture of the organization. In addition, those people involved in the early stages of establishing a new organization have a shared sense of mission, a commitment to the success of the venture.

As the organization grows and develops precedents are set which begin to shape permanent features of the culture. Stories about past successes, characters and problems get recounted to newcomers, and serve to reinforce the established members' identification with 'their' organization.

When the organization reaches a particular stage strenuous efforts are made to preserve the culture, through devices such as recruitment and promotion policies, and indoctrination programmes, the organization only recruits people who are likely to 'fit in' to the established culture; 'like promotes like', so no one who reaches a senior position in the structure is liable to rock the boat. Also training and induction programmes are devised to inculcate into new members the 'right' attitudes and beliefs.

We have seen how the culture of Easton College seemed to emerge from the personal styles of two or three powerful individuals. Staff joining this college from other similar institutions have remarked on the informal, casual and almost reckless manner in which new developments are approached. The atmosphere is optimistic, interpersonal relationships tend to be good and morale is generally high. How much is this due to the leadership of the college? Perhaps other factors are equally significant, like the opportunities for advancement and personal achievement, the newness of the college, and the average age of the staff? The differences in culture between two similar professional bureaucracies cannot, obviously, be explained by the similarity of their work, or their structures. Why is it that another polytechnic of similar size and age projects a cautious, sober and formal atmosphere?

Culture is clearly an important aspect of organizations, especially for the persons working in them. An employee is unlikely to be happy if he or she is fundamentally at odds with the organization's culture. Some people thrive in unpredictable, flexible organizations, where promotion comes rapidly to those with energy and the need for power. For others, the safe predictability of the large bureaucracy suits their personalities – few changes, and a steady promotion ladder available for those who keep their noses clean.

The management style of the founders of the organization does appear to exert a strong influence on the emerging culture. The style can be perpetuated long after the founders have left the organization by the processes of 'myth building', promotion, recruitment and indoctrination.[11] Thus the culture of the organization assumes an existence separate from the particular individuals inhabiting it at any moment. However, new cultures can emerge, or even be imposed, to replace the prevailing one.

3.3 Management

Management style

Figure 4.12 lists a range of style options that a manager may adopt. They have been grouped into two broad categories: *autocratic* styles (where the decision making power resides firmly with the manager), and *democratic* styles (where there is some involvement of subordinates in decision making). We shall work through this 'menu' of styles, beginning with the authoritarian management style.

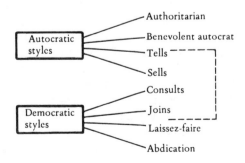

Figure 4.12 *A menu of management styles*

Authoritarian This style is autocratic in so far as decisions are taken by the manager and imposed upon subordinates. Subordinates comply through fear of punishment or because they acknowledge the right of managers to give them orders (they acknowledge their formal power, or authority), or maybe through a combination of the two. Being authoritarian is not the same thing as being autocratic, although authoritarian managers *are* autocratic. It implies that managers either enjoy or feel it is necessary to exercise power over subordinates over and above that required strictly for the accomplishment of the task. It can be a symptom of a lack of inherent leadership qualities in inadequate managers, who resort to the formal powers of their office as the only means they have to influence their subordinates.

Benevolent autocrat Autocracy with a smile! This is the rather paternalistic, 'patting on the head' style of father knows best. It is likely to appeal to subordinates who are genuinely looking for someone else to make the decisions for them, and who respect and admire their boss. It will really grate on subordinates who think they probably know as much, if not more than their manager.

Tells This is the autocratic end of a continuum proposed by Tannenbaum and Schmidt[12] which we have incorporated in our style menu (the dotted lines in Figure 4.12 mark the continuum). Here the manager is simply autocratic, selecting the decision and communicating it to his or her subordinates. There is no overlay of paternalism, or authoritarianism.

Sells Here autocratic managers, sensing the possibilities of some resistance to decisions, attempt to convince or persuade the subordinates of the correctness of decisions. This may well be because autocratic managers perceive their relative lack of power to enforce their decisions, or because it is necessary for the subordinates to *positively* accept their decisions.

Consults This is the first of the styles which involves some participation from subordinates. Managers identify the problem, and invite suggestions from subordinates. Having considered these alternatives, however, they still retain the right to make the decision themselves. This consulting style is about as far as most managers are prepared to go down this continuum, and for most managers this is what 'industrial democracy' and 'participation' is all about. Of course, consultation can backfire on managers. If the group comes up with a solution to the problem which is rejected by managers in favour of their own views, the group may resent the imposition of the decision even more than if it was made autocratically without any pretence of consultation.

Joins Managers still define the problem but they then pass the decision over to the group; they have (in theory) one vote like everyone else. Few managers in a conventional organizational setting are prepared to slide this far along the continuum, except for the most inconsequential decisions, like deciding what colour to repaint the office walls. We should not be surprised at this. For a number of reasons managers will wish to hang on to as much decision making power as they can.

- It took a whole lot getting into a management position, so what is the point of giving away all the power once you get there?
- Managers will be held accountable for the vast majority of decisions that are taken in their sections. They will be reluctant to carry the can for decisions they do not agree with.
- The manager may well be privy to information, or possess knowledge which is not available to subordinates. Without this additional information they are unlikely to come to a 'good' decision.
- The decisions may be ones which only the manager can take, like disciplining a subordinate.

Not-for-profit organizations can sometimes get trapped in ideological twists with inappropriate uses of this type of managerial style, 'sell out' and 'she/he used to be one of us' may be charges and pressures put on managers in such settings.

Laissez-faire Managers consciously, and positively leave the group to get on with it. They trust their judgements, and are there as a source of help or advice should the group require it.

Abdication This is where managers leave the group alone for negative reasons. They deliberately avoid contact, disappear when trouble looms and appear to have little interest in the group or its activities. Again, this may be a symptom of an inadequately trained manager, or one who is not temperamentally suited to the role.

We have explored a range of styles primarily along one dimension; the degree of participation in the decision making process. Other dimensions explored in the literature are the concern for task dimension and the concern for people dimension (e.g. Blake and Mouton,[13] and Reddin,[14] see page 80). At one extreme the manager is obsessed witrh operational matters, and in particular improving the efficiency of the unit. This high concern for task to the exclusion of the human dimension can be found in many managers, but is particularly prevalent in production situations, where a combination of intense pressure to meet quantifiable targets, coupled with the 'engineering' orientation of many production managers encourages a 'hard-nosed' management style. At the other extreme the manager is greatly concerned with process issues, with the encouragement of a friendly, satisfying and hassle-free group climate. An 'ideal type' is suggested by Blake and Mouton, where managers display a high concern for task accomplishment *through* their high concern for people.

Selecting a management style

Is the manager free to choose from the whole range of styles in Figure 4.12 or are there personal and organizational constraints operating to limit the choice? For example, can a manager operating in a large manufacturing organization choose a democratic style of management if everyone else is sticking to an autocratic approach? Creating islands of participation in a sea of autocracy is challenging for both the manager and the subordinates. Being more democratic could be perceived as a sign of weakness by subordinates, superiors and colleagues alike. Dangerous precedents may be set, expectations may be raised in subordinates which cannot be fulfilled. The subordinates might find it almost impossible to respond to the opportunities to participate offered to them. Years of working in a culture in which operators are not considered capable of contributing anything, where managers alone have the knowledge and right to make decisions, is likely to engender a high degree of suspicion and scepticism amongst subordinates.

If the manager is by nature a gregarious and friendly person, he or she is unlikely to be able to convincingly behave in an authoritarian manner. People who find it difficult to be warm and approachable will come across rather falsely if they try to use a style which is highly people orientated. A person's views about human nature can also influence the way they approach the management role.

McGregor[15] postulated two different views of human nature that a manager might hold. One view, Theory X, is based on the following assumptions:

- People have an inherent dislike of work – they will avoid it if possible.
- Because of this most people must be controlled or threatened before they will work hard enough.
- People prefer to be directed, dislike responsibility and desire security.

Managers with this view of their subordinates (of course it doesn't apply to them!), are liable to behave towards them in a particular way. They will assume that as soon as their backs are turned staff will down tools, so they need to constantly cajole them and check up on them. Their subordinates are incapable of exercising any initiative, so they must spell out how to do the job in the smallest details. In other words, he treats them like children.

The key feature of McGregor's theory is the circular nature of these assumptions. If you treat people like children they will behave like children, and thus continually reinforce the manager's Theory X view of people. Once this loop is started up, years and years of experience convince the manager that he is right, which makes it very difficult to persuade him that he might have got it wrong.

Theory Y has a different view and might be a more accurate representation of human nature:

- Work is as natural as rest or play.
- People will direct themselves if they are committed to the aims of the organization.
- Satisfying jobs lead to commitment to the organization.
- People learn to accept and seek responsibility.
- People's imagination and creativity can be harnessed to solve work problems.
- Under most working conditions the intellectual potential of most workers is underutilized.

The manager with Theory Y assumptions will treat staff like adults, and they will respond with these positive traits, thus confirming the original assumptions.

So, assumptions about human nature may go a long way towards explaining the style a particular manager adopts. However, there is in what we have written an implied criticism of managers with Theory X views. If the organizational setting is such that, due to the nature of the production process, operatives are given extremely limited, tedious and repetitive jobs to do – the sorts of jobs that a four-year-old would soon get bored with – is it any surprise that they exhibit responses which seem to fit a Theory X view of the world? Can managers, given the job of controlling these people, be blamed if they adopt a rather jaundiced view of the liberal Theory Y outlook?

Before we leave the issue of management style, we could usefully link back to our discussion of decentralization, where it was suggested that particular organizations would, because of the nature of the tasks they are tackling, be either centralized or decentralized (see pages 69–71). In particular, the professional bureaucracy would inevitably be decentralized. This presumably implies that only democratic styles would be effective in this type of organization. Similarly, autocratic styles would seem to fit the circumstances of the highly centralized machine bureaucracy. This is leading us towards a situational, or contingency approach to management style which we shall take up further in Chapter 6.

Delegation

A manager's attitude towards subordinates is likely to figure significantly in his decision to delegate some of his responsibilities to those subordinates. A manager with Theory X assumptions, for instance, will be reluctant to risk passing on important tasks to subordinates. But, as we have seen, delegation is one of the ways in which an organization copes with a growing workload. Delegation is an essentially dynamic process whereby tasks are passed down the hierarchy, and through it new jobs are created. So in the growing organization, delegation is a necessity, not an option, for the manager.

Managers delegate when they deliberately choose to give a subordinate authority to carry out a piece of work which they could have decided to keep to themselves. So, if the manager would ordinarily order the stationery but he chooses to pass this job on to a subordinate, he is delegating that particular task. Note, though, the important distinction between delegation and *work allocation*. If the same manager gives his secretary a letter to type, that is work allocation, because typing letters is not a task that the manager would ordinarily carry out.

If the subordinate makes a hash of ordering the stationery, who is held responsible? The task itself has been passed on, but the manager still remains *accountable* for the performance of the task. So if, through a mistake made by the subordinate, 400 reams of A5 are delivered, where only 40 reams of A4 were required, the office manager will have to take the brunt of criticism and admonition. He, in turn, may well feel like kicking the subordinate, but in a sense *organizationally* he is still responsible for this task.

Accepting responsibility for actions of subordinates is a very grey area. For example, would you take full responsibility for shoddy work by subordinates if you have no say in their appointment? Can you justifiably be held accountable for the work of inadequately trained staff that were foisted upon you?

The advantages of delegation are firstly, that it relieves the overburdened manager of some tasks. In the context of the growing organization, this is likely to be the strongest motive for delegating. The subordinates, in turn, should benefit from the enhanced responsibility they are being entrusted with. If the subordinates are more motivated through these additional responsibilities, and if the manager's time is freed up to enable him to tackle important planning and improvement projects, the delegation process should enhance the performance of the whole unit.

Why is it, then, that so few managers delegate effectively? Consider some of these explanations:

(a) The manager feels that the subordinate is incapable of doing the job properly, it would take time to train him to do it well, and hence it is quicker for the manager to do the job himself. There is a good deal of sense in this explanation. For delegation to be effective, it must take up time in the *short term*, in the long term the manager should be permanently freed of a routine task.

(b) The subordinate has not got access to knowledge possessed by the manager which is essential for the successful accomplishment of the task. Again, a plausible reason for not delegating as, if we recall the investigations of Mintzberg into the nature of managerial work, a great emphasis was seen to be placed by managers on the *verbal* communication media. A vast amount of information picked up through conversations, informal and formal meetings, telephone calls and tours is stored in the manager's head. Conscious efforts must therefore be made to make this information available to subordinates (e.g. through thorough briefings; involving the subordinate directly in relevant meetings; making notes of phone calls etc.). There are few things more demotivating than to have tried your best to do a good job for your boss, only to be told that your efforts are useless due to some important factor you were not made aware of.

(c) Some equally understandable, but perhaps less justifiable reasons for not delegating are as follows:

- The manager feels he needs to be burdened by trivia, by tasks which he should pass on to subordinates. This could be because he lacks the confidence to actually *manage*, perhaps, because he cannot do it, or because he does not know how to.
- The manager likes to keep all the interesting jobs, only passing on tedious ones to subordinates.
- Managers may feel the need to be *seen* to be busy. Sitting and thinking about ways of improving the department might actually be a very productive activity, but it could look like sheer idleness. In some organizations a frantic culture is encouraged, where the most highly regarded managers are continually rushing around, phones are ringing, people are flying in and out of his office. It's a brave person who, in this environment, turns his chair to the window, puts his feet on the desk and just thinks.
- Some basic fears may be at the root of a reluctance to delegate. Fear that the subordinate would do a better job than the manager; fears that continual delegation will no longer mean that the manager is indispensable; or fear that a promising subordinate will be promoted away from the section through successfully coping with additional responsibilities.

A theme which runs through many of these reasons for a lack of delegation, or for deliberately poor attempts to delegate is inappropriate, or non-existent management development. The 'sink or swim' policy of too many organizations towards systematic attempts to develop staff to assume management positions, has resulted in a lot of unhappy, and poorly performing managers. It is no great surprise that some newly appointed managers engage in a process of *negative delegation*, where instead of passing on tasks to subordinates, they hang on to work which they used to do before they were promoted. This is almost the same as pinching work from subordinate positions;

work which the new manager is good at, which can be used to fill his day and thus leave no time for managing, and which makes him feel good, by boosting his confidence.

Some of the more unpalatable management styles identified in the previous sections could be adopted by the new manager floundering in this uncomfortable new role, e.g. the authoritarian style, relying solely on formal power, or the abdicator who is running away from the responsibilities of management.

A useful model of leadership which addresses the issue of delegation and builds on the earlier theories mentioned is the *situational leadership* framework put forward by Hersey and Blanchard.[16] They agree that there are four basic leadership styles and four typologies of followers. The most appropriate leadership style is dependent upon the nature of the task and the commitment and competencies of the follower. The four styles are in Table 4.3

Table 4.3   Situational leadership – four basic styles

(S1) **Directing**	High directive/low supportive leader behaviour. Leader tells follower what to do, when, how and where. Communication and decision-making is one way and monitoring is systematic.
(S2) **Coaching**	High directive/high supportive behaviour. The leader still sets direction but seeks to hear follower's feelings and thoughts about decision. Leader retains control.
(S3) **Supporting**	High supportive/low directive leader behaviour. Day-to-day control placed with follower. Leader acknowledges follower's input and facilitates problem-solving.
(S4) **Delegating**	Low supportive/low directive leader behaviour. Leader and follower seek joint agreement on tasks. Decision-making delegated to follower.

They examine leadership behaviour in terms of task (directive) related activities (e.g. setting goals, planning, coordinating, monitoring) and person-orientated (supportive) behaviours (e.g. coaching, training and praising).

Hersey and Blanchard found that leadership style was mainly influenced by the 'development' level of the follower.

Development level is defined as competence and commitment to undertake the task without supervision.

■ Competence includes knowledge skills from training, education or experience.
■ Commitment includes motivation and confidence.

Situational leadership identified four development levels: low (D1), low to moderate (D2), moderate to high (D3) and high (D4). The model is depicted in Figure 4.13.

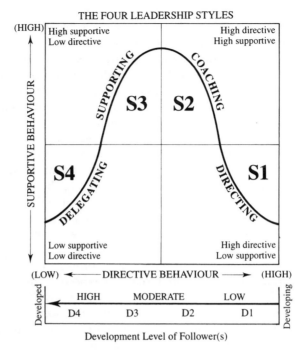

Figure 4.13 *Situational leadership model*

What we see from the model is the following:

1 The four styles relate to different development levels of the followers:

- Directing (S1) to lower development level (D1)
- Coaching (S2) to moderate development level (D2)
- Supporting (S3) to moderate to high development level (D3)
- Delegating (S4) to high development level (D4).

2 Given any task, the leader can use the 'S' curve as a development cycle: taking someone from a low development level (S1), coaching them (S2), supporting them as they gain more confidence and competence (S3) and finally delegating tasks (S4).

3 The simplicity or complexity of the task will mean that some people who are D4 on one task may be D2 or D1 on another task.

4 The implication, which is often contrary to the myth is that leaders need to have style flexibility rather than one constant style.

3.4 Groups

Group size and coordination

Organizations growing up in simple and stable environments can make greater use of standardization to achieve coordination. But extensive standardization of work processes is a feature of maturing organizations reaching large scale operations, where it is worth analysing and redesigning the work methods because the task is repeated thousands of times. Before the organization in the simple and stable environment reaches this point it will need to employ other, non-standardizing mechanisms for coordination. The most appropriate mechanism being direct supervision.

If direct supervision is still the primary coordinating mechanism in the organization, this must place a limit on the size of the formal groups or units reporting to a supervisor. Here the limited span of control concept *does* apply, restricting the potential size of units to numbers of staff that one person can effectively supervise.

Let us turn now to complex tasks. Where the complex work is being undertaken by professionals who can operate *independently* of one another, we can tolerate quite large unit sizes. For example, the accounting practice where each professional serves his or her own group of clients; or in the college, where it is quite feasible for a lecturer to perform lecturing and research duties with the minimum of contact with colleagues. Thus, quite large unit sizes are feasible.

However, some complex work requires professionals to work together very closely. Redesigning a degree course, for example, requires that a team of lecturers from different disciplines get together to share ideas, discuss and agree new proposals. Ideally, this group should involve everyone who is likely to have some involvement in the redesigned course, but this could be upwards of thirty staff members. The coordination mechanism being used in this degree development group is mutual adjustment, direct face-to-face informal communication between the people directly involved in the task. If you have seen committees of thirty plus at work you may well be aware of how ineffective they are. Either everyone who wants a say, gets a say, thus the meetings end up lasting all day; or, to keep the proceedings as brief as possible people cannot, or choose not, to contribute their opinions, in which case they are only participating in a passive, receptive way in the decision process. Consequently, complex tasks which require professionals to work interdependently, using mutual adjustment, can only effectively be tackled by *small groups*.

So, if the organization is growing up in a stable environment, the primary means of coordination being used are likely to influence the size of individual units. Where simple tasks are being tackled and direct supervision is still predominant (because the standardization of work processes has not yet had a major impact), there will be an upper limit on unit size. Where the task is complex and stable, but it can be performed essentially independently by trained professionals, unit sizes can be quite large. But where the work is complex *and* interdependent, the mutual adjustment mechanism is employed which severely restricts the size of the group.

Working against these constraints on unit size is a tendency for growing organizations to add extra staff to existing units to cope with increasing workloads. It is far easier to almost surreptitiously add one extra member of staff to an existing unit, than it would be to create another unit altogether, even though the logic of effective coordination suggests that this would be more efficient. Consequently, almost by default, incremental additions to existing groups can result in unwieldy, over-large units. Divisions of units into subunits may be influenced by the nature of the task and the ability to have clear boundaries about when tasks begin and end. This view is held by those who take a sound technical perspective on organization and suggest the subunits most revolve around compete tasks.

Dynamic environments drive the organization to adopt coordinating mechanisms that are flexible and adaptable to changing circumstances. This rules out any form of standardization, leaving direct supervision as the primary mechanism for simple, dynamic environments, and mutual adjustment as the appropriate coordinating device for complex and dynamic environments. As we have seen, both of these mechanisms tend to put constraints on how large the unit size can be.

Stages of group development

Earlier in the chapter we introduced Greiner's model of the stages of development an *organization* passes through. In this section we explore a similar conception of *group* development devised by Tuckman.[17]

Four phases of development using our task/process model of group behaviour outlined in Chapter 3.

Stage 1: Forming
(a) *Task:* A period of orientation where group members try to establish the parameters of the task, its 'content', and they begin to determine methods for tackling it. Included here are considerations of the group hierarchy, in particular the leadership of the group, the allocation of other roles, and the establishment of codes of conduct.
(b) *Process:* Group members begin to test one another out, to create an impression. Some look to the leader for guidance as to what behaviour is appropriate.

Stage 2: Storming
(a) *Task:* Having embarked upon the task, the organization and methods decided in Stage 1 are put under test. These arrangements are challenged by group members who are becoming increasingly confident in expressing their views.
(b) *Process:* Interpersonal conflict, disagreements about methods, attempts at resisting group influence and outright hostility are

process features of the 'storming' stage. If these disagreements are openly discussed improvements in the group's structures and procedures can result.

Stage 3: Norming

(a) *Task:*   New standards and new roles emerge and are accepted by the group members. There is an open exchange of ideas and opinions, coupled with a willingness to listen to, and accept, alternative suggestions, but potentially controversial aspects of the task are avoided.

(b) *Process:*   The group develops cohesion as conflict and hostility start to be controlled. Norms of acceptable behaviour are developed, and the emphasis is on maintaining the harmony of the group. This development of strong 'group' feelings can be counter-productive if the norms that are set are more orientated to maintaining cohesion rather than to achieving the task (see pages 134–7 on the Hawthorne studies, and pages 181–3 and 229 on Groupthink).

Stage 4: Performing

(a) *Task:*   When (and if) the group reaches Stage 4 a structure of interrelated roles has been established. Constructive suggestions lead through to problem resolution and successful completion of tasks.

(b) *Process:*   In the three previous stages leading to the performing stage a good deal of the group's energy has been diverted away from the task into exposing, and ultimately resolving, interpersonal hassles. Now that these problems have been sorted out all the group's energy can be directed to the task.

The clear implication from Tuckman's model and others like it[18] is that unless the group passes through all four stages, effective task performance will not be forthcoming. The speed at which the newly formed group passes through these stages may determine how successfully the interpersonal issues are resolved. The more rapidly the stages are forced through, the more likely it is that unresolved grievances will continue to simmer. At a much later stage in the group's life these issues may re-emerge to challenge group arrangements, much to the surprise of the group leader, who probably thought everyone was quite happy.

As in the Greiner model of organizational development, a group may collapse at any one of the first three stages, especially if interpersonal conflicts about status and roles persist, or if arguments about working methods raised in the storming stage are not satisfactorily resolved. So there is no necessity for every group to move smoothly through to the 'performing' stage.

In the group organization, where new groups are being established, the crucial lesson to be learnt from the Tuckman model is that positive leadership must be exercised at the *early stages* of the group's development. This is to help the establishment of group norms which are congruent with the aims of the management and that fit in with the 'positive' aspects of the emerging organizational culture. Otherwise the group may well move through to Stage 4 with a set of norms which satisfy the group members, but which are out of step with the wishes of the management. Once norms are established, and the group becomes more cohesive, it is very difficult for other norms to be introduced, and then accepted by the group.

One of the problems of group cohesion experienced in the growing organization is inter-group hostility, conflict, and rivalry. In the very small organization the informal and formal group will tend to comprise the whole organization, so a cohesive group may form which will be working towards the organization's goals. As the organization expands new formal and informal groups are established. These may be professional subgroupings or based on interest groups who have shared life experiences, e.g. class, race, gender.[19] Ideally, these groups should become cohesive, and should share the same goals as the managers of the organization. However, it is a feature of cohesion that the 'we feeling', or group identity, is often established through the group differentiating themselves from other groups in the organization, around, for example, a set of norms which says that 'we're great, and the rest of the factory are useless'. Alternatively the group may form an 'anti' culture – 'look at those idiots working like crazy, they must be simple'.

Resentment towards new group members may emerge especially if the group sees itself as 'special' in some way – through them all having the same qualifications, or through them all being founder members of the organization.

The development of the group's norms should not, then, be left to chance. Inadequate leadership and direction from those in formal positions in the organization will result in groups looking elsewhere for leadership. This, then, exposes the organization to a risk that developing norms will be more influenced by informal leaders than by appointed managers. And ultimately the *organization's* culture, the shared norms and beliefs, will reflect the informal codes of conduct established by the informal organization, not the formal organization.

If we reflect back to Top Gear Driving School for a moment we may recall the strong leadership exercised by Stan Gordon. The fact that he has personally trained the majority of the instructors has helped to bring about a fairly consistent set of norms in the group as a whole. In a sense, the 'norming' process is conducted *prior to* the instructor joining the group, as training takes place in isolation from the group. Although the instructors are not required to work *together* the shared values and cohesiveness of the team must help to sustain morale, even through the individual instructor carries out his task remote from his colleagues.

There are similarities between the TGDS group, and groups in Easton College, as both organizations require trained personnel to perform tasks professionally and independently. However, although staff in the college are all lecturers (so they have that in common) they are increasingly differentiated one from another through their academic specialisms, whereas, the driving instructors perform the same task. With respect to the role of leadership, no manager in the college has anything like the power enjoyed by Stan Gordon. Moreover, individual lecturers are likely to be members of a variety of groups at any one time: some led by people with formal authority, others led by one of their peers. Thus the possibility exists for there to be a wide divergence of group climates with differing sets of norms.

2.5   The individual

A growing organization can be an exciting place to work in. Growth provides opportunities for individuals to take on more responsibilities, to try out new jobs and to learn from new experiences. For a 'growth orientated' person the expanding organization is an ideal environment for him or her to satisfy their needs. However, the pace of change, and the uncertainty can cause some individuals a good deal of stress. Some people are happiest in situations of predictability and stability.

Some particular features of the growing organization have important implications for the individual member:

Fluidity of the structure

If the pace of growth is great there will be little time or inclination to firm up, or define the structure. The scope of an individual's authority and responsibility can change almost overnight. Because of the lack of definition in the structure, some individuals can take it upon themselves to expand their area of authority up until the point where someone else objects. The state of flux and lack of clarity enables status and power-orientated individuals to assume authority without it being formally delegated to them. If you act as if you have authority, and others go along with your suggestions, then you have authority, as the Bellman, a character in *The Hunting of the Snark*, says, 'What I tell you three times is true', you *become* a person with authority.

Generalists become specialists

In the first section of the chapter, on the structure of the growing organization, we indicated that increasing specialization was a feature of growth. Staff who were in the organization when it was very small had to be jacks-of-all-trades. We saw in our example of the college that in the early days a lecturer would teach a variety of subjects – marketing, statistics, management and economics, for example. But increasing size coupled with the growth of more advanced courses, has required each lecturer to specialize in just one of these areas. This narrowing of jobs may well be welcomed by some staff; others are likely to miss the variety of their old job, and might fear that specialization could make them vulnerable to a shift in the organization's priorities.

Opportunities for personal growth

Above all, growth provides opportunities for individuals to take on more responsibilities, to attain management positions and to learn from new experiences. A person can experience more variety in three years in a rapidly growing organization, than in a lifetime spent in a stable bureaucracy. New responsibilities that are coped with successfully can develop great self confidence, enabling the individual to tackle new challenges without trepidation.

So far we have focused on the more positive aspects of growth as they affect the individual. But growth also brings pressures and tensions which can cause disruption and demotivation (see Chapter 9 on the transition curve of change).

Structural imbalances

We have explained that the structure of the organization does not adapt smoothly and appropriately to the growing task. As a consequence increasing workloads may result in some staff being snowed under. When more staff are taken on, floor space may not be increased commensurately, resulting in overcrowded offices and shop floors. And often, along with the growth in the overall size of the organization there are shifts in the nature of the workload, leaving some staff underutilized. This can cause fear of redundancy in the underworked staff, and resentment amongst the overworked staff (see Chapter 9).

Increasing formalization

The informality enjoyed when the organization was small is gradually being replaced by formalization along a number of fronts. Job descriptions emerge as a way of resolving disputes about who does what, and to help in recruiting new staff. But the pace of change may be such that no sooner is the job defined than it becomes a redundant document. Attempts to limit the span of control in the growing organization will inevitably lead to more management layers. So, people who once reported straight to the managing director may find one, or perhaps two managers between them and the boss. 'Staff' specialists in the emerging technostructure begin to 'interfere' in the way the work is carried out, setting budgets, and targets, planning and scheduling the work, and maybe even taking over the disciplining of the operators from the line management.

Increasing formalization of communication may cause annoyance; more meetings (with minutes), more memos copied to all and sundry, and the clarification of a chain of command requiring subordinate staff to communicate only through the formal lines of authority.

The resentment of the old guard

This encompasses not only the new entrants resenting the old established members, but also the old guard viewing the new entrants with suspicion, fear and possibly contempt. The informal group can exert a powerful influence on the individual, and group norms and traditions will be jealously guarded. The old guard will hanker after the old days, when things were simpler and more informal, and when everyone pulled together. They will resent newcomers stepping into management positions. New entrants are unlikely to share the same feelings of loyalty to the organization as the old guard, creating yet another area of potential conflict.

Further reading

Greiner's article[1] could usefully be read in full. Excerpts from Lawrence and Lorsch's study of the links between organization and environment can be read in *Organization Theory*, edited by D. S. Pugh (Pelican, 1985). The machine bureaucracy and the professional bureaucracy are explored fully in Mintzberg's *Structure in Fives*,[3] chapters 9 and 10.

References

1   Greiner, L. E., 'Evolution and Revolution as Organizations Grow', *Harvard Business Review*, July–August 1972
2   Miles, R. E., Snow, C. C., Meyer, A. D. and Colman, H. J., Jr, 'Organisational Strategy, Structure and Process', *Academy of Management Review*, 1978, 546–62
3   Kets, D., Vries, M. R. F. and Miller, D., *The Neurotic Organisation*, Jossey Bass, San Francisco, 1984
4   Burke, W. W. and Litwin, G. H., 'A Causal Model of Organisation Performance and Change', *Journal of Management*, Vol. 18, No. 3, 1992, 525–45
5   Porter, M., *Competitive Advantage: Creating and Sustaining Superior Performance*, Free Press, New York, 1985
6   Lawrence, P. R. and Lorsch, J. W., *Organization and Environment*, Harvard, 1967
7   Greiner, L. E. *Ibid.*
8   Mintzberg, H., *Structure in Fives*, Prentice Hall International, 1983
9   *Ibid.*, Chapter 10

10   Schein, E. H., *Organisational Culture and Leadership: A Dynamic View*, Jossey Bass, 1986

11   Mintzberg, H., *Power In and Around Organizations*, Prentice Hall International, 1984

12   Tannenbaum, R. and Schmidt, W. H., 'How to Choose a Leadership Pattern', *Harvard Business Review*, May–June, 1973. See also Hersey, P. and Blanchard, K. H., *Management of Organisation: Utilising Human Resources*, 3rd edition, Prentice Hall, Englewood Cliffs, 1977, 1982

13   Blake, R. R. and Mouton, J. S., *The New Managerial Grid*, The Gulf Publishing Company, 1978

14   Reddin, W. J., *Managerial Effectiveness*, McGraw Hill, 1970

15   McGregor, D., *The Human Side of the Enterprise*, McGraw Hill, 1960

16   Hersey and Blanchard, *Op. cit.*

17   Tuckman, B. W., 'Development Sequence in Small Groups', *Psychological Bulletin*, Vol. 63, 1965

18   Bennis, W. G. and Sheppard, H. A., 'A theory of group development', *Human Relations*, Vol. 9, No. 43, 1956, 415–37

19   Brown, L. D., *Managing Conflict at Organisational Interfaces*, Addison-Wesley, Reading, MA, 1983

5 The large organization

This chapter looks at the key issues that underpin a large organization: be it bureaucratic, a public organization or a private sector organization. It shows how control systems move to the technostructure and the differing and diverse roles of managers impact on their decision making horizons, authority and realms of decision making. These are compared with the informal group process and the motivation and aspirations of individual workers.

1 Case study: Amalgamated British Brands

'Hey, Carl, have you seen the new capital equipment requisition forms Head Office have sent through? The boss says you've got them.'

Little creep, thought Carl. There was no need to go straight to Palmer, all he needed to do was to ask me. He knows damn fine I've got them; he's just looking for a new way to drop me in it. These graduate trainees were all the same, he decided, although Nigel Rourke seemed even more opinionated and smug than the others who had spent their statutory two months in the finance department.

'Yes, I've got some. Why do you want to see them?' replied Carl, trying not to let his irritation show.

'Oh, it's just that Mr Palmer thought it would be a good idea for me to familiarize myself with the new capital purchase system, seeing as I'm likely to end up in Head Office anyway.'

'OK here they are. I expect you'll have no problems deciphering them.' Carl handed over the sheaf of documents, secretly hoping Rourke would not grasp the new system.

Carl checked his watch. 'It can't possibly be only 10.35. God, one hour fifty-five minutes to lunch.' He reached for another pile of MR32s (the standard materials purchase forms) and began checking them for errors.

Carl had been a clerical assistant in the Accounts Department for eight years now. During that time he had sat behind three different desks in the same office, but although the forms might have changed over the years, the job was pretty much the same. Few people seemed to appreciate how difficult it was to concentrate hour after hour, day after day. One slip, one unchecked total and he would be in trouble.

Carl had various ways of combating the boredom of the job. For instance, if he put in a spurt of effort he might reward himself with a visit to the drinks machine in the corridor. The reward being not so much the insipid, instant coffee but more the change of scene and the opportunity to stretch his legs. But generally he was able to almost split his brain in two, and have one half on automatic pilot checking the forms, whilst the other half was free to daydream. He was, actually, very good at his job, and was capable of halving the standard time set for checking these forms. Not that it made any difference to his pay as the bonus scheme applied to the department as a whole.

Nigel Rourke couldn't wait to finish his six months 'training' period and get on with a real job. But it was important in the meantime to create the right impression. He was sure that going to see Mr Palmer to volunteer to check through the new capital purchase system would clock him up some 'brownie points'. And it would be nice to prove to the others in the office that he was not just a waste of space. Quite why everyone was so wary of him, Nigel couldn't imagine. Carl seemed downright surly. Anyway, tonight he was meeting some of the other trainees for the Graduate Programme Dinner at which all the top brass would be in attendance. A real chance to make my mark, thought Nigel.

Meanwhile Arthur Palmer was firmly closeted in his office, protected from the outside world by Mrs Soames his formidable secretary. He was not a happy man. If he was honest with himself he would admit to being out of his depth in this job of Manager, Accounts Department, Toiletries Division. He knew that everyone thought that Mrs Soames really ran the department.

He was able to cope reasonably well in the job before the takeover. But since they were merged into Associated British Brands life seems to have become much more complicated. Now there are new systems for everything; everyone's using 'spreadsheet packages'; and HQ issue new edicts almost daily. He dreads opening the distinctive beige transit envelopes from Corporate Finance Department for fear that they will reveal yet another clanger that has been dropped by him or his department.

His recent appraisal interview put paid to any lingering ambitions he might have had. They even complained about his suits, albeit in a rather indirect manner. Also he knew that Barbara, his wife, was not considered to be 'up to scratch' by the other senior executives and their wives. If I can only hang on for three more years, thought Arthur, then I can opt for early retirement.

In the meantime it looked like another sleepless night lay ahead of him. He had been instructed by Group HQ to cut expenditure levels on a number of budget headings by 15 per cent in the coming financial year. The first meeting with the production managers to agree next year's budgets had been a complete disaster. He ended up memoing head office to the effect that, rather than a cut in budget, Toiletries Division would need 13 per cent more cash just to maintain operations at the current levels. Arthur shivered in his chair and felt his face flush as he remembered yesterday's phone call from the Corporate Finance Director who, not being one to mince his words, suggested that if Arthur was not capable of following a quite straightforward instruction from his superior, then maybe he should 'reconsider his commitment to the company'. His parting words were 'You're the Finance Manager, get on and manage the bloody finances'. Arthur dreaded the prospect of meeting the production managers again and forcing them to toe the line. What's more, he knew it was a waste of time trying to get the Managing Director of the Toiletries Division to lean on the production heads. The MD was a production manager himself before his promotion and, as far as Arthur could see, always seemed to favour the production departments.

Nigel, Toby and Pauline were enjoying a pre-dinner sherry in the anteroom of the Executive Dining Suite.

'How are you getting on with Palmer?' enquired Pauline in her rather disconcertingly direct manner. 'The word is he's on the way out.'

'Is he? How do you know?' replied Nigel, automatically on his guard.

'One picks up the odd murmur on the twelfth floor, Nigel, so my advice to you is not to be seen to be too pally with him. You don't want to be tarred with the same brush, do you. And have you seen the state of his wife, Betty, or something?'

Later Nigel found himself sitting next to Alan Armstrong, the Group Personnel Manager, at dinner.

'How are you finding your training programme . . . er Nigel isn't it?' asked Armstrong.

'Yes, Nigel Rourke. Oh it's very interesting. I'm learning a lot!'

Nigel continued to put in a good performance throughout the dinner, although he wasn't quite sure he had said the right thing about South Africa – there did seem to be a slight raising of the eyebrows to his expression of support for black trade unions.

After the thin mints and coffee Sir Gordon French, Chairman and Chief Executive of ABB, rose to make his after dinner speech.

'You people are the future of ABB' he began, 'we will be looking to you in the years to come to provide the leadership that will carry us into the next century. . . .'

Nigel settled back in his seat, with a glass of tawny port in one hand, and a cheroot in the other, and let the chairman's words wash over him. 'Yes', he thought 'ABB really do look after their people. And if I pull my weight there's no reason why I couldn't go all the way to the top.'

Issues arising from the case

We can now try to pick out some of the more interesting issues raised by the case, using our established system of analysis.

Environment

1 Not much is explicitly said of the environment but the fact that the company has recently been 'acquired' suggests it may be a competitive, if not hostile environment.

2 The company experiences the 'parent' role of HQ as intrusive and it forms part of the system's context. How might this strategic interface be managed better?

History and resources

1 The change in ownership will have an impact on the culture. Will the new one become dominant or will the old one survive? What impact will this have on performance?
2 The company is seeking to cut costs and a reduction in budgets. Yet the ability to manage these demands from HQ are proving to be difficult. Is this a result of poor management by Arthur or is it much more contextual?

Task

1 There appear to be competing tasks – make as much as we can (manufacturing), but costs (HQ) manage the systems. There are conflicting priorities along the lines discussed in Chapter 4. How can these be resolved. Are they realistic demands?
2 With size it is likely that the task may become more complex.

Organization structure and management

1 There are clear hints that ABB is a very large corporation. It is organized into divisions with a central headquarters which appears to control the divisions. How has ABB grown so large? Why is it organized like this?
2 The case also suggests that each division is divided up into separate departments, and that the Accounts Manager, Arthur Palmer, reports not just to the MD Toiletries Division, but also to the Group Finance Director at HQ. Is this likely to present any problems for Arthur?
3 Specialization occurs in both horizontal and vertical dimensions. Jobs like Carl's are specialized and routinized as well. What is it about the type of task ABB are engaged in that permits this degree of specialization and routinization?
4 Arthur is for the chop, it appears. The management are presumably confident that he can be easily replaced, how come?
5 What sort of decisions can the Chief Executive of ABB possibly take? What decision making processes might he employ? What is the role of the chief executive in a huge diversified company?
6 How much power does the divisional manager have? Is it feasible that he is biased towards production, and, if so, what effect would this have on his decisions?
7 What is the scope of a production manager's job, given that there are probably separate departments dealing with production planning, quality control, incentive pay systems, work study etc.?

8 Systems for budgeting, payment-by-results and graduate recruitment are mentioned in the case. What are the reasons for inventing these systems, and why are they found in this type of organization?

The informal organization

1 Arthur lives in fear of Headquarters and the Group Finance Director. 'HQ' appears to exert a considerable degree of authority and is clearly seen to be very powerful. Is the perceived authority of HQ managers enhanced by their remoteness?
2 The budgeting process requires some interrelationship between Arthur in the role of a staff specialist, and the line managers in production. What problems does this line/staff relationship pose for both sides?
3 How are the standard times for jobs like form checking set? Why is it possible for Carl to undercut them so easily?
4 The case gives us some insights into the culture of ABB which appears to be based on conformity and conservativeness. What informal processes are at work to preserve and promote this culture?
5 The Accounts office seems to have made little effort to include Nigel Rourke into the group; why should this be?
6 The production managers have formed an alliance to pressure Arthur into taking a softer line on the budget cuts. What makes them so cohesive?
7 The group bonus scheme operating in the Accounts Department does not appear to be motivating Carl, although he works efficiently in any event. How could the group exert influence on group members to get them to work harder?
8 The gossip machine is a source of information and possible power. But how does it get used – for good or ill?

Individuals

1 Nigel Rourke sees a whole career path spreading out in front of him at ABB. Is this a realistic vision?
2 In contrast, Carl would seem to be in a cul-de-sac, with no obvious route out. His job is dull and repetitive, so how could his manager hope to motivate him?
3 Why is it of any importance that Arthur's wife Barbara doesn't fit in? Why is Nigel worried about expressing his opinions on South Africa?
4 To what extent can an individual like Carl, buried in the depths of the large bureaucracy, identify with the organization or understand its overall structure?
5 How useful is a 'training' programme which moves people around from department to department?

Outputs

1 It is difficult to tell from the case how far the organization achieves its goals, but it's clear that resource utilization is far from perfect.
2 Adaptation to the changes is fraught with feelings of fear, suspicion and experience of a difficult transition. How might one deal with these worries?
3 Groups are rewarded by results but how effective can they be given the range of tensions and inherent conflict that is unexpressed or avoided.
4 There are different levels of disaffection and feelings of being disliked. What next is waiting around the corner for staff to deal with?

These issues can be partly explored by concepts and theories developed in Chapters 3, 4 and 8, but writers and researchers into management and organizations have tended to concentrate on the problems of the large bureaucracy. Hence there is a wealth of theory to draw upon, and we have, consequently, had to be fairly selective in deciding what material to include. We should direct the reader who is looking for more depth in a particular area to the recommended reading at the end of the chapter.

2 Context

Table 5.1 Summary of key factors in the case

Inputs	
■ Environment	■ Take over/'Acquisition'
	■ HQ experienced as intrusive
■ Resources	■ Need to make cuts but competing demands
■ History	■ Change in ownership
Transformation	
■ Task	■ Increasingly managed from HQ, but also perceived as increasingly complex
■ Individual	■ Roles more clearly defined to sub tasks
■ Organization	■ More systems, forms, clear reward systems and structure
■ Informal	■ Inter-group rivalry, rumour and gossip thrive, pressure for conformity
Output	
■ Goal achievement	■ Uncertain
■ Resource utilization	■ Poorly managed?
■ Adaptation	■ Feelings of uncertainty and not coping
■ Group performance	■ Uncertain but reward by group
■ Individual behaviour and effect	■ Various degrees of intrigue or disaffection

3 Organizational configuration

3.1 Structure

The nature of bureaucracy

We have to be very careful when using the term bureaucracy. In common usage it is almost a term of abuse, with connotations of inefficiency, 'red tape' and the rule-bound rigidity of 'bureaucrats'. However, Max Weber, a German sociologist of the nineteenth century, saw bureaucracy as an organization type which had distinct merits over other forms of organization.[1] For Weber, the great advantage of bureaucratic organizations was that they can persist despite changes in the people that staff them, so bureaucratic organizations can survive long after the founders of the organization have left. The particular features of bureaucracy that permit this are now familiar, and they include the following:

(a) Tasks and duties are divided up and allocated to *positions* in a clear-cut *hierarchy of authority*.
(b) *Rules* and *regulations* are employed to ensure uniformity of action, which assists in the coordination of tasks.
(c) Information is stored in *files* not in heads. This enables the new occupant of a position to pick up the job where the previous person left off.
(d) Jobs are filled on merit, based on the qualifications the person has for the position.

These features provide consistent practice efficiency and most of all in his time, impartiality.

Weber's original work has been subjected to a good deal of criticism, which in many respects stems from a misrepresentation of his position. There is little doubt about the merits of bureaucratic organization; our modern large scale businesses, and government agencies all display to some extent the features listed above. But, there is also general agreement that, no matter how carefully a bureaucracy is designed, it cannot meet all the aspirations of those who control it, work in it or are clients or customers of it.

Most of us are aware of the disadvantages that large scale organizations can display:

- A rigidity in the face of much needed change.
- A tendency to rely too much on rules and regulations, and not enough on initiative, common sense and compassion.
- An excessive concern for secrecy.
- An encouragement of officious, status conscious administrators.

Moreover, the high degree of job specialization (in both the vertical and horizontal dimensions) can result in very boring jobs for people lower down the hierarchy.

Some of these issues will be picked up in this chapter, but first we shall explore the formal structure of a large bureaucracy.

The structure of ABB

We can infer from the case that ABB is a large scale organization. It is, in fact, a hybrid form of organization called a multi-divisional structure. Each division has a machine bureaucratic structure (see pages 67–8), and the divisions themselves are coordinated and controlled by a central headquarters. Figure 5.1 illustrates the structure in the stylized form developed in the last chapter.[2]

The multi-divisional structure is usually found where a firm with a machine bureaucratic form has diversified away from its original product groups. As long as there is no significant requirement to coordinate products or resources between the divisions they can be operated on a fairly autonomous basis. In fact, one form of structure, the holding company, displays not only autonomy of operation *between* the divisions, but also the HQ takes little part in the management or control of each division, except for the setting of broad targets.

ABB does not take this extreme, 'hands-off' approach to the divisions. We have evidence in the case of interference by the HQ in the budgeting activities of the Toiletries Division. Also the Accounts Manager in the division seems to report not just to his Divisional Managing Director, but to the HQ-based Finance Director as well. This relationship may well be depicted as a dotted line on the organization chart (see Figure 5.2).

In effect, then, Arthur Palmer has two bosses. This arrangement violates one of the 'classical principles' of organization which were developed alongside the concept of bureaucracy, most notably by Henri Fayol.

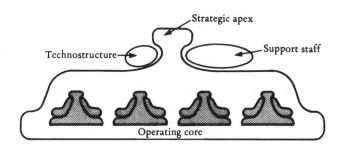

Figure 5.1 *A multi-divisional structure*

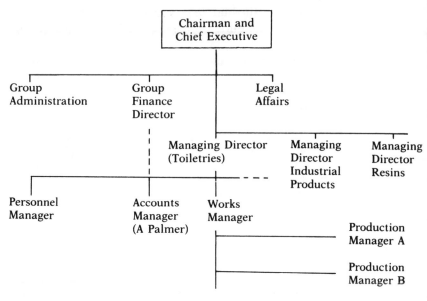

Figure 5.2 *The structure of ABB*

The classical principles of organization

Fayol[3] identified fourteen principles of management and organization; four of the more important of them are:

- Specialization and the division of work confers great benefits in terms of productivity.
- Unity of command; one man should only have one boss. Dual command will lead to conflict.
- Unity of direction; so effort is focused on achieving a single objective.
- Scalar chain; a clear line of authority must link the top of the organization to the bottom.

Similar lists of principles have been drawn up by other writers in the classical tradition (e.g. Urwick,[4] Brech[5]). One problem that arises with these very prescriptive approaches to organization is that they may be slavishly followed by designers of organizations, irrespective of the peculiarities of the environment or tasks facing the organization. In a sense, they are an anti-contingency approach, putting forward the 'one best way' of organizing regardless of other factors such as the size, age, and environment of the organization. The blame for the insensitive adherence to these principles lies not with Fayol, but with later writers and practitioners.

Returning to the situation of Arthur Palmer, it is clear that the 'unity of command' principle is breached in the structure of ABB. Directives from the Toiletries Division Managing Director may well conflict with the budget restrictions being imposed by the Group Finance Director. Arthur is 'piggy-in-the-middle' unable to satisfy both bosses no matter what he does. But the 'two bosses' situation is a minor aberration on an otherwise clear, unified chain of command in ABB. However, in Chapter 6 we will explore organizations where 'two bosses' is the rule rather than the exception.

In previous chapters we have considered the impact of size, growth and the task environment on the shape of the organization. One other important influence on the design of organization structures is the type of production process being used in the operating core. We shall now turn our attention to these links between production technology and structure.

Influence of production technology

Joan Woodward, in a survey of manufacturing firms in Essex, established clear links between the type of production technology used in the operating core of the firm, and the firm's structure. In particular, her results seemed to contradict some of the classical principles of organization, especially the concept of the limited span of control (for instance she found that in mass production firms the control span for first line supervisors could be as high as fifty).

She distinguished three broad types of technical system:

(a) *Unit Production:* Firms that manufactured single units, proto-types and small batches.
(b) *Mass Production:* Firms making very large quantities of standard-ized products often using production line techniques.
(c) *Process Production:* Those firms engaged in continuous produc-tion of fluid substances (e.g. oil refining, chemical processing).

The characteristic organizational features of each can be summarized as follows:

Unit Production
■ Ad hoc, non-standardized outputs meant that coordination between workers was effected by either mutual adjustment or direct supervision, or a combination of the two. Thus these firms did not display the features of a bureaucracy, and as they tended to be small, informal arrangements and relationships predominated (see Chapter 3).
■ Coordination by mutual adjustment and direct supervision placed an upper limit on group size, and hence on span of control.
■ These firms had very few layers of management and had no technostructure to speak of (due to the lack of standardization of outputs or work processes).

Mass production

- These firms exhibited most clearly the features of the classic bureaucracy. The work in the operating core was highly routinized and unskilled; coordination was achieved, then, through the standardization of work processes. This permits very large spans of control at the first line supervisor level.
- Standardization implies a well developed technostructure, which engages in activities like method and time study, scheduling, planning and quality control.
- Woodward discovered three areas of conflict in these firms:

  (i)   Between the mass production system and the 'social system'.
  (ii) Between line and staff personnel.
  (iii) Between the short-range, problem solving orientation of the managers in the lower levels, and the long-range focus of the strategic apex.

We shall pick up these three areas of conflict later in this chapter.

Process production

The pace of production in the mass production firm relies to a large extent on how hard the unskilled operators in the core work. Although these structures are often highly mechanized they are not *automated*. In contrast, the operating core of the process firm is almost devoid of people. The pace of production, the flow of product, is determined by the design of the plant not on the speed at which the operatives work.

As a result, the need to control the workers in the operating core is largely removed. There is no longer a need for rules, disciplinary systems, and work study officers. And the distinctions between line and staff wither away. Hence process firms exhibited very different structures to mass production firms.

We find that:

- Relationships were very informal.
- Support staff formed a significant proportion of the structure.
- Small teams of specialists worked together to solve technical problems, and many decisions were taken by committees. Thus mutual adjustment emerges as a key coordinating mechanism.

We might speculate on the impact that robotized production systems will have on today's mass production firms. As workers on the production line are replaced by machines, will we see a transformation of the superstructure that controls the operating core? In particular, will the obsession with 'control' that characterizes many of the relationships between managers and operators, give way to a potentially more harmonious working environment?

Before we leave the exploration of links between production technology and structure we could usefully return to the example of a multi-divisional structure provided by ABB. Here each division operates more or less independently of the others. This is because there is no significant product or resource connection between the divisions. Consider, however, the divisionalized structure of an oil company depicted in Figure 5.3.

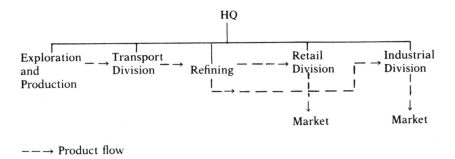

−−→ Product flow

Figure 5.3 *The multi-divisional structure of an oil company*

Here the product flows across divisions ending up in the Retail, and Industrial Divisions. The 'technical system' for the company as a whole is sub-divided between the divisions. This implies, then, a requirement to coordinate activities *between* divisions.

Line vs. staff

Woodward's research pointed out that the relationships between line and staff personnel were a source of conflict in the mass production organization. For our purposes we can define 'line' managers as those that are in the direct flow of formal authority from the apex of the structure to the operating core. 'Staff' people are, then, located in the technostructure and the support staff. It is the staff in the technostructure that conform most closely to the military usage of the term 'staff', as advisors, and specialists that serve the line managers.

Although broad classifications of staff and line groupings in the organization are useful, it is not helpful to push these distinctions too far. For example, the quality control manager may well be classified as a member of the 'staff' but in certain circumstances he or she can and does intervene directly in the activities of the operating core. And, in process production firms with their automated operating cores, it is not easy to distinguish who the 'line' management would actually be controlling.

Nevertheless, large, machine bureaucratic structures have considerable numbers of staff people who necessarily come into contact with those in the line. So what are the areas around which conflict arises? Some suggestions might be:

(a) Line managers may resent 'interference' from specialists who, not only take no responsibility for the decisions (they just advise), but who are often out of touch with the realities of the operating core.

(b) Staff personnel may complain that their advice is often ignored, and that they are not kept sufficiently informed about events in the operating core.

(c) Line managers can often be subjected to conflicting advice from different staff specialists.

(d) Staff may be resented for the apparent absence of performance controls applying to them compared to the close monitoring of production management and supervision.

(e) Line managers may resent the gradual erosion of their powers as more and more areas of discretion are pre-empted by staff in the technostructure.

(f) Staff may be seen as irrelevant, an 'overhead' being carried by the 'line' and adding no value.

In our case example, the Accounts Manager is attempting to enforce budget cuts imposed by group headquarters. His first attempt to bring the various production managers into line has failed, and he suspects the Managing Director of the Toiletries Division would probably side with his production managers if he tried to appeal to his authority. This incident neatly encapsulates some of the significant dimensions of line/staff relationships.

- Arthur Palmer cannot impose the cuts on the line managers; he does not have the formal authority to do so.
- He may well lack the detailed inside information required to critically evaluate the claims for more resources made by the production managers.
- Even where line and staff managers are at the same level in the hierarchy, often the line manager comes out on top, as he is seen to 'carry more weight' than the staff manager.

Before we leave this section on the structure of the large bureaucracy, and in particular the line/staff distinctions within the structure, consider the organization chart laid out in Figure 5.4. This contains the different departments of the Pharmaceutical Products Division of ABB grouped according to Mintzberg's five parts of the organization. Note that the 'line' contains not just the production managers and workers, but it also contains the sales force; and check the way that staff are classified into the technostructure grouping and the support staff grouping.

3.2 Organizational arrangements

Controlling the operating core

We have already noted that a pervasive feature of the large machine

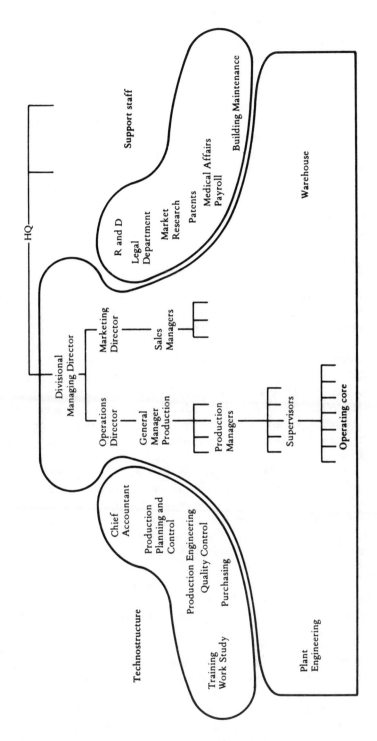

Figure 5.4 *The structure of the Pharmaceutical Products Division of ABB*

bureaucracies is an obsession with control. The benefits of large scale production can only be realized if production costs can be kept to a minimum. Hence strenuous efforts are made by management to keep control of material and labour costs, and to maintain high levels of capacity utilization. In the well developed machine bureaucracy control is largely effected through *systems*. The departments in the technostructure in Figure 5.4 are all concerned with controlling different aspects of the operating core through various systems: quality control, planning and scheduling, budgeting, training, purchasing and production engineering. In this section on Processes in the large bureaucracy we shall be concentrating on two main groups of control systems:

- Those concerned with the *control of work processes*.
- Those concerned with the *control of people*.

The control of work processes

This group of control systems includes systems for controlling quality, work methods, and costs. Before we look at these systems in more detail we can make some general points about the control of work processes. Together the systems are trying to meet the often conflicting objectives of delivery dates, cost levels and quality standards. So the first point to recognize is that these control systems are essentially *fragmented*.[7] They are also largely *impersonal* in nature, as they do not tend to rely on the personal authority of the line manager; the control is exercised via an intermediary system – the works delivery schedule, the job card, the standard costing, the quality standards or specifications.

The often conflicting objectives that each system is trying to meet tend to push the production managers, supervisors and operatives in different directions depending on what happens to be 'flavour of the month'. One week all hell breaks loose because they are behind schedule on delivery of a big order; next week there is a panic about quality after some contaminated products are discovered in a batch awaiting shipment.

It is not uncommon, however, for the production manager to order these objectives into a hierarchy, placing delivery at the top, largely because this is the most obvious and easily measured performance criterion.

As these control systems tend to require large amounts of information, and, in order for them to be effective this information needs to be up to date, computers are increasingly used to process the data. The processing speed of the computer, and the ability it offers, via dispersed terminals, for many people to access the information, are enormous advantages. But, where people are converting from a manually operated system (e.g. record cards) onto a computer based control system, they need to have confidence in the information displayed on the screen. The system is only as good as the information fed into it, so if some staff are sloppy, or late in inputting information then others will mistrust, and then ignore or bypass the system.

Controlling quality

The emergence of large scale manufacture had a profound impact on the quality control system, in so far as it resulted in a shift of responsibility for quality away from the production operative. In the era of craftsmen, and long apprenticeships, each craftsman was personally responsible for the quality of his work. But as specialization and the division of labour began to replace craftsmen by semi- and unskilled labour, a further horizontal specialization spawned the 'inspection' role.

The inspector acted as a quality policeman, often seen to be working *against* the production workers and managers by, for instance, insisting on reworking, scrapping sub-standard items and refusing to grant concessions. The inspection system as a whole acted as a safety net to prevent rubbish leaving the factory.

As production processes became more horizontally specialized, and as the products themselves became more complex, inspection stages were built into the process, to ensure that quality problems were picked up early before more value had been added to the product. Also statistical methods began to be employed, like sampling, process capability analysis, and vendor rating to improve the quality control system. But, despite these growing sophistications, the perception on the shop floor still seemed to be that quality was the inspector's problem.

Prompted in part by the success of Japanese firms in penetrating our home markets with high quality products, and partly by the insistence of major purchasers like the Department of Health and the Ministry of Defence on an improvement in quality systems, a significant shift in attitudes to quality has taken place in recent years. Now the emphasis is increasingly on the *quality assurance* concept. Quality is everyone's responsibility, and the guiding philosophy is 'if you look after the systems, the systems will look after the product'. So the emphasis shifts from the inspection of the *products* in the process of manufacture, to the evaluation of the *systems* that produce the products, and hence determine quality. The narrow focus of product inspection broadens into the assessment of areas like:

- Training
- The control of technical drawing updates
- The organization structure
- Maintenance procedures
- Materials control, e.g. quarantine arrangements
- Operatives attitudes
- Work methods
- Calibration of machinery and measuring instruments.

Ultimately, if the management can assure themselves that they have got the systems right, they might be able to abandon many of the traditional inspection activities. Typically organizations seek to get their quality processes externally validated through BS 5750/ISO 9000 in manufacturing and service settings or 'investment in people' for human resource development processes. In any event, the increasing sophistication of products, especially those with electrical and electronic components, has meant that even 100 per cent inspection cannot guarantee quality. You can test an aircraft navigation instrument before it leaves the factory, but this will only tell you that it works *now*. It won't necessarily reveal a poorly soldered connection which may well cause the instrument to fail within a few hours of installation.

Shifting the responsibility for quality back to the operatives has also had some useful spin-offs in improving the operative's job. In particular, the introduction of quality circles and the concept of job enrichment have conferred benefits on both workers and management. We shall consider these developments later in this chapter.

Control of work methods

As we have seen, then, an important feature of large scale manufacture is the tendency to de-skill jobs. The organization needs, therefore, to develop systems which can ensure that the required standards of product quality, costs, reliability, delivery etc. are maintained alongside the process of replacing skilled labour with unskilled labour. These control systems can take a variety of forms and can usually be found operating in parallel within the machine bureaucracy.

(a) Work simplification, the breaking down of tasks into easily definable elements, is an essential first step in the de-skilling process. Method study, a branch of work study, uses particular techniques of recording and analysing tasks with the aim of defining more efficient work processes. These can then be specified in the form of procedures, standard working practices and job process sheets.

(b) The production engineer can design the production system to help reduce variability, and to ensure that the pace of production is dictated by the machine rather than the operator.

(c) Production planning and scheduling systems can be designed to ensure that the different production activities are coordinated so as to achieve delivery targets, and to help achieve efficient utilization of machinery.

The simplification of work, and the replacement of relatively scarce and expensive craftsmen with cheaper operatives (and, ultimately, with machines) has not only been experienced in the production area. Large bureaucracies have emerged in other stable task environments, which are more concerned with processing information. Take, for example, an insurance company, the Department of Social Security, a high street bank, or even the Toiletries Division Accounts Department. Consider what happens when you pay a cheque into your bank. The cashier immediately slips into a familiar routine to deal with the transaction. He or she stamps it, records it and files the paying in slip in a particular tray. If we followed the route of the cheque we would appreciate the full extent of the elaborate system employed to cope with this very routine task. This task has all the elements which make proceduralizing it worthwhile: it is encountered thousands of times a day; the management need to ensure each cheque is dealt with in a uniform way; and rather than employing an expert in finance to cope with the task, it is much cheaper to employ a relatively unskilled person and teach them the routine to be followed.

Control of costs

Two particular management accounting systems are employed in bureaucratic structures: budgetary control, and standard costing. Budgetary control involves the setting (agreeing?) of target levels of spending in particular budget headings, e.g. office equipment, direct labour costs, travel expenses etc. Once the budget limit is set, often on an annual basis, spending against the budget is monitored more frequently (e.g. monthly). Thus variances from the planned levels of spending can be highlighted and 'corrective action' can be taken.

Standard costing operates in much the same way as budgetary control, except in this case costs levels are set, for example, for a particular component, and variances from this standard are monitored and investigated.

Some problems with the control of work processes

All the systems that have been set up to control work processes are indirectly designed to control *people*, or, in the case of automation, to eliminate altogether the variability caused by people. As such, these control systems are likely to cause resistance and resentment amongst workers, supervisors and managers in the line departments. These systems are effectively causing a power shift from the 'personal' control system of the craftsman, supervisor or production manager, to the impersonal control systems designed by the specialists in the technostructure. That is not to say that the analysts in the technostructure are given *formal authority* over people in the line and in the operating core, rather they have acquired a degree of *informal power* over the line personnel.

Resentment of the systems imposed by the technostructure can take different forms:

Battles over budgets Production managers are likely to resist attempts to reduce their budgets, managing is always easier if resources are not in restricted supply. Formal and informal pressures will be as applied by politically skilled managers to preserve or increase their budget allocations. Managers and budgetary controllers will both play the system: managers, by greatly overestimating required expenditure levels (knowing that they will be reduced by the budgeting committee); budgetary controllers by asking for almost impossible budget cuts in the expectation that they will be revised upwards. But perhaps the most justifiable complaints against budgetary control systems occur when managers are chastised for variances which are outside of their direct control.

Resistance to work study Work study officers face an uphill task in bringing about changes in working methods in the operating core. Unless they are specifically invited in to investigate a particular problem by the line manager, their 'interference' is likely to be seen as an unnecessary intrusion into the line manager's domain, and it may also be viewed as an implicit criticism of the way the manager is presently running his department. This problem may be compounded by the tendency for officers to tackle problems they can reasily solve, rather than areas that are causing concern to the line management.

It is hard for work study officers to gain the cooperation of workers in giving information as staff are unlikely to trust the process or its consequences. Even when work study officers are able to reach the stage where the improved method is ready to be 'installed', their problems are not over. Supervisors and operatives might like to think that *they* know more about the job than the outsider with the suit and the clipboard. New methods are unlikely to be free of problems, and if the operatives have not been involved in designing the improved method, they may well delight in pointing up every little snag in the system. And a lack of commitment to the change is liable to lead to a reversion to the old methods as soon as the work study officer turns his back.

Constraints on initiative Frederick Taylor,[8] the 'father' of scientific management and work study, was concerned to remove all possible brain work from the shop floor in the interests of efficiency. However with the emergence of more and more systems to control the operating core we have also witnessed a removal of decision making discretion from the line managers and supervisors to the technostructure. So as the machine bureaucratic form has developed, decisions about what to make, how to make it and about levels of quality were firstly removed from the shop floor worker up the hierarchy to his supervisor and manager, and then the power to decide these matters has gradually been shifted *sideways* to the staff in the technostructure. So the scope for exercising initiative on the shop floor is limited.

Now this state of affairs suits some shop floor workers. They prefer to be directed, and they like the stability routine work provides. But others find the constraints placed upon them irritating and demotivating. Take, for example, Carl in our case study. And, unfortunately, there appear to be too few of the former group of workers to staff all our machine bureaucracies. As a consequence, other systems are employed to control people directly. We shall now consider some of them.

Managing people

Traditionally, the functions relating to staff record systems, job descriptions training and the like have been in the 'staff' function of personnel. Now these functions are being devolved to the 'line' and form part of a broader human resource strategy or development programme. Thus, the elements of control on one side and development on the other sit in tension with each other. These tensions can be creative or dysfunctional. How senior management handle, respond and lead will often determine the outcome.

We can make a useful distinction between 'external' systems that are employed to control people, and 'internal' systems that are attempting to bring about self-control, or self-regulation of behaviour. Figure 5.5 lists some external and internal control systems. The external systems are grouped into those that are usually operating across the whole organization, and those that are more specifically related to the job the individual holds. When considering the internal systems we can distinguish between efforts that are made to deliberately influence behaviour, like indoctrination and training, and the staffing system (the way the organization selects new members) which operates in an indirect way through the selection of people who, hopefully, already possess the skills, personality and attitudes that the organization requires. The culturalization process is another indirect system, one which moulds attitudes and sets norms of behaviour. These processes are particularly relevant in the large organization. While present in others, these control methods will be more informal or less apparent.

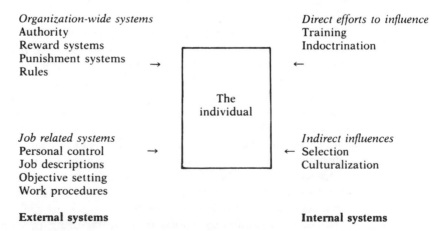

Figure 5.5 *External and internal control systems*

External controls – organization-wide systems

The system of authority has already been explored in Chapter 3. Here we should recall that authority is the formal power vested in the position a person holds. In order for it to be effective as a control system it requires subordinates to recognize the right of managers to give instructions and orders. In most large bureaucracies formal authority is by far the most powerful control system. The mere presence of a 'senior manager' can reduce many staff at the lower levels to a quivering mass! The authority system can also be used in indirect ways to persuade people to fall in line. Consider, for example, the use of the 'courtesy copy' – or 'cc' system. Manager A sends a critical memo to Manager B, who is on the same level in the hierarchy. In order to beef up the impact of the memo, Manager A also sends a 'courtesy copy' to Senior Manager X, expecting that this political technique will add weight to his position. In the case study, casual but deliberate references to the 'twelfth floor' dropped into a remark about Arthur Palmer's future with ABB, give considerable force to Pauline's comments.

But, as we pointed out in Chapter 3, in any given example of a subordinate's compliance to an instruction from a manager, we cannot know the specific reasons for compliance. It could be because of the subordinate's acceptance of the boss's right to give orders; it could be because of the possibility of a reward, or the fear of a punishment of some sort. Let us now expand the reasons for compliance by considering the reward and punishment systems that operate in most large bureaucracies.

Reward and punishment systems   Crudely, these systems, which often work in tandem, reward compliance and penalize non-compliance. The reward system includes not just pay, but also the prospect of promotion (more pay, plus status and power!), fringe benefits (overtime, company cars, health care insurance), and the praise of the respected manager.

For most members of the large bureaucracy there is only a loose link between pay and performance. There is also evidence that pay rises only have a short term effect on motivation,[9] employees pretty soon gear up their expenditure to the higher income, and hence the new pay level becomes the norm. So for all those staff who cannot see a clear link between pay and performance, wages or salaries are a poor motivating device. Few employees rush around saying or thinking 'I'm paid £X,000 therefore I must work as hard as I can'. Moreover, when comparisons *are* made by employees between their pay and others, it is rare for them to select a lower paid comparator group. When people *do* think about pay it is usually to complain about it. (See the motivation model of Porter and Lawler in Chapter 3.)

However, payment-by-results in manufacturing or Performance Related Pay (PRP) schemes in the service sector, have been around for a long time in organizations. The essential ingredient is for there to be an output that can be measured, and that the achievement of that level of output can be clearly tied in to the efforts of the individual or small groups. Attempts to spread PBR/PRP to embrace senior managers' performance, large groups and even to the work force as a whole are unlikely to encourage greater effort, because the link between effort and reward for the *individual* is far too vague. These factory-wide bonus schemes can even have a demotivating effect if they engender conflict between different groups; between those who consider they are 'pulling their weight', and others who are seen as letting them down.

In large organizations, PBR can, though, operate to good effect in areas where output is more measurable, like production and sales. Piece rate systems and commission payments, can encourage employees to put in extra effort, especially where the intrinsic rewards from the job are negligible. Some points worth noting with PBR schemes are as follows:

Problems in setting the rate: We have already suggested that employees may not respond well to being observed and measured, especially where this time study activity is likely to hit them in their pay packets. It is not difficult to find evidence in firms that use PBR of abuses of the system. For example, sometimes rate fixers set impossible rates, or more often, the rate fixer is coerced or conned into setting very 'loose' times that can be easily achieved. To combat some of these problems there are quite sophisticated 'synthetic' time study systems which can be used to build up a time for a job if all the separate operations are known.

Non-response to PBR: Some workers are not motivated by the prospect of higher pay for more output, preferring instead to earn a 'reasonable' wage by putting in a 'fair day's work'. Social pressures can also be brought to bear on the individual by workmates ensuring that the individual does not work 'too hard' as this may well prove to the management that the rates are too loose.

Distortion of effort: If pay is tied to measurable output this will encourage people to produce larger amounts of whatever it is that the management measure. A lowering of quality standards can result if the output measure does not have a quality dimension. Similarly, material costs may rise if no account is taken of costs when measuring performance. Lastly, and perhaps more worryingly, safety standards can be compromised by PBR schemes.

But there is a view that, despite these difficulties, PBR systems offer the only half way reasonable solution to the problem of motivating people in the repetitive, excruciatingly boring jobs found in the large bureaucracy. This issue will be considered again later in the chapter in the section on individuals.

We said that reward and punishment systems often work in tandem, so the threat of the withdrawal of a potential reward operates like a punishment. It is surprising how the long term prospect of promotion can operate to exert a profound influence on the individual with career aspirations. The fear of 'blotting your copy book' continually keeps pressure on the individual to comply with the management's wishes, even if, in fact, his promotion prospects are extremely slim. Of course, this system would have no effect on the individual who has no interest in climbing the promotion ladder. This tends to reinforce the argument we put forward in Chapter 3 that it was not helpful to generalize about the aspirations and motivations of individuals.

But punishment systems which operate to take away something the worker already has, are found more typically at work in the operating core. Here we can find pay deductions being made for clocking in late, verbal and written warnings for absenteeism, insolence or poor performance, leading ultimately to dismissal. In too many machine bureaucracies the disciplinary systems on the shop floor are far more rigorously enforced tham in other areas of the organization. This rightly causes resentment amongst shop floor workers.

Apart from PBR, the reward and punishment systems are blunt and potentially expensive. More finely tuned systems (in addition to the control of work processes considered earlier) exist such as the personal control exercised by the manager through the decisions he makes, and the more focused systems of target setting and management by objectives.

External controls – job related systems

Personal control   Here the manager directs the subordinate by issuing instructions and orders. This very direct form of control can be based on one or more of the control systems we have already mentioned, like authority, or the reward and punishment systems. It could also, though, be based on the respect the subordinate has for the manager as a person; for his technical expertise, managerial skills, integrity etc. Less precise than direct orders are decision guidelines that the manager may give to the subordinate, thus leaving some discretion to the subordinate. Looser still as a form of personal control is the allocation of resources (via budgets) to subordinate managers. The more favoured managers being rewarded with bigger budgets.

Objective setting   A widely known and applied job related control system is Management By Objectives (MBO).[10] The process runs as follows:

■ The subordinate drafts a written statement of his continuing objectives, and specific goals for the year ahead. Included in the statement are suggestions for how performance may be measured.
■ Then the subordinate and boss meet to discuss, negotiate and finally agree a set of objectives for the coming year.
■ The objectives, and progress towards them are reviewed at regular intervals during the year, until at the year end a formal evaluation

takes place. Here the focus should be less on recrimination about non-achievement of agreed objectives, and more on setting new targets for the future.

We can see a link between MBO and the Theory Y view of human nature described in Chapter 4. For MBO to work, managers must have a high degree of trust in subordinates, and the subordinates themselves must respond positively to the involvement in target setting and the increased autonomy the system gives them. However, some firms have tried to adopt MBO without much success. This could be due to the state of the organization at the time of the introduction of the system. For example, if the prevailing climate is characterized by hostility and suspicion, MBO is unlikely to flourish unless a major shift in attitudes precedes its introduction. Some senior managers, desparate for 'off the shelf' panaceas, have jumped at MBO, forced it into the firm and have sat back waiting for the promised benefits to emerge. Consequently, some line managers have resented the system from the start, regarding the whole exercise as a waste of time. We have already noted the problems of setting inappropriate targets, of using performance measures that distort activity away from the true purpose of the organization, and of systems that do not link rewards to performance. To some extent all these problems can be associated with MBO.

In large, stable bureaucracies quite specific objectives can be agreed, which are likely to remain relevant for the year ahead. Where there is instability, however, only very broad guidelines should be agreed, and more discretion will need to be granted to the subordinate.

Different pieces of research[11] have shown that objective setting can be more effective where:

■ The objectives are clear and precise (and, hopefully, are measurable).
■ They are neither too easy nor too difficult to achieve.
■ Subordinates have regular feedback on their performance.
■ Rewards are linked to the achievement of objectives.
■ The objectives have been genuinely agreed with the boss, they have not been *imposed* upon the subordinate.

Job descriptions   A useful starting point in determining objectives in the MBO process is a written job description. This is a formal document which defines organizational role and specifies the content, responsibilities and the authority placed in a particular job. Job descriptions can be very lengthy documents, but more usually they focus on the major responsibilities of a position. In some large bureaucracies job descriptions are collated together in the form of a comprehensive manual for the organization as a whole.

Specifying the content of a particular position in such a form is only really appropriate if there is a high degree of stability in the organization. Otherwise, the job description would soon become redundant as circumstances force changes in the job. They have advantages in so far as they can provide guidance to job holders about their duties, they can also help resolve demarcation issues about who does what, and they can help point out tasks which are falling between two positions and are hence not picked up. In addition to providing a good guide in the assessment of the job holder's performance, the job description can assist in selection decisions, and in highlighting training needs.

On the other hand there are aspects of job descriptions that are not so positive. They can be used in a defensive way by the job holder to fend off additional tasks, or they can be so worded as to render them almost meaningless. A good illustration of this point is the clause which is often inserted at the end of the job description which requires the job holder to undertake any reasonable tasks that may be asked of him or her from time to time by the manager.

Rules and precedents

In our diagram of external and internal control systems (Figure 5.5) we included rules and precedents as two other external control systems. Rules require that specific actions be taken, or not taken, with respect to a situation. Examples might include: 'no smoking'; all requisitions must be countersigned by a Grade 3 (or above) manager; apprentices are not allowed in the works canteen. Rules permit no discretion, and they operate continually until they are changed. Precedents are a much looser form of control, as they are not necessarily binding on the individual. However, in a stable environment they can take the form of 'quasi-rules', resulting in a situation where only a brave individual would go against the established way of doing things. Precedents are, then, a force for stability, acting as a form of organizational inertia.

Internal controls – direct influences

We now turn our attention to the control systems which are attempting to bring about 'internal', or self-control of behaviour. We have classified training and indoctrination as direct attempts by the organization to influence the individual.

Training   Training is the process through which job-related skills and knowledge are developed. In most of the routine and simple jobs that are often found in the operating core of the machine bureaucracy little training is required. Simple assembly tasks, packing, loading, etc. involve little in the way of specialist skills or knowledge. Once the task has been explained, the operative can usually perform it to a reasonable standard within a few hours of starting the new job. Practice, and learning from other colleagues should enable him or her to rapidly achieve performance levels in line with the older hands at the job.

Where the job requires the exercise of a clearly defined set of skills, or the application of a certain body of knowledge, training can take place prior to the individual taking up the job. This training can take many years (in the case, say, of an aeronautical engineer), it can occur in another, separate organization (like a college), or, if the firm is large enough, it may take place in the firm's own training department (e.g. for craft apprentices). But where the firm does not carry out the training activity itself, it must inevitably surrender some control over the process.

Training is most obviously seen to be successful where job performance can be easily assessed. For instance, you either can or cannot operate a capstan lathe, fly an aeroplane, or replace a gearbox (although, clearly these tasks can be performed with varying degrees of competence). Training is perhaps seen to be least effective where there is no clear agreement about the specific knowledge or set of skills that are trying to be developed. Into this category we can place sales training (other than straightforward product knowledge), fashion design and, most relevant to this book, management development. We shall pick up the particular problems of training managers in the next chapter.

Nigel, our graduate in the case study, is on a structured training programme which involves formal one or two week residential programmes at ABB's Training Centre at Bath, which are interspersed with periods of time spent in different parts of the organization. The expressed purpose of the 'on the job' part of the training is to help the graduate familiarize himself with the way ABB works. But, in addition to the 'technical' knowledge that the graduate acquires the training programme has a more subtle role to play in preparing him for a career in ABB. That part of the process which is trying to instil ABB's norms and values we shall call indoctrination.

Indoctrination By indoctrination we mean the formal processes deliberately employed by the organization to ensure that the new recruit adopts the desired set of norms, values and attitudes. This can take many forms, ranging from the 'basic training' of the army recruit, which involves techniques which try to strip away undesirable outside identifications and to replace them with strong loyalty to the regiment, to less obvious means used in the business corporation. We can note that Nigel attended a formal dinner, addressed by the Chairman of ABB, as part of his training programme. The event has few merits as a 'training' device; but it can be explained if we view it as being part of the indoctrination process.

Other indoctrination techniques that are employed by large organizations include: in-house magazines and newspapers; statements, and repetitions of key corporate values (like 'the customer is Number 1'); rallies and conventions (e.g. to launch a new product); and even the singing of company songs! In some cultures, getting employees to identify with the company's goals seems to be easier than others. You rarely find an employee of an American company bad-mouthing it in front of 'outsiders', and loyalty to the corporation seems the norm rather than the exception in Japan.

The desired values and attitudes can more easily be preserved and reinforced if adherence to them is seen to be rewarded by promotion. Furthermore indoctrination is made far more effective if the selection process ensures that new recruits naturally identify with the aims of the organization.

Internal controls – indirect influences

Selection A distinction can be made between *recruitment* and *selection*:

■ *Recruitment* is the process whereby the organization generates a pool of applicants for a position.
■ *Selection* is the subsequent assessment of the individuals from the pool with a view to appointment.[12]

Recruitment devices range from the 'Wanted: bright lad, apply within' notice on the factory gate, to sophisticated 'head-hunting' trawls organized by specialist agencies. More typically, the large organization will employ a variety of recruitment strategies depending upon the positions to be filled. Nigel was initially recruited via the 'Milk Round', a process where large firms (and organizations like the Army) send recruitment specialists around the Universities interviewing final year undergraduates. Promising candidates are then usually offered a second, more in-depth interview and assessment programme at the firm's HQ.

But the selection process itself is full of hazards for both the firm and the potential employee. In essence, the firm is trying to predict how the recruit will perform in the organization on the basis of very limited information. The standard panel interview is often augmented by various tests – of numeracy and literacy, or personality. *Attainment* – what the candidate can do already, can be gauged on the basis of the formal qualifications he presents, backed up by references. *Aptitude*, however, is much more difficult to assess. Here we are looking for what the candidate might be able to do if he was developed and trained. We might be more interested, then, in more subjective aspects of the candidate's abilities like drive, outgoingness, diligence, attention to detail, steadiness, and social skills. These attributes can be assessed using personality tests (like 'Personal Profile Analysis'),[13] but few managers would rely solely on these techniques in making selection decisions. This is why the interview plays such an important part in the process.

Although selection interviews have been criticized as being unreliable predictors of job performance they are nevertheless the predominant, and usually the decisive selection method used by organizations. Reasons for this are:

- The manager needs to assess certain intangible aspects of personality in deciding whether the candidate will 'fit in' to the organization.
- The process is usually two-way, permitting the candidate to ask questions of the panel, and to seek clarification of the job, prospects etc.
- People *expect* to be interviewed, and the interview itself is therefore seen as an important ritual.

Whether or not the candidate will 'fit in' (e.g. conform to the organization's culture) can be a critical aspect of the selection process which is often made difficult to assess if the interview is excessively formal. Formal interviews ensure that the candidate is on his guard. Great efforts are made to project the right image (whatever the candidate perceives this to be) and to give the answers that will impress. However, this tough type of interview technique may well tell you little about the 'real' person behind the defensive barriers he or she has carefully erected. Very few jobs require people to perform well in pressurized, highly formalized situations, so it may be much more helpful to conduct the interview in a moderately relaxed manner. Once the candidate is reasonably relaxed, the barriers start to come down, and the personality can begin to come through.

There are systems designed to help interviewers bring some objectivity into the process. For example, lists of important attributes (such as necessary skills and confidence) are used, either as a checklist, or as part of a point rating system. This technique might be especially useful if a sequence of interviews, with different panels, is being used, and where there are a large number of candidates. But it can backfire if the group is not clear about the criteria and if there is not a shared understanding about the system of rating.

In the large bureaucracy selection decisions for many positions in the operating core and lower levels of the staff departments were made solely by specialist personnel staff. Hence line managers tended to 'get what they're given' as they had no real say in the selection process. This lack of involvement caused resentment in both the manager and the subordinate. However there were good reasons for leaving the difficult task of selection to specialists. They develop expertise in selection that the line manager cannot. Centralizing the recruitment and selection process can also help the company to achieve a uniform standard of new recruits. Similarly, centralization permits a consistent approach to the induction and culturization processes. More recently line managers have been given more responsibility for recruitment decisions with 'staff' acting as advisors on the selection process.

Culturization In Chapter 4 we explained how the culture of the organization emerges, and how it is perpetuated. In addition to the formal methods employed by the management to indoctrinate the new recruits there are various subtle influences at work which attempt to mould the individual to 'fit' the culture of the organization. These pressures operate informally, and our case study gives us a couple of examples to illustrate the culturization process. Arthur Palmer's wife Barbara seems not to 'fit in'. This could be due to her personality, her education or possible her class background. Because she differs from the dominant image of what an ABB executive's wife should be like, she, and Arthur, are probably made to feel quite uncomfortable at ABB social occasions. This 'problem', however unfair, could seriously impair Arthur's career prospects. Similarly, Nigel worries about whether the opinions he voiced on South Africa may count against him in his aim to establish a career with ABB. A cultural consensus can emerge within the management group of a large corporation where political opinions, modes of dress, codes of behaviour and even social and leisure activities conform to an acceptable model. This consensus can be so pervasive that members of the management group would implicitly assume that others shared these attitudes.

For those individuals who naturally identify with the cultural consensus, the subtle pressures to conform would not even be noticed. For others, whose opinions and life style seem at variance with the prevailing culture, these pressures will be all too obvious. For these individuals the choice can be between conforming and internalizing these more acceptable attitudes and norms of behaviour (thus letting them lead a peaceful organizational existence), or leaving the organization. It takes a very strong and determined personality to continually resist these pressures.

Communication in the large organization

Communication systems can be viewed as the glue that binds the organization together. For effective coordination of the diverse parts of the large organization, information about such things as outputs, costs, new innovations, potential customers and changes in the grading system must flow effectively through the structure.

It is useful to distinguish between formal and informal channels of communication that operate in the organization. Information which takes a written form (memos, reports), which is passed on in formal settings (meetings, speeches), which passes down the chain of command, and which is routinely collected and processed can be regarded as part of the formal communication system that has been deliberately set up by the management. Informal communications, in contrast, are more often verbal (telephone conversations, chats in the canteen), often cut across departments and hierarchical levels, they can bypass the 'official' channels, and are often viewed as a source of problems by the management. The 'grapevine' is the most notorious informal channel, one which is essentially outside the control of senior management and which can spread rumours, pass on inaccurate data, and leak 'secret' information. The role of the informal processes and groups comes into its own here.

The existence of informal communications is in part a necessary response to inadequate formal channels. Even where a lot of thought is given to the setting up of formal communication systems, problems seem to arise which force people into the informal systems. Consider some of the following communication problems associated with the large bureaucracy.

Tall hierarchies Some large organizations have five or more tiers of management. Despite the fact that *downward* communications have the force of authority driving them, messages can become distorted, or reinterpreted as they filter down the chain of command. This problem is exacerbated where verbal instructions only are given. Also, the tall hierarchy separates the senior management from the shop floor leading to the senior managers to be seen occupying 'ivory towers' or 'mountain tops in the clouds'. Both groups thus tend to misunderstand each other, and remain unaware of each other's problems.

Blocks on upward communication There is no authority relationship driving upward communications. So grievances, or even positive suggestions emanating from the shop floor may only reach the first or second level in the hierarchy. There are other reasons than the authority relationship for these blockages.

Supervisors may be reluctant to pass on information which places them in a bad light with their superiors. In many large organizations the prevailing atmosphere is one of barely suppressed hostility, fear and mistrust – this climate not only discourages openness and honesty, it is actually reinforced by the withholding of information, and the use of information for political ends. Quality circles, TQM and similar formal processes are geared to reduce these negative effects (see pages 143–4).

Information as a source of power Individuals can enhance their power in the organization if they have access to 'privileged information', or if they possess specialist knowledge which makes other members of the organization dependent upon them. For example, take the operative who is the only person who knows how to repair a particular machine, or the staff analyst who can use his or her superior knowledge to outwit, confuse and bamboozle the line manager.

Departmental 'silos' An overemphasis on the formal, vertical channels of communication, coupled with the tendency of people to identify with a smaller grouping in a large organization can create 'us and them' attitudes between functions. This can be made worse by efforts to build strong team feelings and cohesiveness within departments. This is because one device used by managers to unite a group is to pit it against a 'common enemy', which, in the large organization, may well be another function. So, inspection fight with production, sales staff see the accounts and commercial department's paperwork as preventing them from doing their job, and line managers see the staff people as being out of touch with reality. In such circumstances the free flow of information across the organization can be interrupted and the organization becomes a series of departmental silos.

Large spans of control Where managers have spans of control which are too large to enable them to communicate carefully with their subordinates problems will arise. This is not just down to the absolute numbers of people directly supervised by the manager, it is also affected by how many other demands are placed upon him. The more he or she is diverted into, say, doing technical work, attending meetings with other managers, going away on visits to other parts of the firm, the less time that is available for communication with subordinates. This state of affairs can arise through poor time management or can result from the fact that the manager is so uncomfortable in face-to-face communications with subordinates that this type of contact is avoided as much as possible.

Communication overload Communication problems can arise in organizations through people having too much information foisted upon them. In the large bureaucracy communication overload can have a number of causes: over-use of the courtesy copy system (so everyone gets copies of everything), badly designed reporting systems which make it difficult for the recipient to sort out the wheat from the chaff, and long circulation lists which deliver information to those low down on the list weeks after the information was initially received or generated. The keeping of multiple records in different parts of the organization also causes difficulties when the data needs to be updated.

Communication problems – some solutions? If we accept that the large, complex bureaucratic organization is likely to defeat any attempts to design 'ideal' communication systems which will meet all the problems listed above, then we are into a process of looking for partial solutions to these problems. For example, take the issue of the lack of communication between the senior managers and the shop floor. There are ways of getting around this blockage, but they in turn can create additional difficulties.

The top-down bypass Here chief executives go direct to the shop floor or front-line workers. They mix with the troops, listen to them and maybe even muck in and do some of the work. This kind of action can have beneficial effects, not just in improving the communication flow between top and bottom of the organization. Chief executives can enhance their standing with the people on the front line, they are seen to be 'human', and 'one-of-the-lads'. But, this direct communication bypasses all the levels in the hierarchy in between the top and the bottom. It can undermine line managers' authority, especially if chief executives overturn decisions or policies they have established. So whilst it might do some good to chief executives' reputations this may be at the expense of line managers' relationships with the shop floor. However, this action might not even benefit chief executives; if they are not naturally gregarious personalities or if they are ignorant of much of what happens in the operating core, such a direct intervention can make them appear at best rather silly, at worst the whole exercise could be viewed as an elaborate and cynical charade.

The bottom-up bypass   One way the shop floor can get senior management to listen to them is to go in for some collective action. Individually, shop floor workers have no *formal* power, collectively they can exert quite considerable *informal* pressure on the management. Trade union organization seems to be a feature of the large corporation, not the small firm. Maybe this is a response to the communication problems highlighted above. And maybe there is a size of organization, which, when exceeded, significantly increases the chances of collective action emerging as a response to shop floor dissatisfaction.

Developments in information technology have gone a long way in improving the formal communication flows in the large bureaucracy, especially where the needs of the *user* of the information have been paramount in the design of the system. However, these technological approaches cannot solve the problems of communicating feelings, values, ideas and opinions, nor can they improve *listening* in the organization. Some management solutions to the problems of improving the flow of this qualitative information are listed below.

Briefing groups   The briefing group system is designed to ensure that important information is communicated formally down the chain of command. The cascade begins with the chief executive briefing his team of senior managers, who in their turn, brief *their* senior managers, and so on down to the first line supervisor who briefs his team. Clearly, the process described is necessarily sequential in nature, and delays at any point in the cascade will seriously reduce the impact of the information. Also, the manager is given some discretion in deciding what to pass on to his team, which can mean that some parts of the organization end up better informed than others. Some managers also use the formal briefing sessions to encourage a two-way flow of information, which should be beneficial.

Encouraging informal links   We noted in the issues arising from the ABB case study that Arthur Palmer may feel more intimidated by 'Head Office' because he does not know these people. Some of the greatest benefits of company-wide management development courses result from the informal contacts established between managers located in different parts of the organization. If you know the person on the other end of the telephone it is likely that better communication will take place because the conversation will tend to be less formal. Moving staff around the organization (like Nigel, the graduate trainee) can also help in the establishment of useful informal networks. If managers encourage and promote situations where informal links can be developed between different departments then not only should communication flow be improved, but also improvements in co-operation and decision making can result. These informal links help staff to see the organization's problems from other people's perspectives; actions and decisions by department X which were perceived by staff in department Y as being either crazy, or due to bloody-mindedness, can now be seen in a different light as staff in department Y get to understand the problems facing the staff in department X.

Reorganization   It may be that a reorganization is the best way of improving the communication between staff. Problems may be solved if staff are regrouped under a common manager, or if they are located together in the same office, or building.

3.3   Management

The work of the manager in the large bureaucracy varies a great deal depending on the part of the organization in which the manager is located. We shall pick three types of management position which should help us to get a picture of these variations in management work. These are:

- The chief executive
- The staff manager
- The line manager

In our exploration of these three management positions we shall use Mintzberg's ten role set which was outlined in Chapter 3.

The chief executive

From our case study we know one duty that chief executives of large corporations perform, and that is the delivery of a formal speech to new graduate employees. Here they are acting out the *figurehead* role. Their presence is more symbolic than functional, their speech more inspirational than factual, but they are nevertheless signalling something very important to the new recruits. Just the chief executive being there is evidence of ABB's commitment to these graduates.

Other roles which feature prominently in the work of chief executives are the *liaison*, *spokesman* and *leader* roles. As chief executives are the most powerful people in organizations they have a fair amount of choice about what they do with the job. The personality and personal preferences of chief executives will largely determine which roles they choose to emphasize. So one chief executive may well favour the ceremonial, and external liaison roles, whilst another who cannot help interfering in new projects being developed within the organization, favours the entrepreneur role.

There is also evidence that chief executives delegate some roles to one or two other senior managers, so they work together in informally created small teams.[14] For instance, the chief executive may choose to pass on the internally focused roles, like resource allocator and disturbance handler to his second-in-command, and retain the external roles (liaison and figurehead) himself.

Generally, the work of chief executives in large organizations displays the following characteristics:

- A large amount of time is spent in formal meetings.
- The chief executive tends to have a well developed set of external contacts.
- A relatively small amount of his time is devoted to internal operations.
- The job tends to be unstructured, and unspecialized with a long range orientation.
- A large degree of work managing ambiguity, uncertainty and discretion.

The chief executive in control of the machine bureaucracy is specifically concerned with keeping the whole structure altogether. The conflicts and problems that seem to be an inevitable feature of these organizations mean that tight control over people (through the exercise of the chief executive's formal powers) is a major feature of the chief executive's work. We have already noted the strong tendency for vertical communication flows, this, coupled with the blockages on lateral communication means that disputes and coordination problems between functions are passed up the hierarchy to the only *generalist* position in the whole structure, the office of the chief executive. So disturbance handling is, perhaps surprisingly, a significant element in the work of the machine bureaucratic chief executive.

The staff manager

Arthur Palmer, the manager of the Toiletries Division Accounts Department is a typical example of a staff manager. Other similar positions would be: the head of corporate planning, the personnel manager and the chief production engineer. These management positions are located *outside of* the 'line', in the technostructure and the support staff groupings. The roles which tend to be to the fore in these staff management positions are those of spokesman, negotiator, monitor, disseminator and liaison personnel.

These managers often act as nerve centres for specialist information, they find themselves having to negotiate with line managers (e.g. the budget cuts that Arthur Palmer has to get agreement on) and they are often required to represent a particular specialism in dealings with other parts of the organization.

Generally, the work of the staff manager exhibits these characteristics:

■ They spend more time alone in their office than other middle managers.
■ They demonstrate the least amount of fragmentation and variety in their work.
■ They often get involved in *doing* specialist work themselves, rather than just managing the other specialists.
■ Staff managers therefore have to be experts themselves in order to successfully manage other experts.
■ They may not have had formal training in a managerial role but have gained such positions due to their 'expertise'.

The line manager

In the *small* organization the line manager engages in a wide variety of activities. Take production managers, for example, who are responsible for planning and scheduling the work in the shop, for sorting out problems with quality, component supplies and machinery; they are also responsible for leading, disciplining, appointing, promoting and rewarding the supervisors and operators who work under them. We can contrast this broad scope of responsibilities with those of line managers in large bureaucracies. Most of these activities have been removed from the line manager's job description. Planning and scheduling is now carried out by specialist production planners, quality is the preserve of the quality assurance manager, the machinery is maintained, and replaced by the plant and production engineers, and decisions about discipline, hiring and firing, pay and promotion have either been completely removed from the line manager, or tight procedures and rules have been set to constrain and guide his decisions. So, much of the power, and a good deal of the interest in the line management job has shifted away to staff in the technostructure. The major tasks left to the line manager are:

■ Trouble shooting, or disturbance handling.
■ Liaising with the staff in the technostructure.
■ Supporting the vertical flows of communication – passing data upwards and converting plans sent down to him into detailed sequences of actions.

Line managers (e.g. works superintendent, regional sales manager) tend to be on the go from the moment they begin work. They seem to be bombarded by problems, crises and orders. Their day is fragmented, and due to the ad hoc nature of the demands made upon them, they rarely have the opportunity to sit back, reflect, and plan. Coping and firefighting best describes the job. The two examples we have picked, the works superintendent, and the sales manager are both responsible for activities where the measurement of performance is quite straightforward. If delivery dates are not met, if sales targets are not fulfilled, the senior management can quickly jump on the manager responsible. Contrast this with some staff management positions e.g. the training manager; how closely can his performance be monitored?

By definition, the line managers are engaged in the core task activity of the organization, and although this responsibility carries with it some of the problems highlighted above, it also has its compensations. The line is where the action is, where 'real' results are achieved. This sense of immediacy and importance can be attractive as it also confers on the line manager a certain amount of informal status vis-à-vis the rest of the organization.

To sum up, then, the line manager's main activity is centred around the decisional roles of disturbance handler and negotiator.

Managerial decision making

One of the most direct ways in which the manager impacts on the organization is through the decisions he takes. It will be easier to understand the nature of decision making at both the apex of the organization and in the middle line if we are familiar with a general model of the decision making process. Figure 5.6 presents a framework which can help us pick out some of the more interesting aspects of decision making; it is a *descriptive* model, as it does not purport to tell managers how to make decisions. We shall work through the model from the top, explaining first the pressures on managers for decisions.

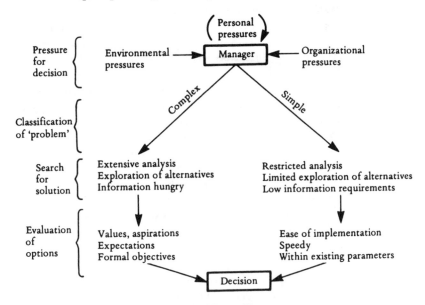

Figure 5.6 *A model of managerial decision making*

Pressure for decisions There are three sources of pressure on the manager to make decisions. The first source of pressure is the *environment*, and the type of task the organization is engaged in will largely determine how dynamic and complex the environmental pressures facing the manager are. In addition, the level at which the manager is operating can give us a guide to the extent of exposure to outside influences he will be subjected to. Generally the higher the level, the more environmental interaction takes place and the greater the degree of discretion invested in the role.

Organizational pressures come at the manager from all sides. Demands for decisions from the boss, from other managers and from staff experts in the technostructure, have to be prioritized alongside pressures from the unit or department the manager is in charge of. These pressures can result from disturbances to systems and routines, the need to allocate (or reallocate) resources, and demands from subordinates. The manager's staff can generate the need for decisions of a 'technical' nature (to do with the work of the unit), or for decisions which are more to do with personal or organizational issues.

The third source of pressures are those that managers put on *themselves*. This can depend on their personalities, how confident and 'proactive' they are about the job and their reactions to pressure and stress. Do they actively go out and look for problems to solve, systems to improve? Or do they hide in their offices hoping no one will bother them? Also, this can depend upon how *responsive* managers are to requests for decisions. A negative response, or no response at all, will not encourage people to come to them; they may well be bypassed or ignored.

Lastly, pressure can depend upon how sensitive managers are to signals of disquiet, or disequilibrium in their units. The more sensitive they are, the more decisions they will get involved in.

Problem classification Having been presented with a problem, the manager is then faced with having to make a decision about how to proceed with this decision. This stems largely from how the manager initially perceives the problem being posed. A simple problem will not justify some extensive search for a good solution, and, conversely, a problem judged to be complex will call for fairly extensive search activity. To take a very simple example, suppose Arthur Palmer's secretary popped her head round his door and asked 'Tea or Coffee?'. This is clearly a simple problem requiring the very minimum of thought prior to a response.

Although this is a trivial example we can nevertheless use it to make some important points about problem classification. Why was it such a simple decision?

(a) *Only two options were posed:* If she had asked 'would you like a drink?' the decision becomes more complex. Hot or cold? Alcoholic or nonalcoholic? Is she inviting me out to the pub?

(b) *The consequences of a wrong decision were minimal:*   He asks for tea, when Arthur gets it he perhaps wishes he'd chosen coffee as he'd forgotten how awful her tea was. Thus the risks attached were very low.

(c) *Considerable experience in the decision area:*   A lifetime of tea and coffee drinking informs Arthur's decision.

In contrast, what about Nigel's decision to join ABB? If you scan the list of three variables in the tea/coffee question and apply them to this job selection decision, we can see a clear difference in the two decisions. Nigel may well be faced with any number of career routes to pursue – business or the professions? public sector organizations or private sector? small organizations or large? The consequences of a wrong decision, although not exactly catastrophic, could be quite far reaching if he joins a firm he is not happy with. Furthermore as regards previous experience of this decision, Nigel has none; little from his own experience can be brought to bear on this decision.

Other problems facing the manager may not be so easy to classify. Consider how the wrong classification of a problem can cause great difficulties to the manager. A subordinate requests a day off next Thursday, and you the manager immediately say yes. It turns out that he has already exceeded his holiday entitlement for the year; or that next Thursday is when the auditors will be in so we need everybody available; or that, because last week you turned down a request from another man in the same section, you are now being accused of favouritism, and there are rumblings of discontent at your inconsistency.

Again, it is drawn to your attention that some staff are arriving often ten or fifteen minutes late in the mornings. A simple problem calling for a simple solution? Get each supervisor to note down arrival times and to discipline those who are late more than once in a week. By initially perceiving the problem as a simple one, the manager has jumped to a simplistic solution. But there may be many complex issues involved in this situation. For example, perhaps they are late because the bus timetables have changed; perhaps they all stay longer at the end of the day. It could be that the lateness is merely a symptom of poor morale in the section, maybe in response to the section supervisor's management style. Now if this latter situation was in fact the case, the solution to the problem would be far more difficult to find.

So faulty problem classification can trigger off an inappropriate search for solutions.

Search for solutions

Problems classified as complex warrant a fairly extensive search for alternative solutions. Often these are one-off problems which require novel approaches, calling upon both quantitative and qualitative information. Judgement, experience and intuition married to sound and logical decision processes should improve the quality of these complex decisions.

In contrast, simple problems can be solved using past precedents, procedures and fairly 'mechanical' routines.

Evaluating options   This stage matches the alternative courses of action with the values and objectives of the decision maker. Managers often like to make out that they take 'rational' decisions. This belief is based around the notion that there are a set of agreed and understood objectives against which alternatives can be evaluated. For example, the rational decision is the one involving least cost, or the one that will potentially yield most profit to the firm. This view of rationality can be taken to an extreme where a decision is seen to be more 'rational' than another even without referring explicitly to a set of objectives. This is a mistake, as decisions can only be judged 'rational' or not, against some frame of reference. Now, in some manager's minds the paramount objective is the profitability of the firm, and therefore it is 'rational' to sack 200 staff as this helps restore profit levels. But there are other frames of reference which are more to do with the manager's *personal* objectives and values. Will this decision make me look good in the eyes of my boss/subordinates/family? Will it involve me in some psychological discomfort? (e.g. will *I* have to tell them they've been sacked?). What might the impact be on the local community?

Even where the decision maker says he is being rational and objective, this is often an illusion. A study in the United States showed that graduates making decisions about their future careers did so in a subjective way even though they perceived their decision to be objectively rational.[15] For example, the MBA student really wants a job in Vermont because that is where his girlfriend lives, but he *tells* people he's looking for a job with a small, rapidly growing high tech outfit, because he knows XT Inc. who are small, high tech etc. are based in Vermont.

Two last points should be made before we leave this section on managerial decision making. Firstly, we need to make a clear distinction between being *decisive* and being a good decision maker. Decisiveness often implies spur of the moment decision making. This impresses some people as it demonstrates quickness of thought, and clarity of judgement, and in some corporations, this shoot-from-the-hip, seat-of-the-pants decision making is the dominant management style.

But there are few decision situations which require *immediate* responses, and the quality of the decision can usually be improved even with just a couple of minutes reflection. The trick is to avoid being pressurized into quick decisions without at the same time being perceived as being indecisive.

The second point concerns a whole array of social and psychological influences on management decision making, which can operate at all the four stages in the decision making process outlined in Figure 5.5. For example, look at the following two groups of biases and perceptual distortions and see if they make sense in relation to your decision making.[16]

(a) *Social position/organizational position:* Your social position influences the way you see the world. Some of us are quite isolated from alternative life styles, attitudes and values. We can deliberately filter the media (by choosing a particular newspaper, for example), choose where to live and who to mix with, so that we rarely come across people who do not share our view of the world. Secondly, if you are promoted into a management position do you still see the organization from the same perspective you held as a subordinate?

(b) *Preference for simplicity:* The world is a complex place. We use a range of techniques to simplify it like categorizing people as either all 'good' or all 'bad'; like assuming other people think the same way as we do; like taking more notice in decision making of the concrete things, and the measurable things that are nearest to us in time and place; and like looking for straightforward explanations of causation.

Armed with these general insights into managerial decision making we can now focus on decision making at two distinct levels of the large organization: decision making at the strategic apex, and at middle management positions.

Decision making at the apex

The time horizons tend to be long term at the apex, and hence decisions taken today might affect the health of the organization far into the future. The chief executive, being the most powerful person at the apex is able to make decisions about most aspects of the organization. He can decide where to allocate new investment, he can create a whole new department, close down the regional sales offices, and scrap the payment-by-results system. So the breadth of his decision making power is formidable, but although the chief executive *decides*, it is up to other people in the organization to *implement* his decision.

Some of these very big decisions (or 'strategic' decisions as they are often referred to) may be made more or less on the spur of the moment. But, many of them will only be taken after a fairly extensive analysis of a number of alternatives, and their advantages and disadvantages, has taken place. This logical and systematic analysis will probably be done by staff specialists who advise the managers at the apex. They are likely to engage in many, if not all, of the strategic processes outlined in Table 3.2.

We might take as an example of a strategic decision, whether ABB should launch a new range of deodorants. Initial approval to begin development work was given by thc Toiletries Division Board three years ago. This amounted to an increase in the research and development budget in the first year of development of £240,000, a sum which was just within the division's approval limit of £250,000.

If the budget increase had been in excess of this sum, approval from the main board of ABB would have been required. After three years of research, development and test marketing the development team have come to the Divisional Board with a proposal to launch the range of deodorants nationally in three months time. As part of the case they have presented to the Board they have included a comprehensive market research report, an analysis of the present competition in the industry, details of postings, production schedules, advertising campaigns and profit forecasts. These analyses have been carried out by internal researchers and external consultants.

On the basis of this information, the Divisional Board, chaired by the Managing Director, have to come to a decision. In reaching their decision as to whether, and if so when, to launch the deodorants, the Board, guided by the Managing Director will have to weigh the evidence presented with other, less quantifiable aspects of the decision such as:

- What if the launch is a flop? How will this affect our reputation? (Or even our jobs?). A classic example is the disastrous launch of Ford's Eisel car, despite its comprehensive marketing and development.
- What if our major competitor beats us to it? Can we afford to delay the decision? as IBM's slow response to the PC.
- If we commit resources to this range of products, this might mean other potentially profitable developments may be starved of funds i.e. what are the opportunity costs?
- If we are not seen to be innovative, will we be criticized by ABB main board? i.e. how do we see ourselves?
- Will we look daft if, having agreed to the development funding over three years, we are now seen to pull out of this project?
- Can we trust the profit forecasts? i.e. what are the bases and assumptions about revenue flows?
- How demotivated will the team be if we delay, or turn them down? Will this affect morale in the whole division?, i.e. trust and innovation – what really is the company culture?

This launch decision helps us to highlight some important aspects of strategic decision making and the attendant subtext and risks. Where there is some relative stability in the organization's environment, and where the consequences of a wrong decision would be very serious, it is usually worthwhile investing time and resources in improving the quality of the decision. Corporate planning, which is an elaborate and systematic approach to making strategic decisions, takes a number of forms, one version of which is outlined in Figure 5.7.[17] During the process of corporate planning the external environment is analysed and the strengths and weaknesses of the firm in relation to its environment are assessed. Alternative strategies are generated and evaluated, before the 'best' strategy is selected, and implemented.

1 Clarify corporate objectives
      ↓
2 Set Corporate targets
      ↓
3 Forecast future performance with
   existing strategies
      ↓
4 Identify differences between targets
   and forecasts
      ↓

5 Appraise the   Assess the
   external   ⟷   firm's strengths   6
   environment   and weaknesses

7 Identify competitive advantages
      ↓
8 Revise targets
      ↓
9 Generate alternative strategies
      ↓
10 Evaluate alternative strategies
      ↓
11 Select strategy
      ↓
12 Implement strategy

Figure 5.7 *A corporate planning process*

This structured and logical approach to these important strategic decisions has distinct advantages:

■ It ensures that as far as possible all feasible options are explored.
■ It forces the decision makers to consider the firm's resources, and to evaluate these in the light of an assessment of the external environment.
■ The process itself generates important information which can be used for other purposes.
■ The process should improve the decision maker's confidence in the strategy finally selected.

So logical approaches to strategic decisions would seem to be beneficial, but how can we incorporate into this process some of the less 'objective' considerations we have suggested could be the concern of the decision makers in ABB? In the evaluation and selection of different strategic options (e.g. launch in three months; launch in six months; abandon the project) these qualitative considerations will be brought to bear on the emerging decision. When it comes to the crunch, the chances are that the Divisional Board will go ahead with the launch, because by that time abandoning the project would be more difficult (more embarrassing?) than going ahead.

We can conclude that even where a logical and systematic decision making process is used to make a strategic decision, qualitative, value-laden considerations still play an important part.[18]

The successful implementation of this decision to launch depends on two factors:

(a) *Stability:* The decision has been taken at the top on the basis of analyses presented to these decision makers, and on their assessment of the evidence. The product launch date, and the budget allocations agreed upon will only remain feasible if no significant internal, or external changes take place. So this type of centralized planning and decision making is only viable where stability obtains.

(b) *Commitment:* The decision takers are not the ones who have to make the plan work. The launch will only be successful if the managers and staff lower down the hierarchy are committed to its success. *Compliance* can be achieved by the use of the authority system, but changes like this new product launch invariably generate unpredicted problems which require more than compliance for their resolution. Genuine commitment can be gained through the exercise of inspirational leadership from the apex, or through some involvement in the decision making processes by those who will have to actually see the project through. (See Chapter 6.)

(c) *Personal anxiety* – the dynamics of personal risk – fears of rejection, humiliation, failure and disapproval – also play a part in how the top team takes up its role and its desire for risk aversity or grandiosity in its strategic deliberations. These unconscious dynamics will impact on their decision making.[19]

To summarize, we can say that decision making at the apex of the large bureaucracy exhibits the following characteristics:

- A long range, corporate-wide perspective is usually required of the strategic decision makers.
- Decision makers often call upon staff specialists to provide analyses to support the decision process.
- Strategic decision making and planning in the machine bureaucracy is a highly centralized, top-down process.
- Although 'rational' decision making techniques are often employed by the decision makers, their decisions will still reflect important, non-quantifiable considerations.
- Risk and uncertainty can generate feelings of anxiety and unconscious emotional effects.

Decision making in the middle line

Middle managers in the large bureaucracy are only required to make decisions within narrow, specified domains. This reflects the high degree of horizontal specialization that is such a feature of the large, stable organization. So in stark contrast to the chief executive, the scope of the middle manager's decision making is very limited indeed. We have also noted the seemingly incessant demands that are made on the line manager, especially in the production area. Other features of decision making in the middle line are:

(a) *Short Time Horizons:* Decision making tends to be over short time horizons, months and weeks, rather than years. In production areas especially the immediacy of the task often demands very rapid decision making.
(b) *Closer Control – less autonomy:* In contrast to the chief executive, the middle manager usually has to work within quite limiting constraints imposed by his or her immediate boss. Also rules, precedents and procedures limit freedom of action.
(c) *Limited scope for Innovation:* The large bureaucracy emerges in a stable environment, and in turn the nature of the structure militates against change. Hence the scope for innovation is severely curtailed as changes will inevitably interfere with established systems, and they are likely to impact upon someone else's territory engendering resentment and resistance.

Problems with planning

We have already mentioned some problems that corporate plans may encounter which could prevent their implementation (instability, and lack of commitment), but attempts at planning can come unstuck for other reasons.

(a) *Responsibilities not clarified:* It is essential to clearly allocate responsibilities for the implementation of the planned course of action, otherwise the chances are that everyone will think it's someone else's problem.
(b) *Unrealistic targets:* Setting ambitious but attainable targets (like delivery dates) can be a useful motivating device, but unrealistic targets can turn people against the whole plan.
(c) *Plans too rigid:* Even the most stable organizations are subject to some unforeseen events. A plan which cannot cope with even slight hiccups is unlikely to be successfully implemented.
(d) *Lack of control information:* In order to monitor whether the plan is being achieved, some control information must be generated and fed back to the managers responsible.

Successful plans tend to have the following features:

(a) *Workable:* They are realistic, not overambitious. This often rules out major shifts in the organization's activities. Plans which work are ones that involve incremental moves, rather than wholesale changes.

(b) *Resistant:* Plans need to be able to survive some unanticipated events. This often means that only *general* issues are decided upon initially, leaving the detailed implementation to evolve to match the changing circumstances.

(c) *Acceptable:* Those responsible for implementing the plan must accept it. This means that the plan must not only be *understood*, it also needs to be agreed rather than imposed.

3.4 Groups

In Chapter 4 where we considered the process of group formation, attention was focused on the importance of leadership in guiding the efforts of the cohesive group. In this section, this issue shall be further explored through the examination of a classic series of research projects that have become known as the Hawthorne experiments. We then look for reasons why 'negative' informal leadership emerges, and examine some of the conditions which can make this phenomenon a problem for the management of the large organization.

The Hawthorne studies

These investigations, at the Hawthorne Works of the Western Electric Company in Chicago, were carried out between 1927 and 1932.[20] The experiments began in the best traditions of scientific management with an investigation into the effects of illumination on output. Two groups of workers were isolated; the lighting conditions for one group were varied, those for the other held constant. The surprising result emerged that no matter how the lighting was altered productivity increased for *both* groups. This prompted the industrial engineers at the plant to look for some academic help in explaining these results. A team of researchers from Harvard University led by Elton Mayo,[21] and including F. Roethlisberger and W. Dickson, then took over the investigation.

Mayo set up a second experiment which involved segregating six women whose job it was to assemble telephone relays. In their Relay Assembly Test Room, the women were subjected to a variety of changes in their conditions over a five year period. These involved alterations to:

■ The group bonus scheme
■ Rest pauses
■ Refreshment breaks
■ Hours worked

Before the changes were implemented the researchers spent time discussing them with the women. As with the illumination experiment, nearly all the changes resulted in an increase in output. Then the six women were returned to their original conditions, whereupon their productivity rose to the highest level yet recorded.

The researchers offered a number of explanations for these results.

- The women experienced a new freedom in their work which led to greater satisfaction.
- The women had formed a highly cohesive group.
- The open communication with the researchers had acted as a kind of positive leadership encouraging the women to deliver what they felt the researchers required.
- The investigators took a personal interest in each woman.

Such explanations were only arrived at some time after the Relay Assembly Test Room experiments had ended. At the time the investigators were puzzled by the results and in an attempt to shed some light upon the findings they embarked upon a second phase of research. This consisted of mass interviews throughout the factory and was to reveal an apparent clash between the workers' emotionally based attitudes on the one hand and the managers' 'logical' concerns for efficiency on the other hand.

The third phase of the investigation was the observation of a group of workers in their 'natural' setting, i.e. not in a specially segregated test room. Men engaged on wiring, soldering and inspecting banks of telephone switchgear were observed, as unobtrusively as possible, going about their normal business. These findings were in stark contrast to the Relay Assembly Test Room. The investigators found that:

- The men deliberately restricted their output to what they considered to be a reasonable day's work.
- The men were indifferent to the company's incentive scheme.
- The group was highly cohesive with its own social structure and codes of behaviour.
- The group set norms of output for each individual which should not be overshot, or undershot and penalties were imposed on 'rate busters' or 'chisellers' (e.g. ridicule, ostracism, and physical punishment).
- The group displayed solidarity against the management.

Subsequent studies into the conduct of the Hawthorne investigations have revealed very serious weaknesses in the experimental approaches used.[22] For example, two of the six women originally selected for the Relay Assembly Test Room experiment were replaced at an early stage due to 'uncooperativeness'. Hence, the original conclusions drawn by Mayo, and separately by Roethlisberger and Dickson, have had to be re-evaluated.

It could be argued that both the Relay Assembly group and the Bank Wiring group were highly cohesive, and that the differences in their performance stemmed largely from the type of leadership the group accepted. With the women the leadership came from the investigators, and, from a strong, production orientated informal leader that emerged within the group of six. The men were not led by their supervisor, who only appeared to have fleeting contacts with them, so they looked within the group itself for leadership. It happened that in this case the leadership that was exercised seemed to work against the interests of the management. Nevertheless, the studies highlighted the importance of the informal group in the workplace and began a new era of investigation into the Human Relations side of enterprise.

So informal groups are powerful, and it is in the interests of the management to try to ensure that they are 'positively' led. Some reasons why negative leadership from within the group may emerge are as follows.

- No effective leadership is being provided by the manager or supervisor. This could be due to excessively large spans of control, or poor (or non-existent) management development.
- The organization is so huge that the worker finds it difficult to identify with the aims of the organization and experiences a sense of 'alienation'. This can be exacerbated by a many-tiered hierarchy separating the worker from the management at the apex.
- 'Walls' emerging which separate one group of workers from others, or which separate workers from management. The us-and-them feelings can encourage group members to look for leadership which echoes and supports these views.
- Genuine fears and grievances in the group may emerge. The emotional and 'illogical' attitudes discovered by Mayo may look quite reasonable viewed from a worker rather than a management perspective. The experience of tedious and tiring work, and fears of redundancy are likely to override even the most enthusiastic leadership provided by the supervisor.

Groups and dependence

Michel Crozier's research into the French nationalized tobacco industry revealed the importance of the informal power a group can exploit due to the organization's dependence upon them.[23] The cigarette industry was comprised of a large number of essentially identical factories employing between 350 and 400 people spread throughout the country. The French tendency for centralization meant that finance, raw materials procurement, sales and distribution were all controlled from Paris. All aspects of this stable operation were controlled centrally, with the exception of machine stoppages. These were common because in addition to the usual breakdowns, adjustments had to be made fairly frequently to cope with variations in tobacco leaf.

The only group in the organization able to cope with this important

problem (no machines working means no output) were the maintenance men. They alone knew how to set and repair the machines. They
also avoided any attempts to reduce the organization's dependence
upon them by retaining their expertise in their heads.

So the ability to cope with the last remaining source of uncertainty
in an otherwise completely routinized organization confers informal
power on the maintenance workers. Whether or not they choose to
exploit this power for their own ends would depend upon their
attitudes, morale and the informal leadership of the group. But as soon
as the organization's dependence is removed, the power base withers
away. New computer controlled machines could virtually render the
maintenance workers redundant, if they could automatically re-set
themselves by sensing the changes in tobacco leaf, and if advances in
design made the machines much more reliable. The power of the
workers could also be removed by making their specialist knowledge
available to the machine operators.

3.5 The individual

We have already looked at individuals in *management* positions in the
large bureaucracy, so in this section we shall focus on employees
working at non-management jobs. One message that comes through
clearly in this chapter is that large organizations have many highly
specialized jobs. The differences between vertical and horizontal job
specialization were explained in Chapter 3, but the matrix in Figure 5.8
might help to clarify this distinction.

It is the jobs in quadrant 1 that we are particularly interested in.
These are highly specialized in both dimensions, which implies that
the work is not only narrow in scope, but that the job holder has little
say in how the work should be done. These are the routine, repetitive
and proceduralized jobs found in the operating core of the machine
bureaucracy. There are few opportunities for the employee to exercise

Horizontal specialization

		High	Low
Vertical *specialization*	High	*Unskilled jobs* in the operating core and staff units 1	Some *low-level* *management* jobs 4
	Low	*Professional jobs* 2	All other *managerial jobs* 3

Figure 5.8 *The two dimensions of job specialization*
Adapted from: Mintzberg, H., *Structure in Fives*, Prentice Hall, 1983

initiative, change the method, sequence or pace of work. For many people the lack of challenge and variety in the job leads to de-motivation.

Bob Geldof gives us a good example of this type of work in his autobiography *Is That It?*[24]

> It was a boring job, sorting peas on the conveyor belt. You would fall into a trance, occasionally flicking a blackened pea off the line. Chlorine stung your eyes and dried your mouth and nose. Your ears were assaulted by the constant clatter of empty cans rattling down the runners on to the hoppers, then on to loading racks to be boiled. When we got bored, we turned a can sideways on the runners and the line would stack up behind the overturned tin until it ran back and jammed the machines. We'd hang around until the fitter came to fix it.
> It was mind numbing.

As we noted in the earlier section on structure, Woodward argued that in the machine bureaucracy there is an irreconcilable conflict between the technical and social systems. The technical systems of production are designed with objectives like efficiency and low unit costs in mind. Little thought seems to have been paid to designing production processes that are 'operative friendly', that take the needs and aspirations of those who have to work the system into account. Let us now take a brief look at the needs of the individual, an understanding of which may help us to see more clearly why conflict can arise between the individual and the design of the job.

The individual's developing needs

Chris Argyris suggests that, in the development of the individual from childhood to mature adulthood, changes take place on seven dimensions.[25]

Child	Adult
Passivity	Activity
Dependence	Independence
Limited behaviour	Many behaviours
Erratic, shallow, brief interests	Stable, deeper interests
Short time perspective	Longer time perspective
Subordinate social position	Equal/superior social position
Lack of self-awareness	Self-awareness and self-control

The mature adult who has developed fully along all these dimensions is capable of rising to challenges which can make full use of his potential.

The problem for many people is that the work that they are required to do in the machine bureaucracy prevents them from progressing from the infantile behaviours listed above. These routine jobs require passivity, limited behaviours, short time perspectives, and the individual is subjected to close external controls. They thus tend to display 'childlike' behaviour, which spurs the infuriated management into exerting even more controls on the individual in an effort to 'correct' these behaviours. We thus have a vicious circle of control: people are treated like children; they then behave like children; and they are therefore punished and controlled even more. The same has been described in public sector settings which can reduce autonomy and responsibility.[26]

We should, though, make two important qualifications to this line of argument. Firstly, we should not assume that all individuals are capable of displaying the same level of 'maturity' on Argyris' seven dimensions. Additional responsibilities and independence in their job might overwhelm them. Secondly, we should bear in mind that the job is only one portion of an individual's 'life space'; it may even be the least important to him or her (see Chapter 3). The individual may have more than enough opportunities to develop mature behaviours outside of work, through family responsibilities, hobbies, or work for voluntary organizations. They may even come to work looking for a rest from these demands!

Nevertheless, industrial relations problems seem to be a feature of the large machine bureaucracies which suggests that there is a significant degree of dissatisfaction in the operating cores of these organizations. There appear to be four options which could help reduce the conflicts between the needs of the job holder, and the demands of productive efficiency:

(a) *Abandon mass production technologies:*   One way this could be achieved is through a wholesale change in consumer attitudes away from preferences for cheap, disposable products to higher cost, more durable products, which can be produced on more of a 'craft production' basis.

(b) *Change the reward systems:*   Accept that boring jobs are here to stay, but reward productivity directly through acceptable payment-by-results systems.

(c) *Automate the operating core:*   This has happened in many *process* industries. The operating core is, in essence, just one huge machine, where the pace of output, and its quality are determined by the design of the system, not on the efforts of operators.

(d) *Redesign jobs:*   Rather than abandoning the enormous productivity of the mass production systems, make adjustments to the *content* of jobs to make them more intrinsically rewarding.

It is this last alternative which has attracted most attention from practitioners and researchers. However, before looking at the redesign of jobs in more depth, a consideration of the theoretical work which stimulated much of the debate in this area is required.

Herzberg's two-factor theory

Frederick Herzberg, an American psychologist, is regarded as perhaps the most influential advocate of job redesign.[27] He and his colleagues conducted a series of surveys of employee attitudes at work. Employees were asked to recall times when they felt exceptionally good about their jobs, and when they felt really bad about them. The investigators then probed for reasons why the employees felt as they did.

The key result from these studies was that events and factors that caused satisfaction at work were quite different in kind to those that caused dissatisfaction. Factors that caused satisfaction at work were as follows.

- Achievement (e.g. demanding, complex tasks accomplished)
- Recognition
- The work itself (challenge; autonomy; the sense of 'wholeness' in the job)
- Responsibility
- Advancement

But it transpired from the surveys that the *lack* of these factors in the job did not significantly explain *dissatisfaction*. A different set of factors seemed to be associated with dissatisfaction at work:

- Company policy and administration
- Supervision (technical, and interpersonal relations)
- Salary (and fringe benefits)
- Working conditions
- Communication channels

Herzberg suggests that improvements to these factors will reduce dissatisfaction but they will not promote positive feelings of satisfaction in the job holder. It is the motivator, or 'growth' factors, that cause job satisfaction. The clear message from this research is that the jobs in the organization that are highly vertically and horizontally specialized should be redesigned to inject more responsibility, challenge and interest into them. Only this way will the job holder display positive motivation at work.

However, Herzberg's research has not been without its critics.[28] Specifically, different researchers have levelled these criticisms at the 'two factor' theory:

- Attempts to replicate the research have not produced the same result.
- Satisfaction and dissatisfaction can be caused by the job content, or the job context, or both, depending on the *expectations* of the respondent.
- Respondents are likely to take credit for 'good events' and to blame others for 'bad events': this may explain why people associate the job they do with feelings of satisfaction, and associate feelings of dissatisfaction with what 'others do to them'.

■ The research method, being largely based on views, was susceptible to bias in the coding of subsequent interpretation.

Job redesign

Figure 5.9 shows three alternative methods of redesigning jobs.

Job enlargement involves re-allocating the work in such a way that the job holder does a more meaningful, or 'whole' portion of the task. So instead of separate workers machining and assembling pump bodies, the work is re-allocated so that each worker machines *and* assembles his own set of pumps. The intention of this form of horizontal job loading is that it will reduce 'alienation' and increase the job holder's ability to identify with the task, as a more complete and understandable portion of the job is now under his control.

Job rotation leaves the definition of the job unchanged. Here it is the *job holder* that moves between different jobs all at the same skill level. This is not, strictly speaking, a form of job redesign, but it has the merit of introducing some variety into the work of the individual employee. However, if there is a significant level of specialist skill involved in the jobs, productivity (and quality) may suffer as the operatives change on to a new job. Some firms have introduced *group* job rotation, so teams of workers who have formed themselves into cohesive groups are rotated en masse through the factory. This preserves the all important benefits of informal group membership. Critics of job rotation describe the process as the worker moving from one boring job to another equally boring job.

A widely quoted example of this form of job redesign is the group working approach adopted by Volvo in Sweden.[29] Here, in place of

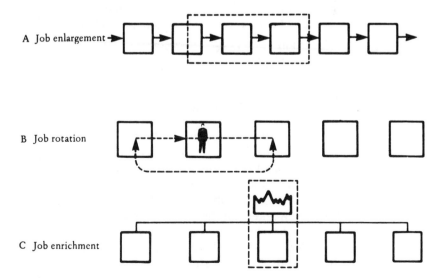

Figure 5.9 *Job redesign*

the traditional production line, a system was devised which allowed the car to be moved from work station to work station. Small teams of people then worked together to assemble a sizable proportion of the car. The teams operated their own form of job rotation, and they controlled many aspects of the work process themselves. Mixed results seem to have emerged from this experiment. Absenteeism and labour turnover, which were a big problem in the Swedish car industry, seem to be reduced significantly at Volvo's new plant, but the longer term viability of the system has yet to be established.

The Volvo experiment introduced elements of enlargement, rotation and enrichment into the design of work. Enrichment involves loading the job *vertically*, by introducing more control and discretion into the job. We have seen how, as the machine bureaucratic form of organization has developed, more and more decision making power has shifted away from the shop floor – to the line managers, and then sideways into the technostructure. Job enrichment is an attempt to reverse this flow using a number of methods.

- *Adding responsibilities*, for example, make the machine operator responsible for checking the dimensions of the components himself, resetting the machine, and carrying out routine repairs and maintenance of the machine.
- *Giving autonomy* to determine the pace, sequence and method of work.
- *Providing feedback*, so that the operator can monitor his own performance in terms of productivity, costs and quality.
- *Providing growth opportunities* where the operator can develop and exercise new skills.

Hackman and Oldham[30] have suggested that the 'motivating potential' of a job can be assessed objectively using this formula.

$$MPS = \frac{\dfrac{Skill}{variety} + \dfrac{Task}{identity} + \dfrac{Task}{significance}}{3} \times Autonomy \times Feedback$$

(MPS = Motivating Potential Score)

Task identity refers to the 'wholeness' of the work, task significance is defined as the degree to which the job is seen to impact on the lives and work of others. These two coupled with the variety of skills involved combine to give an average score of the job's meaningfulness. Autonomy gives the job holder feelings of responsibility, and feedback allows the worker to judge his effectiveness. But, in their review of the relevant research, they concluded that the link between job design and motivation depends crucially on the strength of the individual's growth needs. This in turn is related to their age, intelligence, place of work etc.

So even a job yielding a high MPS will not necessarily motivate a given individual. In fact, a high MPS job may well *demotivate* an individual who may be completely overwhelmed by the demands of the job.

In concluding this section on job enrichment we should make two important points.

(a) Job enrichment may benefit the *organization* if the gains from better motivated workers outweigh the losses from abandoning the most technically productive form of work organization (e.g. the production line).
(b) Job enrichment may benefit *workers* if they have high growth needs, and are capable of responding to the increased challenges and responsibilities of the redesigned job.

Quality circles

The reason we have held over our consideration of quality circles (rather than deal with them in the section on controlling quality) is that, for most of the organizations that introduce them, they represent much more than merely a technique for solving quality related problems. In fact, it would not be overstating the case to argue that, for some organizations, quality circles represent a major shift in management and employee attitudes, a culture shift. Moreover, where circles have failed, it is largely due to people not recognizing the extent of the attitude shifts required for the system to succeed.

Quality circles are small groups of employees who work together to agree ways of improving quality, productivity and other aspects of their work. They are led either by a supervisor, or by someone chosen from the circle.

Although the basic idea originated in the United States, Japanese manufacturing firms were the first organizations to really exploit the potential of the technique. Quality circles are both a form of job enrichment, and an extension of participative management, which can bring significant tangible and intangible improvements in the work-place. In addition to measurable benefits (e.g. elimination of scrap, reduction in reworking of components), a successful circle programme can result in greatly improved morale and motivation.

However, like some other management techniques (MBO, briefing groups) quality circles have sometimes been 'forced' into organizations without proper preparation. Often, where they have failed, management blame the technique itself rather than the ham-fisted way it was introduced into the organization. Some problems that can prevent the successful introduction of quality circles include:

■ Inappropriate management styles (e.g. authoritarian).
■ Shop floor suspicion and mistrust.
■ Lack of senior management support.
■ Inadequate training of circle leaders.

■ Unwillingness to support/implement solutions proposed by circles.
■ Lack of appropriate facilities (and time), for holding meetings.

However, where the organization is ready for the introduction of circles, and where the appropriate training has taken place, they have been successful. UK companies that have benefited from the technique include Jaguar, Rolls-Royce (Aero Engines) and Ford.

Careers in the large organization

In this, the last section in the large organization, we shall be raising issues about the nature of careers, and career 'progression' within the organization. Few answers are provided, but posing the questions should stimulate some useful reflections.

Does career progression imply promotion? Can individuals see themselves as progressing in their careers in any way other than movement up the hierarchy into more and more senior management positions? Can organizations cope with the concept of career progression in other ways? As most large organizations are pyramid structures, everyone cannot expect to be promoted. Individuals with career aspirations will be frustrated and demotivated if these expectations are not fulfilled. Do processes like graduate recruitment, and special graduate training schemes raise expectations which the organization cannot deliver?

Does everyone want a 'career'? A mistake some managers make is to assume that their subordinates are all interested in promotion. The prospect of promotion can operate, for some individuals, as a type of control system, but for others this carrot holds no attractions. This could be due to their perceived inability to 'hold down' a management position, or that the efforts required to get promoted do not match the rewards, or that they are more interested in the 'technical' aspects of the job, or, maybe, that the prospect of joining 'the management' is viewed with horror as selling out to 'the enemy'.

Can a career be planned? Someone joining a large stable organization has a better chance of satisfying their career ambitions, than an equally talented entrant into a small organization. Bigness provides opportunities, and stability within the organization's structures and processes also helps the individual identify the behaviours, qualifications and experiences that tend to lead to successful career progression. Whereas instability changes the rules on which promotion decisions are based, leaving some individuals well qualified for positions that no longer need to be filled.

Although a well planned career is more achievable in a large stable organization (e.g. the Civil Service) even these leviathans are not immune to the forces of change. Technological developments, reductions in funding, economic recession, oil price movements and changes in government can disrupt the large bureaucracy, leading to cutbacks, blocks on recruitment, and redundancies.

What are the costs to the organization of the career/promotion link?
If progression implies movement into management positions, the organization operating this policy may encounter some unanticipated side effects. The organization may lose its best designers, engineers and accountants either to other organizations not operating this type of policy, or they will be 'lost' as they replace technical work with management work. Also the quality of management may suffer if good specialists are rewarded by promotion to management positions to which they are not suited. For example, the qualities required of a good systems analyst (e.g. diligence, ability to work independently, attention to detail, stubbornness) may not be ideal attributes in a *manager* of a team of systems analysts.

Most large organizations operate policies of promotion from within, so that only certain specialist positions in the hierarchy are filled through external recruitment. Promotion from within has distinct advantages for the organization.

- *Authority:* If all managers began their careers on the shop floor (or its equivalent) they would have a better chance of earning the respect of their subordinates. They would have been 'at the coal face' so they would be able to relate more easily to the problems and concerns of their subordinates. Thus the authority of the individual manager, and of the management group as a whole could be enhanced.
- *Preserving the culture:* Where the loyal and staunch supporters of the organization's norms, values and ways of doing things are rewarded by promotions, strong forces exist which help to preserve the organization's culture.
- *Familiarity with systems:* In the large and complex bureaucracy it can take years for individuals to familiarize themselves with the systems and procedures employed in the organization. Promotion from within helps, then, to enhance the administrative competence of the management.
- *Reducing labour turnover:* If individuals with career aspirations see that there are opportunities for advancement within the organization they will be encouraged to stay.

However, if the overwhelming majority of management positions are filled by internal promotions, the quality of decision making can be affected. In particular, over time a narrowing of organizational thinking can occur and the culture become inward-looking.

With like tending to promote like, the ambitious members of the organization may feel that their best chance of promotion lies in conformity, compliance and not rocking the boat. One dominant function in the organization (e.g production, sales or finance) often supplies the people who fill the more senior posts (especially that of the chief executive), thus encouraging a function-orientated view of corporate decisions.

Further reading

A comprehensive and up to date survey of management and organization theory is provided by L. J. Mullins in *Management and Organizational Behaviour* (Pitman 1985). Most of the more popular management and organization theorists's contributions to our understanding of large organizations are succinctly summarized in *Writers on Organizations* by D. S. Pugh, D. J. Hickson and C. R. Hinings (Pelican 1989).

References

1 Weber, M., *The Theory of Social and Economic Organization*, Free Press, 1947
2 Mintzberg, H., *Structure in Fives*, Prentice Hall International, 1983
3 Fayol, H., *General and Industrial Management*, Pitman, 1949
4 Urwick, L., *The Elements of Administration*, Pitman, 1947
5 Brech, E. F. L., *Principles and Practice of Management*, Longman, 1975
6 Woodward, J., *Industrial Organization: Theory and Practice*, Second Edition, Oxford University Press, 1980
7 See Reeves, T. K. and Woodward, J., 'The Study of Managerial Control' in Woodward J. (ed) *Industrial Organization: Behaviour and Control*, Oxford University Press, 1970
8 Taylor, F. W., *Scientific Management*, Harper and Row, 1947
9 Herzberg, F., *Work and the Nature of Man*, World Publishing Co., 1966
10 See Drucker, P. F., *The Practice of Management*, Pan Books, 1968 and Humble J. W., *Management by Objectives*, Management Publications Ltd. (BIM), 1972
11 See Webber, R., *Management*, Irwin, 1979
12 See Lewis, C., *Employee Selection*, Hutchinson, 1985
13 Thomas International
14 See Mintzberg, H., *The Nature of Managerial Work*, Harper and Row, 1973
15 Soelberg, P., 'Unprogrammed Decision Making' in *Studies in Managerial Process and Organizational Behaviour*, Edited by Turner, J. H., Filley, A. C. and House, R. J., Scott Foresman and Co., 1972
16 See Katz, D. and Kahn, R. L., *The Social Psychology of Organizations*, Second Edition, Wiley, 1978
17 See Argenti, J., *Practical Corporate Planning*
18 See Bowman, C. and Asch, D., *Strategic Management*, Macmillan, 1987
19 See Kets de Vries and Associates, *Organisations on the Couch*, Jossey-Bass, 1991 and Jarrett, M., and Kellner, K. 'Coping with Uncertainty: A Psychodynamic Perspective', *Journal of Management Development*, March, 1996
20 Roethlisberger, F. J. and Dickson, W. J., *Management and the Worker*, Harvard University Press, 1949
21 Mayo, E., *The Human Problems of an Industrial Civilization*, Macmillan, 1933
22 See Rose, M., *Industrial Behaviour*, Penguin, 1978

23 Crozier, M., *The Bureaucratic Phenomenon*, Tavistock Publications and University of Chicago Press, 1964
24 Geldof, B., *Is That It?*, Penguin Books, 1986
25 Argyris, C., *Personality and Organization*, Harper and Row, 1957
26 Diamond, M., 'Psychological Dimensions of Personal Responsibility for Public Management: An Object Relations Approach', *Journal of Management Studies*, Vol. 23, No. 5, 1985, pp. 543–62
27 Herzberg, F., Mausner, B. and Snyderman, B. B., *The Motivation to Work*, Second Edition, John Wiley & Sons, 1959, and Herzberg, F., *Work and the Nature of Man*, World Publishing Co., 1966
28 See House, R. J. and Wigdor, L. A., 'Herzberg's Dual-Factor Theory of Job Satisfaction and Motivation. A Review of the Evidence and a Criticism', *Personnel Psychology*, Vol. 20, Winter 1967 pp. 369–90 and King, N. 'A Clarification and Evaluation of the Two-Factor Theory of Job Satisfaction', *Psychological Bulletin*, Vol. 74, July 1970, pp. 18–31
29 See Rowe, C. J., 'Visiting Volvo: New Developments in Car Production' *Industrial Management and Data Systems*, January/February, 1983, pp. 8–12
30 Hackman, J. R. and Oldham, G. R., *Work Redesign*, Addison-Wesley, 1980

6 The flexible organization

In this chapter different aspects of flexibility will be explored. The central theme is the flexible organization, and the case study describes a structure which is designed to be 'permanently flexible'. But organizations which do not require this capability still need to change and adapt periodically. They need to be flexible at certain times to cope with the demands of change. In addition to issues concerning change in organizations, flexibility is also considered in relation to managers, and individuals. Ideas about flexibility in management style, and the need for individuals to adjust and adapt their skills are developed in the latter half of the chapter.

1 Case study: Pearson, Merriman

It was 9.45 on Tuesday morning in the second week of January. Rob Hearne moved around the conference room, adjusting the seating arrangement. He checked that coffee cups were available on the table in the centre of the ring of easy chairs he had formed. He was nervous. This was the first meeting of the project team that had been assembled to carry out the airport extension appraisal requested by the County Council. He had been given the job of Team Leader, his first real role since joining the firm a month before from Sussex County Council. There he had spent four years in the Planning Department having qualified in town planning at Liverpool University.

Pearson, Merriman had recruited Rob because they were expanding their management consultancy business. In the past five years the firm had trebled in size, largely through the enormous demand for consultancy. The core of the business was still chartered accountancy, but increasingly the emphasis was shifting to new areas of work. The consultancy business centred around three broad areas: financial management; management information systems; and project appraisal. It was this last area of business that Rob was earmarked for; the senior partners in the firm believed that recruiting someone from the public sector would help them move into the lucrative large scale project work required by local authorities and national governments in the UK and abroad.

Although this was ostensibly a briefing meeting, Rob was aware that this was an important opportunity to bring the new team together and to establish himself as project leader. The team was comprised of Rob and four specialists from different departments in the firm:

John: A cost and management accountant recruited from Unilever.

Pauline: An operations researcher by profession, specializing in modelling transport systems.

David: A computer programmer/systems analyst recruited from Logica.

Peter: An ex-government economist with expertise in cost-benefit analysis and environmental impact assessment.

By 10.05 a.m. the group had assembled and Rob tried to bring the meeting to order.

Rob: 'OK, thanks for coming everyone . . . er . . . Peter, David can we start the meeting, please?'

Peter: 'Sure, why not?'

David: 'Sorry, Rob.'

Rob: 'Well, if I could begin by bringing you all up to date on our discussions with the council . . .'

Rob proceeded to fill the team in on the meetings he had held over the last ten days with officers from the council.

Rob: '. . . so, to sum up, they want us to carry out a full appraisal of the runway extension, using the consulting engineers' estimates of capital costs and construction lead times, but we are to carry out the demand forecasting and environmental impact analysis ourselves.'

Pauline: 'Sounds fine, Rob, but when do we have to deliver the report?'

Rob: 'Ah, well, they rather pinned me down on this one . . . I said we'd deliver the final report by the end of February.'

At this point, Peter, who had been making the odd aside comment to David throughout Rob's presentation, interjected forcefully.

Peter: 'Impossible. There's no way I can do a sensible environmental impact assessment in less than three months, and to do that I need the air traffic forecasts. So a February deadline is just not feasible. The earliest we could manage it is June.'

Rob, who was clearly rattled by this sudden, critical reaction, tried to negotiate with Peter. But he was getting nowhere. Peter stuck to his original assessment of the time required for the job, and, in arguing his point made sarcastic references to Rob's lack of project management experience. Eventually, after Rob had sensed that the other members of the group were becoming increasingly irritated with this prolonged argument, he said:

Rob: 'Look, I'm in charge of this project and in my judgement it is feasible to carry out the environmental impact analysis in the time we have available. So, I must insist that . . .'

At this Peter rose from his chair

Peter: 'Insist? Insist? Oh, I see, so you *Insist*!'

Then he visibly relaxed, and, addressing no one in particular said 'somebody ought to make sure in future that project leaders have some idea about how to manage a project team.' And with that, he left the conference room.

David, who was obviously uncomfortable with the turn of events then made some excuses and left the meeting. John, apologizing to Rob, pointed out that without Peter they couldn't do the project, so Rob had better try to 'bring him round'.

That left Rob and Pauline together in the conference room.

Pauline: 'Rob, I think you should have contacted each of us before agreeing the delivery date with the council. I know Peter went over the top, but he's got a point.'

Rob: 'But I tried to call a meeting last week. You and John were still tied up with another project, and Peter was in Frankfurt all week! What else could I have done? And anyway, what's Peter working on that's so important that he can't spend more than two days a week working on this project?'

Pauline: 'Well, you'll have to sort that out with Peter.'

Rob: 'After his performance this morning I can't say I'm inclined to go to him waving an olive branch. He's in the Economic Analysis Department, isn't he? I think I'll have a word with his boss.'

Pauline: 'I don't think that's a good idea, Rob. If you take my advice you'll try and solve this problem yourself. Believe me, if you go running to the head of department expecting them to wield a big stick on your behalf, you'll be disappointed. Worse still, it'll really count against you. They'll think that you're not up to the job.'

Issues arising from the case

Environment

1 Pearson, Merriman is operating in a growing and therefore dynamic environment.
2 The demands for their consultancy services have increased.
3 There is an increasing interest and potentially lucrative new market in the public sector.

History and resources

1 The company started and still retains its core business in chartered accountancy.
2 The last five years has seen an increase in size by a factor of three fold.
3 The rapid expansion and the development of new markets suggests a resource base capable of supporting these changes. However,

caution is also necessary as like the growing times (Chapter 4), 'overtrading' can cause cash flow difficulties.

Task

1 The core task of the business was the provision of consultancy services in the hold of management accounting – presumably to increase the quality of client's decision making, risk assessment and returns on investment.

2 The particular project task in the case focused upon forecasting and making an environmental impact assessment.

3 The specific tasks under the broad business activity were likely to be complex (both routine and non-routine) and have varying degrees of uncertainty that needed to be managed. Thus, the quality of skills, competencies, experience and expertise required from the project team would be paramount to its success. This diversity of skills base was certainly reflected in the group.

Structure and management

1 The evidence in the case points to the existence of a quite complicated structure. There are departments, like Economic Analysis, where Peter is located, and presumably John comes from an accounting group of some description, David would be in with the Systems Analysts and so on. So Rob is managing a team of people who come from separate departments, each headed by a departmental manager. We therefore have individuals (like Peter) who report to at least two bosses. What difficulties is this likely to present to the management and the individual?

2 The management consultancy projects would appear to be demanding tasks requiring technical sophistication for their successful completion. Also the amount and type of work coming into the firm is fairly unpredictable. To what extent is the structure of Pearson, Merriman a natural response to this type of task?

3 A central issue in the case is Rob's ability to manage his team. Does he have much formal authority over team members? On what bases can he hope to influence them?

4 What skills and expertise should the project leader have? How can they be developed?

5 If a lot of decision making is dispersed, how is the strategy of the organization determined?

The informal organization

1 Communication across the organization is a feature of Pearson, Merriman. This is encouraged both by the Project Team concept, and frequent meetings. Are there other ways of effecting cross-departmental liaison?

2 There are hints in the case of an informal working environment in Pearson, Merriman (or, at least, in the consultancy part of the firm) with staff on first name terms. Does this informality make the management and control of staff easier or more difficult?

3 The firm seems to recruit staff who have already established themselves in other organizations. What might be the effect of this policy on the culture of the organization? Would it encourage individualism at the expense of a 'corporate', or 'group' ethic?

4 Hiring is done on merit, and firing on the basis of poor performance. Are organizations like Pearson, Merriman more likely to sack inefficient staff than large bureaucratic firms?

5 Decision making power appears to be widely dispersed in the organization, flowing to those with the expertise and information to make good decisions. If this is the case what decisions are left to the senior managers?

6 How can you establish cohesive, cooperative groups when they are continually being disbanded and reformulated, and when they are composed of a heterogeneous collection of individuals?

7 Meetings seem to be an important feature of this type of structure. How can they be made more effective? Are there any problems when groups rather than individuals take decisions?

8 Is there the right blend of people in the team to help make it function effectively?

Individuals

1 The unpredictability in the flow of work must create uncertainty for the individual about what (if anything) he will be expected to do next.

2 Two bosses, and multiple projects present the individual with often conflicting demands on his time and loyalty. How does the individual cope with this?

3 Where does Peter's informal power come from? Is it due to his expertise, his force of personality or perhaps it stems from his 'connections' with senior members of the firm?

4 The skills, competencies and experience of staff appear to be of a high level in this case study. What are the implications of managing such diversity?

Outputs

1 The major issue for this project based system is time. The deadline is considered to be too tight. Furthermore, while the resource of expertise is available, people's time is not. Thus, meeting the February deadline is unrealistic. How can one manage time better in this situation?

2 The ability of the group to manage adaptation and be flexible is uncertain from the case. What conditions do you think would be necessary to help flexibility?

3 Rob's initial meeting has done little to promote the 'spirit d'corps'. In fact, he may well have damaged relationships already. Thus, reducing the group's performance from its inception. What might he do to increase performance or at least limit the 'fall out'?

Table 6.1 Summary of key factors in the case study

Inputs

■ Environment	■ The market is increasingly interested in the company's services with a new and growing market in the public sector.
■ Resources	■ Assume to be financing expansion but caution about cost flow.
■ History	■ Established core service is chartered accountancy. Grown by three fold in 5 years.

Transformation

■ Task	■ Company task chartered accountancy and consultancy. Project task consulting on project. Appraisal.
■ Individual	■ Task requires high skills/competencies and authority, based on expertise.
■ Organization	■ Based on project teams, matrix structure *intended* to be flexible.
■ Informal	■ Power bases and alliances exist. Personal authority can usurp delegated authority like managing cats.

Output

■ Goal achievement	■ Project leader sets unrealistic time scale.
■ Resource utilization	■ Time and 'opportunity cost' of one project over another seems to be the key constraints.
■ Adaptation	■ Uncertain
■ Group performance	■ Looking poor
■ Individual behaviour and effect	■ People's ego at stake.

2 Context

The consultancy side of Pearson, Merriman is operating in a changing and exciting market environment. It shares many of the features of the growing organization. However, in the latter case, the growing organization is dealing with change from one organizational configuration to consider: or form one relatively stable position to another.

In the case of the flexible organization it operates in a rapidly changing environment and therefore needs to be able to constantly respond quickly. Such an environment suggests that for companies to retain a competitive edge they need to be 'proactive' in their strategy, 'prospectors' of business and in the extreme case 'innovators'. While not all companies can be the post-war innovators of Sony or Hewlett Packard,[1] they certainly need to share some of their strategic principles. These have included:

■ product and market focus – including high awareness of market trends

- a need for quality goods
- high level specification in the product or service
- research and development investment
- valuing employees and relationships with clients
- a willingness to take risks
- clarity about the organization's philosophy and culture without being 'closed'
- a willingness to adapt and change
- commitment by employees and managers to the organizational task and new product/service developments or improvements.

Furthermore, under such conditions, the task is more often not that complex. In the case of Pearson, Merriman that is certainly true. Thus, the context of this organization can be seen as dynamic and complex as described in Chapter 4, summarized in Table 4.1.

3 Organizational configuration

3.1 Structure

Mechanistic and organismic structures

A useful starting point in our exploration of the flexible organization's structure is a study by Burns and Stalker into change in the electronics industry.[2] This innovative work highlighted deficiencies in the bureaucratic structures of some Scottish electrical firms which prevented them coping effectively with changing markets, and, particularly, with changing technology. Burns posited two 'ideal types' of structure, a *mechanistic* structure which is adapted to relatively stable conditions, and an *organismic* (or organic) structure which is adapted to conditions of change.

The mechanistic structure has most of the features we have described as pertaining to the large bureaucratic organization, including:

- A high degree of specialization, where individual jobs are difficult to relate to the overall task of the organization.
- Precise definition of jobs, responsibilities and work methods.
- Hierarchical structures of control, authority and communication.
- Knowledge located at the apex of the organization.
- Vertical interaction predominates.
- Insistence on loyalty to the organization and obedience to superiors.

Where the environment of the organization remains stable this mechanistic structure is quite successful. It can produce standardized products cheaply. But conditions of increasing instability which call for adaptation and innovation, sometimes of a sophisticated and complex nature, put the mechanistic structure under pressure.

Burns commented that:

> The ideology of formal bureaucracy seemed so deeply ingrained in industrial management that the common reaction to unfamiliar and novel conditions was to redefine, in more precise and vigorous terms, the roles and working relationships obtaining within management, along orthodox lines of organization charts and organization manuals. The formal structure was reinforced, not adapted!

Faced with the need to adapt to changing circumstances, mechanistic firms adopted three types of bureaucratic response.

Informal pairings   The normal procedure for dealing with anything outside of one's clearly defined job would be to pass it on to someone else. This assumes that new roles have been created to deal with the new tasks as they have arisen. In the absence of these new specialist positions the only recourse would be to pass the problem upstairs to the boss. Unstable conditions will lead, then, to the senior management being overloaded with demands for decisions. One way of coping with the overload adopted by some of the chief executives in Burn's survey was to establish ad hoc relationships with individuals at various parts of the hierarchy. The chief executives thus began to delegate decision making in such a way that the official line of authority was often bypassed: a case of crisis management.

New positions and departments   Burns referred to the creation of more positions and departments as the 'mechanistic jungle'. Communication problems were dealt with by creating liaison positions, and new, specialist departments. Hence new jobs and whole new departments were established which depended for their survival on the perpetuation of the problem. The need for liaison posts was exacerbated by management cultures which expected people to stay in their places, at their work. So if communication with another part of the organization was required, rather than allowing the engineer to 'wander round the factory', a liaison person was appointed to wander round the factory for him.

Committees   Not many firms opted for this response, partly because it was perceived as a characteristic disease of government administration. Committees are a way of dealing with temporary problems which cannot be solved by an individual without upsetting the balance of power. However as a permanent solution it posed difficulties for the individual, whose career interests and loyalty were tied to his function and department, not to the committee.

So, mechanistic structures were not capable of adapting effectively and naturally to the changing circumstances facing the firms. Burns concluded that it is the organismic form which is appropriate in changing conditions, where fresh problems and unforeseen requirements for action cannot be broken down or distributed automatically to existing parts of the functional structure. The organismic structure is characterized by the following features:

- The contributive nature of special knowledge and experience to the common task of the firm.
- The adjustment and continual redefinition of individual tasks through interaction with others.
- Problems are not easily passed upwards, downwards or sideways.
- A network structure of control, authority and communication.
- Knowledge located anywhere in the network, and this location becoming the centre of authority.
- Lateral rather that vertical communication.
- Communication consists of information and advice rather than instructions and decisions.
- Commitment to the task, expansion and technological progress valued more than loyalty to the organization.

The almost complete failure of the traditional mechanistic structures to absorb electronics research and development led Burns to doubt whether a mechanistic organization can change itself into an organismic form. This can largely be explained by the resistance to change which is endemic in the highly structured organization. If adaptation means that old departments are disbanded, and new activities are established which divert resources from existing functions, change will be resisted.

The environment of the flexible organization

From Burns and Stalker's work we can conclude that the bureaucratic form of structure is ill suited to changing environments. But can environmental instability, or dynamism, be coped with by the simple form of organization described in Chapter 3? You may recall that this structural form had few staff specialists, and decision making was centralized at the apex of the organization. The great advantage of the simple structure, though, is flexibility, but the structure can only successfully adapt if the tasks facing the organization are essentially simple. Simple tasks can be coped with by centralizing decision making, where changes can be implemented by the boss issuing new instructions to his subordinates.

However, Pearson, Merriman are tackling quite complex and sophisticated tasks in their developing consultancy business. This suggests that more experts will need to be involved in decision making, so a highly centralized structure would not be an appropriate response. Where the environment facing the organization is dynamic *and* complex, a new structural form is required, something that contains the features of the organismic structure posited by Burns and Stalker.

The flexible structure needs to allow experts to come together to solve complex problems. These teams cannot however be permanent fixtures or departments (like in the professional bureaucracy) because the problems they are tackling are continually changing. What is required is a structure that can permit the forming and re-forming of expert groups, whilst preserving the expertise of the individual professional. One solution to this problem is the matrix structure.

The matrix structure

This structural form deliberately violates the 'one-man-one-boss' principle of organization design (see Figure 6.1).

This organization chart is unlikely to be on the wall at Pearson, Merriman because as soon as it was drawn up it would probably be out of date. The only relatively permanent features of the chart are the functional departments. These are the 'homes' for the technical experts, each one being led by a departmental manager. All staff are allocated to a functional department, including the project managers. Rob has been pulled out of the Project Appraisal department to head up the airport project. The other team members are temporarily seconded from their functions to work in Rob's team. You should note that this project is not expected to occupy all the time of each team member; Peter, for example, will continue to work part time finishing off a project led by another project manager, Dick. It is also possible for a project manager to be a member of another project team.

The advantages of flexibility that the matrix structure brings should

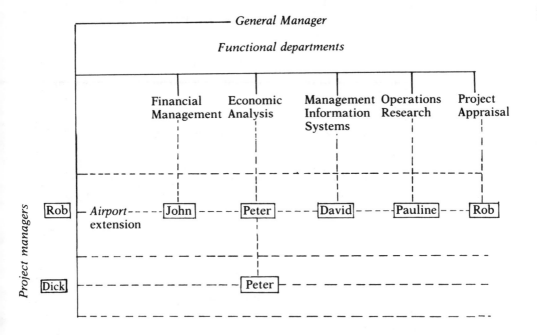

Figure 6.1 *The management consultancy division of Pearson, Merriman*

be clear. However, in some respects this flexibility is achieved at the expense of the individual specialist. Whilst some stability is provided for individuals in the functional 'homes', where they can work on longer term developments, update their knowledge and share experiences and problems with a group of like minded experts, tension and conflict can arise where a person is reporting to more than one boss. Another difficulty presented by this structure is that individuals' performances at their jobs are seen by the project managers, but their pay and promotion prospects are determined by their functional bosses.

The matrix drawn up in Figure 6.1 has the functional managers and the project managers reporting directly to the General Manager. Organizationally, this is a device to *equalize* the formal authority of both sets of managers.

Thus, when conflicts arise between project and function they cannot be resolved by one or other manager imposing his preference through the exercise of formal authority. By equalizing formal power, in theory, such power becomes irrelevant. Conflicts and problems must therefore be resolved through other means, like discussion, negotiation and the exercise of goodwill. We need to stress that formal power is balanced *in theory only* in the matrix structure. It is likely that in the real organization one or other of the groupings will be seen to have the upper hand. This is usually the *function* for these three reasons.

(a) *They were there first:*   Where a matrix structure is introduced it usually takes the form of an overlay on top of an existing functional structure. Staff who are used to the organization are likely still to perceive the functional heads as being more powerful than the project managers.

(b) *They are more permanent:*   Projects, and hence project managers, come and go. Functions are much more stable, and hence staff are more likely to perceive their interests being best served through loyalty and compliance to the functional boss's wishes. Moreover, the function head has a permanent pool of staff which can act as an informal power base in negotiations with the manager of the transitory project team.

(c) *They are the source of professional identity:*   Often, the experts are praised and rewarded because of their professional contribution as an accountant or architect. This is where the status, recognition and sense of value is obtained and thus a high degree of identification with the task is invested through professional identity. This contrasts strongly with the temporary and equalizing nature of a project or matrix team – which in the extreme can be seen as an alienating structure.

It may be worth noting that the matrix structure has been tried in a three-dimensional form. Some very large multinational corporations have experimented with a structure with functional, geographic and product groupings operating simultaneously. Here, a brand manager may find him or herself reporting to three different bosses! Peters and Waterman in their book *In Search of Excellence* have this to say about the matrix structure:[3]

> Virtually none of the excellent companies spoke of itself as having formal matrix structures, except for the project management companies like Boeing. But in a company like Boeing, where many of the matrix ideas originated, something very different is meant by matrix management. People operate in a binary way: they are *either* a part of a project team and responsible to that team for getting some task accomplished (almost all the time), *or* they are part of a technical discipline, in which they spend some time making sure their technical department is keeping up with the state of the art. When they are on a project, there is no day-in, day-out confusion about whether they are really responsible to the project or not. They are.

The matrix structure is described in Greiner's model of organization growth[4] and adaptation which was introduced in Chapter 4. Table 4.2 highlights management practices that are features of Greiner's Phase 5 organizational structure. This advanced phase of development is appropriate where the management focus is on problem solving and innovation. Participation and mutual goal setting are significant aspects of Phase 5.

Adhocracies

Mintzberg,[5] borrowing a term coined by Alvin Toffler in *Future Shock*,[6] describes these flexible structures as *adhocracies*. He distinguishes two types of adhocracy: the *operating adhocracy*, which would describe Pearson, Merriman; and the *administrative adhocracy*, a structural form identified by Woodward in the process industries she surveyed.[7] In some process industries the operating core is largely automated (e.g. oil refining, chemical processing), but because the production system is technically sophisticated, highly trained staff are required to maintain, improve, and redesign the system. The problems are complex and interdisciplinary, requiring experts to work co-operatively in teams for their resolution.

Whereas the operating adhocracy takes on projects on behalf of its clients, the administrative adhocracy undertakes its projects to serve itself. Also, in the operating adhocracy there are no clear distinctions between line and staff, or more significantly, between the management and staff groupings on the one hand, and the operating core on the other. In Pearson, Merriman the 'operating core', 'support staff' and 'line management' merge into one integrated effort. In this respect, however, the administrative adhocracy differs from the operating adhocracy.

The administrative adhocracy makes a sharp distinction between its administrative component and operating core. The operating core exists as a separate, often completely cut-off part of the overall organization. This truncation of the operating core can occur in three ways.

An automated operating core The process industry, where the core virtually runs itself, is an example of this. Routine operating matters are of minor importance, but what is critical for the health of the organization is that change and innovation take place to maintain a technical lead over competitors.

The need for innovation coupled with a machine bureaucratic operating core If competition in the industry is based largely on frequent product improvements, but the demands of volume production require the benefits of a machine bureaucratic core, the organization faces a dilemma. We have chronicled at length the rigidities and conflicts of the large machine bureaucracy. This is not an atmosphere that is conducive to creative and innovative work. So, one option is to separate out the operating core, manage it in an appropriate way, and prevent the culture 'leaking' into the organically structured, creative administrative component. A good example of this type of truncated structure can be found in the newspaper industry. The editorial part needs to be creative and innovative, responding to an intensely dynamic environment, but the actual printing of the paper is a standardized procedure, which is managed in a machine bureaucratic way.

A subcontracted operating core The adhocracy concentrates on innovative design, and leaves the production process to another organization. Sinclair is a good example, here. The production is subcontracted, leaving a small, talented team of researchers to carry on innovating, unencumbered by the demands of administering volume production processes. NASA, in the USA, did much the same with the Apollo and Shuttle developments.

The tendency to bureaucratize

It can be argued that adhocratic structures are inherently unstable. Can an organization be perpetually innovative? The ambiguity and fluidity of the organization can eventually exhaust the employees, and there may be pressures from clients and customers to improve efficiency in solving *their* problem. Maybe Pearson, Merriman will find a 'niche' in the consultancy market that they choose to develop; one where they have some particular advantage over their competitors. For example, say they were getting a lot of business in the area of job evaluation and the design of remuneration schemes. The first one or two contracts required a great deal of creative effort and research, but after seven or eight similar projects an 'approach' to the task emerges. Rather than continually re-inventing the wheel, a more or less stable team of staff begin to specialize in this area of work. A standard set of questions is derived which seem to apply to most organizations they are called in to assist. The 'Pearson, Merriman job rating scale' becomes recognized as a job evaluation package. So, over time, novelty and innovation is replaced by standard systems and packages. Ultimately, there is little point in employing highly skilled experts to administer the question- naire; the standardized procedures can be carried out by semi-skilled assistants.

This transition from operating adhocracy to a professional bureau- cracy may be quite successful, as long as the market for the standardized product continues to expand. However, an administra- tive adhocracy that ceases to innovate and settles into a machine bureaucratic form may well find itself destroyed by competitors who have continued to adapt and improve.

3.2 Organizational arrangements

Coordination across the organization

Coordination in the flexible structure is achieved predominantly through the process of mutual adjustment. This coordinating mechan- ism is a feature of both the simplest and the most complex forms of organization.[8] In the flexible structure great efforts are made to facilitate face-to-face communication between specialists, whereas in the simplest form of organization mutual adjustment occurs spon- taneously.

The matrix structure is designed to enable different specialists to come together to solve problems, and by forming them into small teams mutual adjustment can be easily effected. Thus the matrix structure is an elaborate liaison device. Other, less complex forms of liaison have been introduced into organizations to encourage lateral communication. We have come across one of these already, the 'liaison man' as seen in Burns' study of a mechanistic electronics firm. He was supposed to be the contact between two or more parts of the organization who needed to communicate. To rely on the formal channels would involve a lengthy process of routing questions and responses up and down the chain of command. The liaison position, although by no means a perfect solution, is a formal acknowledgement of the need for lateral communication. Of course, prior to the appointment of the liaison man, contact was still being made between departments, but it was unofficial and informal in nature.

The person occupying the liaison position has a certain amount of informal power as a result of the information he can control. Nevertheless, a liaison position can be a frustrating role to fill. Take, for example, design engineers attached to production departments. They are there as experts in their own right, but also as conduits channelling queries and decisions back and forth from their 'home function', design. However, the range of their expertise is necessarily limited so they cannot always advise the production staff without first referring back to their functional colleagues. This diminishes their standing as 'experts' in the eyes of the production people. And all the time they are out of the design function they are missing out on new developments, and promotion prospects. They don't fit into the production culture, and they lose contact with their former colleagues in the design office.

Another way of effecting liaison, short of the full-blown matrix structure, is the use of committees. These are formal devices for assisting the mutual adjustment process. They can be issue-specific, set up to tackle a one-off problem (like organizing a move to new office accommodation), or they can be permanent devices, like a production review meeting which takes place every week to discuss common concerns across a number of departments.

A further step in the formal recognition of the need for lateral communication is the project or brand manager concept. This is not quite the same as the full matrix organization because no staff are explicitly allocated to work on the project, or for the brand. Rather, the brand manager has formal authority to manage a single product. He or she has to ensure that all aspects of its planning, production, distribution and marketing are being carried out effectively. The degree of power that the brand manager possesses will vary according to formal arrangements, and informal processes. Formally, the brand manager may control the budget for the product, or at least some proportion of it, e.g. the promotion and advertising budget. This gives the manager a significant degree of power to influence other departments in the organization. The brand manager may also have the right to veto decisions, to prevent poor quality products from leaving the factory, and to determine pricing policy. Informally, the senior management can invest the position with considerable power by creating a climate in the organization that values brand managers. This can be encouraged if the brand manager position is seen to be a stepping stone to senior management positions, and where the brand managers are more often than not supported in their recommendations and wishes when they are at odds with various functional departments. (Note that this is not the same as the brand manager *personally* having the authority to tell functional staff what to do.)

So, more or less elaborate formal arrangements can be made to facilitate mutual adjustment, but without an atmosphere of co-peration and trust even the best designed matrix structure will not deliver the required amount of horizontal communication. Staff must be prepared to compromise and negotiate, and to work through problems, rather than use them as excuses for non-cooperation. Goodwill is particularly essential in the ambiguous structure of the flexible organization, where, almost daily, weaknesses can be exposed in the organizational arrangements. A commonly shared commitment to accomplishing the task can overcome these structural defects; positive cooperative attitudes can make even the most inappropriate structures work.

Decision making and culture

It may appear strange to link decision making processes and organizational culture together, but there are important connections between the two. Centralized decision making (the system favoured in most large machine bureaucracies) goes hand-in-hand with power and authority concentrated at the apex of the organization. Authoritarian (not just autocratic) management styles may also, but not necessarily, fit these conditions of centralization. If, however, the tasks facing the organization require a large degree of decentralized decision making, power must accordingly be dispersed to the experts with the knowledge to make the decisions. In these circumstances authoritarian styles are glaringly inappropriate and are more than likely to be ineffective.

The need for flexibility, the uncertainty of the work and the strong requirement for informal liaison will discourage more 'traditional' notions of work and management control. Management cannot expect to see designers sitting at their boards from 9.30 to 5.30 every day. It must be accepted that there will be slack periods followed by periods of intense activity. The staff must be conceded the freedom to relax in the troughs, if they are expected to put in unpaid overtime in the peaks. First names are likely to be the norm, and the conventional trappings which distinguish management's working conditions from those of the 'workers' become increasingly irrelevant (now everyone has a mobile phone!).

We should not, however, confuse informality with inefficiency. In the flexible organization there are few places to hide, because individual contributions can more easily be identified. Flexibility extends to attitudes towards hiring and firing. Flexible organizations can be quite ruthless in shedding inefficient, or not needed staff. In fact, some firms actively encourage staff to move on after a few years service. Some computer and systems consultancies prefer to continually recruit new graduates to replace staff whose expertise may be becoming outdated.

The process of change: adapting the organization

As the theme of this chapter is the flexible organization, we have concentrated our attention on structures which are designed to be 'permanently flexible'. But if we view stability and flexibility as two ends of a continuum, there will be organizations between these extremes which need to adapt to changing circumstances, but their environments are not so dynamic that adaptability needs to be an inbuilt feature of the organization.

Managing change is discussed more fully in Chapter 8. However, it is also relevant in the content of the flexible organization so the relevant aspects are briefly covered here. We have used the example of a major change in the electronics industry to explore the relationship between the structure of the organization and the impact of technological developments and we have examined change processes associated with the growth of the organization (Chapter 4).

Greiner's model of organization growth suggests that the process of adaptation is not continuous but occurs in spasms of 'revolutionary' change. A period of upheaval and turmoil is experienced during which the structure and processes of the organization are adapted to match the requirements of increasing size. The extent to which the organization successfully negotiates this transition is crucially affected by the quality of the decisions the management group make. Inappropriate reorganizations implemented on the basis of inadequate analysis and insight can lead to stagnation and ultimately, the demise of the organization. IBM's restructuring in the 1990s to a divisional structure was quickly reorganized when the new CEO, Gerstner, saw it was not working.

We have made the point quite strongly already in this chapter that the culture of the organization should 'match' or 'fit' the decision making structure. Indeed, the central theme of the book is that structures, processes and management practices should match the particular contingent conditions facing the organization, i.e. there needs to be 'congruency'. The advisability of this perspective is underlined by a significant piece of research carried out in the UK coal industry. This study broke new ground by pointing out, and stressing the importance of, the interconnections between the tasks, the technical system, the organizational structure and the informal social systems of a complex organization.

The process of change: the socio-technical system

Eric Trist, a social psychologist, in collaboration with K. W. Bamforth an ex-coal miner, examined the impact of mechanization in the UK coal industry.[9] They compared the 'hand-got' system of coal getting with the new 'long wall' mechanized system introduced around the time the industry was nationalized. Using the model of groups introduced in Chapter 3, we can compare the two production systems on the three dimensions of: the *content* of the work; the *methods* employed; and the interactions between the individuals in the group. Table 6.2 describes the traditional 'hand-got' method of coal extraction.

Table 6.2 The 'hand-got' method

Content	Coal extraction from underground seams. Environmental conditions: dark, potentially dangerous, unpredictable, changing.
Methods	Extraction by hand, small teams (two/three) working short faces. Teams often subcontracted to the colliery management. Autonomous teams responsible for the whole task. Men are skilled, flexible. Payment-by-results.
Interactions	Intimate, dependent relationships. Self-regulation and internal leadership. Self-selection of workmates. Stable relationships.

The working methods, the structure and the informal interactions in the hand-got method had evolved over a considerable period of time, producing a stable and integrated socio-technical system. The small, tightly knit teams were appropriate to the demanding and dangerous underground conditions where each miner depended for his safety on his colleagues.

The new, mechanized long wall system is analysed in Table 6.3.

Table 6.3 The 'long wall' method

Content	Coal extraction from underground seams. Environmental conditions: dark, potentially dangerous, unpredictable, changing.
Methods	Highly mechanized mass production system working long coal faces (200 yards). Task specialization and three shift working. Teams of forty–fifty men split into cutting, ripping and filling groups who work in sequence spread over the three shifts. Shotfirers and deputies in supervisory roles. Payment-by-results.
Interactions	'External' supervision/control. Little chance of informal communication due to noise and isolation of the individual. Groups are dependent on the previous shift performing well to enable them to earn bonuses.

By comparing Tables 6.2 and 6.3 we can note that, although the content of the task has remained the same, namely extracting coal in difficult and dynamic environmental circumstances, the methods employed have changed radically. A mass production technology has been introduced, and the organizational structures and processes have been adapted to fit the demands of the mechanized production system.

However, the anticipated productivity gains from the new system did not materialize. In addition to low productivity, other symptoms of poor morale were exhibited: increased stoppages, absenteeism, scapegoating (blaming the previous shift), suspicion, hostility and increased labour turnover. To use Trist and Bamforth's own words:[10]

> The crises of cycle stoppages and the stress of the deputy's role are but symptoms of a wider situation characterized by the establishment of a norm of low productivity, as the only adaptive method of handling, in the contingencies of the underground situation, a complicated, rigid, and large scale work system, borrowed with too little modification from an engineering culture appropriate to the radically different situation of the factory.

So the mass production approach that was introduced clashed not only with the environmental problems encountered underground (like faults, water etc.), but it also destroyed the social systems of the organization. The highly cohesive, autonomous working group was replaced by a large, fragmented 'team' operating across shifts, never meeting together and expressing alienation. Moreover, they were subjected to external control from supervisors, the machine technology and the bonus system.

A third system was developed which attempted to marry the benefits of the mechanized production process with the virtues of the 'hand-got' social system. In this 'composite long wall' system groups of miners were responsible for the whole task, they allocated themselves between the shifts and to jobs within the shifts, so a 'group' actually spanned the three shifts. As a result scapegoating, and leaving poor work for the next shift were replaced by inter-shift cooperation. For example a shift group who had completed their task would carry on with the next task in the sequence to help their fellow group members on the next shift. Hence, the redesigned system was not just determined by the demands of the new technology, it was also accommodating some aspects of the social relationships in the mine.

This study illustrates an important lesson regarding change in organizations. The organization is a complex, interrelated sociotechnical system, and change in one part of the system will have ramifications for the rest of the organization. Figure 6.2 represents these interconnections.

The process of change: the organizational context

Before considering ways of managing and implementing change, it is useful to think about the organizational context in which change takes place. The Trist and Bamforth study clearly illustrates the need to consider the social systems within the organization when contemplating changes, and Burns and Stalker's investigations highlight some of the links between the structure of the organization and how it copes with change. Here are some additional aspects of the organizational context which are relevant to the problems of change.

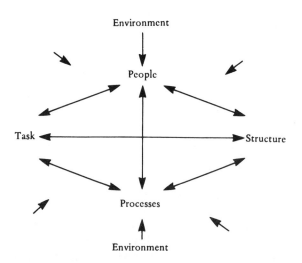

Figure 6.2 *The organization as a complex system*

Past record of change If the organization has a recent history of successfully managed change, attitudes towards more changes are likely to be positive; managers and staff will be confident in their ability to cope. Conversely, changes that have been poorly implemented, that have had a traumatic impact on staff will create hostile, distrustful and fearful attitudes to more proposed changes. In organizations that have experienced great stability over many years staff may fear change because it is unknown.

Expectations about change processes In centralized, autocratic organizations staff lower down in the hierarchy will have no expectations that they would be consulted and involved in designing or implementing changes. They expect to be told of the changes decided by senior management. Authoritarian management cultures may make changes easier to implement if fear of reprisals provokes no opposition or resistance to new proposals. However, authoritarian styles can actually provoke resistance, almost as a reflex reaction in the work force. In contrast, in organizations like Pearson, Merriman staff will be expecting some involvement in changes mooted by the management, and if they are not involved or consulted they may display indignation and dissatisfaction.

Formal and informal power structures If power is centralized, then changes can be decided autocratically and can be imposed upon the rest of the organization members. Where power is dispersed in the organization, those people and groups with significant formal and informal power can choose to resist changes, and can do so successfully.

Strategies for managing change must take account of these contextual factors if they are to be effective. These are discussed in Chapter 8.

3.3 Management

The power of the project manager

In the 'pure' form of matrix structure where both project and functional managers have equal formal authority, conflicts and differences between the project and function managers must be resolved without the exercise of formal power. In the case study Rob Hearne's authority over the project team was put to test by Peter walking out of Rob's meeting. Rob's position as a project manager is in stark contrast to that of both Stan Gordon in the small owner/managed firm (Chapter 3) and Sir Gordon French the Chief Executive of ABB, the large conglomerate (Chapter 5). Both these managers had a great deal of authority; in Stan Gordon's case, the fact that he both owned and managed the business gave him a considerable amount of power over his staff. Sir Gordon

French, Chairman and Chief Executive of ABB, does not own the company, but his *position* is vested with immense formal power, delegated to him from the Board of Directors. The Chief Executive is the most powerful position in the structure, and, depending on their level in the hierarchy, other managers share a proportion of this formal power that has been similarly delegated to their position.

If Rob tries to resort to his formal powers as a means of controlling his team he is liable to run into problems. In a way, he does this in the case study when he tries to *insist* that Peter should cooperate with him on the project. This tactic clearly did not work with Peter, who then left the meeting making remarks about Rob's managerial abilities.

The project manager, brand manager or 'liaison' manager cannot rely, then, on formal authority, or on powers to punish and reward as a means of controlling other staff. They have to look elsewhere for means of influencing others, to their personal skills and qualities rather than to their position. The project manager needs to have the respect of those he wishes to influence.

In Chapter 3 we suggested that any manager has two routes to earning his subordinate's respect:

(a) Respect for his 'technical' abilities.
(b) Respect for his managerial abilities.

Generally, project or brand managers would have some technical expertise which could form the basis of some respect for them as individuals. However, in the multi-disciplinary team it is rather more difficult for the individual specialist to earn general recognition for his abilities, as other team members may not be familiar with his technical area, or it may be that some members have a low regard for his specialism. If this is the case, the manager would need to shift the basis of his influence away from technical competence towards managerial competence. It could be that, of all the management positions considered so far in the book it is the project manager that most obviously needs to have managerial skills. In other organizational settings, managers can rely on formal authority, and other external control systems to back them up; when the project manager looks behind for support there is not much there. It is for this reason that we have held back our consideration of management development to this chapter.

Management development

Where can the project manager (or any other manager, for that matter) pick up the management skills he needs? Most managers are promoted on the strength of their technical competence, in the hope that they will display managerial abilities in their new posts. Very few managers go through a formal development process prior to their appointment.

So most managers learn from experience, either by picking up ideas and styles from other managers, or by learning from their own successes and failures. This is potentially a very expensive way to learn. No one would think of training a cost and management accountant by a process of trial and error, but it is deemed appropriate for managers. A cost and management accountant's training takes a number of years; people who are then promoted to the job of *managing* a team of accountants are lucky if they get sent on a two-week management course.

Learning from experience inevitably limits the range of options available to managers. If their only perspectives of management are picked up from their peers and bosses in the organization, their approach is unlikely to differ a great deal from that of their peers and bosses. There are benefits here, in so far as a consistent management style emerges in the organization. Problems arise, though, where managers pick up styles and practices that are inappropriate to their situations and their personalities. Moreover, McGregor's Theory X (Chapter 4) illustrates how managers' experiences can lead them into making unhelpful generalizations about their subordinates.[11]

Some organizations have recognized a need for a more structured approach to management development. They have set up in-house training courses, or sponsored and encouraged their managers to attend seminars and courses offered by specialist private management development consultancies, or local colleges and universities. Unfortunately, these enlightened employers are in the minority, and the quality and effectiveness of courses and programmes designed to help develop managers can vary considerably. An assumption that underpins most 'general' management development programmes is that there are 'good' and 'bad' management practices. Little account seems to be taken of the personality of the manager, or the particular demands of the situation facing him at work. A further problem arises from an inappropriate model of the learning process.

Consider the two diagrams in Figure 6.3.

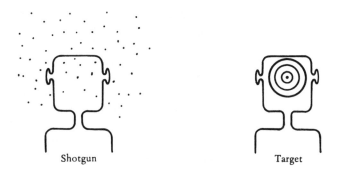

Shotgun   Target

Figure 6.3 *Two approaches to management development*

The 'shotgun' approach to management development bombards the individual with a wide range of theories and techniques covering most aspects of management, from industrial relations law to financial management, from operations research to organizational sociology. This can have a very beneficial effect on individuals as it should broaden their perspectives and they may pick up some useful techniques along the way. However, what appears to happen with the shotgun approach is that only a few pellets hit the target; only a small proportion of the material brings about any real change in the manager. Moreover, different managers will engage with different parts of the course.

The 'target' approach is quite different. It takes as its starting point a view that individuals need to be motivated to learn before the learning process begins. If we link back to the shotgun method, what seems to determine which pellets hit the target are the current problems, concerns and interests of the individual. The manager facing a discipline problem with one of his staff is motivated to look for solutions. Similarly, the sales manager promoted to the board finds that he needs to understand the rudiments of the balance sheet. Unfortunately, even if the sales manager had attended a management course in the past, the finance lectures were probably amongst the pellets that passed him by.

Focusing and tuning the development process to the manager's motivation to learn is very difficult. The target approach must be a flexible, and more or less continuous development process. This implies that it needs to be managed inside the organization by people in close contact with the individual manager. Perhaps the conclusion to be drawn here is that the organization needs to have 'coaches' constantly available for consultation, discussion and advice. But ultimately, managers must be in a position to manage their own learning.

A big problem in deciding on the appropriate training and development process for a manager or group of managers, is that it is extremely difficult to assess the effectiveness of these alternative approaches. With the shotgun method, some benefits in terms of improved managerial performance may well not emerge for several years, until the manager is in a position to exercise his enhanced capacities. The targeted development process may yield more directly attributable improvements as it can be focused on a particular area of weakness (e.g. understanding basic finance; conducting appraisal interviews). Generally, though, money invested in management development is largely an act of faith, which leaves the training budgets susceptible to savage cut-backs when senior management are looking for cuts in overheads. Strategic management development should be the focus for such interventions, with performance and organizational development goals also being objectives.[12]

A contingency approach to management style

Fred Fiedler published a book in 1967 which challenged many widely held views about management styles.[13] In the 1950s and 1960s the 'human relations' school was in its ascendancy. Democratic, participative styles were favoured, autocratic styles were thought inappropriate to the needs of the individual. Writers like McGregor, Likert and Argyris were widely quoted advocates of this movement.[14] It must be remembered, however, that there was a world of difference between these academic developments and management as it was practised in the overwhelming majority of organizations. Because of the paucity of structured management development programmes, few managers were familiar with these business school trends. The situation in the USA was probably different, though, reflecting the more advanced state of management and business education in that country.

Fiedler was interested in the links between leadership style and the performance of the group. The emphasis in his work is quite clearly on the group's accomplishment of the task, rather than concern for the wellbeing of the individual group member.

He identified two basic leadership styles:

■ *Relationship-motivated leaders* who are concerned about group members' feelings, and their attitudes towards them as leaders. They encourage participation.
■ *Task-motivated leaders* who, in contrast, are concerned about task accomplishment. They prefer clear guidelines from their bosses, and in turn prefer to implement them through tight procedures and precise instructions.

Using an ingenious questionnaire Fiedler was able to classify leaders on a dimension with high relationship-motivated leaders at one extreme, and high task-motivated at the other. He emphasizes that both these styles can be effective in appropriate situations. Thus he favours a contingency approach to leadership style, where the most effective style is determined by the nature of the task, and by the situation in which the leader is operating.

The situation leaders find themselves in can be categorized as either favourable or unfavourable in terms of the degree to which they have power and influence over the group. The more power leaders have the less they need to depend upon the goodwill of the group. The favourableness of the leader's situation is defined on three dimensions.

■ *Leader–member relations:* This is the most important of the three dimensions. Leaders who are liked and respected will have more influence than those with poor relationships with the group.
■ *Task structure:* Vague, unstructured tasks create problems for the leader. Clearly defined tasks give the leader more influence.

■ *Position power:* This is the least critical dimension of the three. It refers to the formal power and authority vested in the leaders position; the more position power the leader has, the more favourable his or her situation.

These three dimensions combine to produce situations that vary from being extremely favourable to extremely unfavourable. Where the leader–member relations are good, where the task is highly structured and where the leader's position power is strong, the leader faces an extremely favourable situation. Conversely, poor relationships, an unstructured task coupled with weak position power produce the worst possible situation for the leader.

Having defined the favourableness of the situation, Fiedler was then in a position to relate the situation to leadership style. The graph in Figure 6.4 summarizes Fiedler's empirical findings. The most interesting outcome is that task-motivated leaders tend to perform better in situations that are either very favourable or very unfavourable. Relationship-motivated leaders perform best in the intermediate situations between these two extremes.

So, according to Fiedler there is no one best style of management, it all depends on the leader's situation. In the very favourable situation the group are looking to be led by their respected and powerful boss. An example might be the surgeon in the operating theatre. A concern for the task is a more appropriate style than one where the surgeon is more concerned about not upsetting the anaesthetist, or the theatre

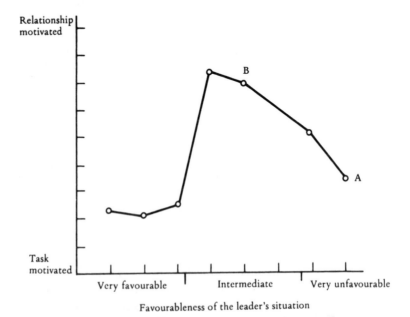

Figure 6.4 *Fiedler's leadership effectiveness model*

sister. A good example of an unfavourable situation would be a young teacher, fresh out of college trying to teach history to a non examination class of demotivated fifteen year olds. On all three dimensions the leaders situation is very unfavourable. Fiedler suggests that a participative leadership style ('What shall we discuss today, class?') would not be as effective as a more task-oriented approach ('Do the worksheet exercise, and then we will have an unseen test'). This is not to say that the leader in the unfavourable situation will perform *well* with the task-motivated style, merely that he will be more effective than if he adopted a relationship-motivated style.

Fiedler has pointed out some implications of his theory for management development. He believes that the leader's motivation towards tasks or relationships is too stable a characteristic to be easily shifted. You cannot 'develop' managers from one orientation to the other as their style is too closely tied in with their personality and attitudes. Training and development can, though, give leaders more administrative know-how which can enable them to increase their influence and control. This can move them into a more favourable situation in terms of Fiedler's graph. This is represented as a shift from point A to point B in Figure 6.4. The problem then is that this new situation may call for a different management style (relationship-motivated) to the one they are more naturally comfortable with (task-motivated).

This is a 'horses for courses' approach to management style. If you cannot easily shift the manager's style, move him to where his style fits the situation. Perhaps a task-motivated style is most effective in certain production situations; a relationship-orientated approach being more suited to the new product development unit.

Let us now use this model to examine the situation that Rob Hearne finds himself in at Pearson, Merriman.

- *Leader–member relations:* He has only been with the firm a month, which is possibly not long enough for him to have made any great impression on his colleagues. Moreover, some members of the project team may not have even met him prior to the first meeting he formally convened.
- *Task structure:* This is fairly clear, given that these experts are familiar with this type of project work. Group members have some structured techniques to bring to bear on the problem.
- *Leader's position power:* The project leader does not possess a great deal of formal authority, nor is he in a position to reward or punish group members.

Rob's position then is middling on leader–member relations, fairly good on task structure, and poor on position power. Fiedler's model would recommend he use a more relationship-orientated, consultative style of leadership in this intermediate situation. If he did slip into an autocratic, task-motivated style he may well, strangely enough, end up with the most appropriate style for the situation. By adopting such a style he would more than likely lose any goodwill and respect he might have had. Members prepared to give him the benefit of the doubt would react unfavourably to being treated in this unfamiliar style. Rob could then end up confronting an even more unfavourable situation, one in which the only way he could get anything achieved would be through a task-oriented style.

The managerial grid

Blake and Mouton, the inventors of the 'Managerial Grid',[15] challenge the assumption implied in Fiedler's model that managers cannot develop and change their styles. Although they do not reject the concept of a contingency approach to management style, they maintain that appropriate programmes of organizational development can significantly improve the individual manager's performance.

They adopt a two-dimensional concept of management style, not dissimilar to Fiedler's. Managers can be rated on the dimensions of 'concern for production', and 'concern for people'.

The purpose of the grid is to establish *how* the manager expresses concern for either production or people. This point can be explained if we consider the five basic combinations of concern for people and concern for production that are generated on the grid (see Figure 6.5).

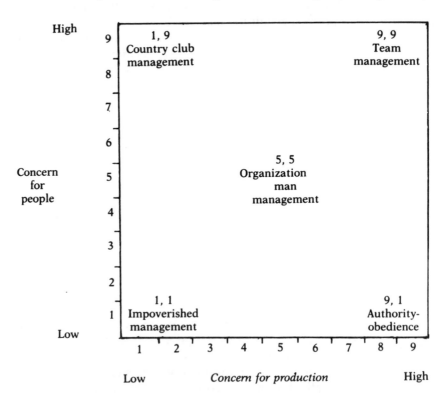

Figure 6.5   *The management grid*

Impoverished management (1, 1) This style is characterized by avoidance of responsibility, minimal effort, commitment and contact with subordinates. This style can be a symptom of a frustrated, passed over, or poorly developed manager.

Authority–obedience management (9, 1) These are autocratic and authoritarian managers. They do not respond favourably to staff challenging instructions or procedures. Disagreements and conflicts are suppressed.

Country club management (1, 9) Managers who are concerned solely for people. They avoid disagreements and criticisms of performance. Harmony is rated above task achievement.

'Organization man' management (5, 5) These managers have middle-of-the-road, live and let live attitudes. Managers try to balance concern for production and for people with a fair but firm style.

Team management (9, 9) Has the following characteristics: A high concern for production *through* a high concern for people. Morale is task-related, staff achieve their personal objectives through attainment of the organization's objectives. Management involve staff in a team approach to decision making. Problems are confronted directly and openly.

Blake and Mouton see the 9,9 manager as an ideal that is worth striving for. They believe that this desirable fusion of concern for production *and* concern for people can be achieved through structured development activities. Individual managers can fill in self-assessment questionnaires which, when processed, locate them somewhere on the grid. Managers' dominant styles revealed through the question- naire are influenced by a number of conditions: the organizations they work in (especially the extent of bureaucratic rules and regulations); the particular situations they face (routine work, or frequent crises?); their values and personalities; and the extent of their exposure to alternative styles, and to different assumptions about people at work.

Given these situational influences on the manager's style, Blake and Mouton have designed, and successfully operated, a development programme which uses 'group dynamics' techniques to move the manager towards the 9,9 ideal.

While a useful model, Blake and Mouton's approach has been criticized as idealistic, suggesting that it would be too tiring to constantly operate at 9,9 and that frankly, it depends on the situation.

The work of Hersey and Blanchard (introduced in the management Section 3.3 of Chapter 4) builds on the concepts implicit in the managerial grid. If you recall they identified a range of styles depending on the situation: the task, its complexity and the staff member's competence and willingness to engage in the task.

The four styles were:

- directing
- coaching
- supporting
- delegating.

Hersey and Blanchard have designed the situational leadership questionnaire which can also be used for management development purposes. It provides feedback to the delegate on their dominant style, style flexibility, areas of weakness and style effectiveness.

These questionnaires, along with others that form part of any development experience, provide feedback and a point of departure for further development. Each emphasizes different or particular parts of the manager or the managerial process. But none of them alone can tell the whole truth about the complex nature of the role of the person in it.

Strategy formation in the flexible organization

Where the organization is confronting an essentially simple task, strategy making can be centralized at the apex of the structure. The more complex the tasks facing the organization the more decentralized the strategy making process must become. On pages 65–8 a distinction was made between two types of flexible structures: the operating adhocracy, established to solve novel problems for its clients; and the administrative adhocracy which is established to solve complex problems generated internally. Strategy formation in these two situations is decentralized but takes slightly different forms.

Strategy making in the operating adhocracy In the machine bureaucracy a distinction can be made between the formulation of strategy and its subsequent implementation. No such clear dichotomy can be identified in the strategy formation processes in the adhocracy. If we take Pearson, Merriman as our example of an operating adhocracy we can see how the strategy of the firm *emerges* from a stream of separate decisions. Consider how the present consultancy strategy of the firm evolved.

1976 Two trainee chartered accountants were taken on who had completed MBA courses.

1980 Request received from a major client for advice on changing their grading system. Normally clients were directed to other organizations. This time the MBA graduate agreed to help and was encouraged by a senior partner.

1983 Pearson, Merriman are establishing a reputation in management consultancy. Partners agree a policy of responding as far as possible to clients' requests for consultancy, as long as it does not compromise the core business of chartered accountancy.

1985 Consultancy business has expanded, and the staff base has grown accordingly. Requests for additional appointments are invariably approved if they are justified in profit earning terms.

1986 Three consultants discover that they have a complimentary set of skills and experience that could be applied to public sector project appraisal. For the first time Pearson, Merriman aggressively tout for this lucrative business.

1987 Project appraisal business takes off. The need for more staff results in a separate department being established.

A combination of chance and a willingness to respond flexibly to new opportunities have resulted in a major shift in the firm's strategy. This was not a 'top-down' decision to move into a new market; the strategy has emerged from initiatives taken in the operating core which were supported by the apex. A variety of people were involved in the formation of this strategy, and we might reasonably suppose that not one of them has consciously thought about their part in the process as leading up to a definite *strategy*. In this type of structure what little guidance there is in determining strategy takes the form of broad policy statements decided and promoted from the apex. These guidelines do not *determine* a particular strategy, they merely provide some shape, direction and constraints on the thinking of the other members of the organization.

Strategy making in the administrative adhocracy   The administrative adhocracy set up to run, for example, a large chemical processing plant, does not have to cope with the same variety of projects as the operating adhocracy. The problems are, however, still of a complex nature, and require a number of specialists to work together to resolve them. Because of the complexity, and the unknown problems that might be encountered, a considerable amount of discretion must be given to these multi-disciplinary teams. In the design, construction, and commissioning of a new processing facility a host of complex problems will need to be resolved; compromises will have to be agreed; and scheduling and action planning will need to be approached in a flexible way. Hence, although the broad strategic decision to expand capacity can be taken centrally, that is about all that can be specified in advance. The resulting design, location and capability of the new facility emerges from a stream of incremental, trial-and-error type decisions made by line and staff people cooperating in teams.

Thus the strategy making role of the strategic apex takes on a very different form in the adhocracy. The managers at the apex will be required to sort out conflicts between strategic alternatives emerging from lower down in the structure, and, because of the ambiguity in the structure, they are also called in to referee political battles. These managers need skills of persuasion and negotiation, they need to be good 'people managers'. The facilities to listen, to counsel and to liaise with the external environment are also desirable.

3.4 Groups

The case study featured the first, rather unsuccessful, meeting of a project team. This setting was appropriate because in flexible and changing organizations formal and informal meetings take up a fair amount of management and staff time. It is the vital need for liaison and coordination through mutual adjustment which makes such meetings significant in these structures. We shall be employing our model of groups again here, to help sort out the important issues. Thus the section is separated into three parts: the *content* of meetings, which lists some of the more common reasons for holding meetings; the *method* of the meeting, where the attention is focused on the organization and management of the meeting; and lastly, *interactions* in the meeting, where some interesting interpersonal and group behaviours are discussed.

The content of meetings

Meetings can be called for a number of reasons some of which may not be immediately apparent. For example the meeting called by Rob Hearne had a number of objectives, some related to the task, and some which were more orientated to the group process.

Task related objectives included:

■ Bringing team members up to date on the progress in the negotiations with the council.
■ Confirming and agreeing decisions taken by the project leader.
■ Discussing and agreeing the future programme of work.
■ Allocating responsibilities.

Process related objectives were:

■ To bolster the authority of the project leader.
■ To encourage a 'group feeling' and unite the group.

The task related objectives are the least contentious and can be made quite explicit at the meeting. The process related objectives may not be generally accepted by all the group, and are not likely to be explicitly stated by anyone.

Formal reasons for convening a meeting might be:

■ Exchanging views and information.
■ Generating ideas.
■ Explaining a course of action already decided.
■ Solving problems, designing changes.
■ Enquiring into a past event.
■ Negotiating.

It would appear from the above list that meetings are called for positive reasons. However meetings can be used as substitutes for action, and as a way of avoiding taking personal responsibility for a decision. Earlier in the chapter we noted that in the Burns and Stalker study committees were regarded with suspicion in some of the firms as they were seen as symptoms of 'government bureaucracy'.

Methods of managing meetings

Meetings can be managed efficiently or they can degenerate into aimless talking shops. In this section we shall look first at some examples of poor meetings management. Then, a few suggestions for making meetings more effective are presented.

Examples of poor meetings management:

- Poor control of discussion.
- Crowded agendas.
- Too much information tabled at the meeting.
- Poorly kept minutes.
- Bad presentations.
- Unclear tasks.
- Inappropriate seating arrangements, location and timing.

These and other bad practices can not only lead to a particular meeting being ineffective, but, if meetings are generally badly run in the organization people will be reluctant to spend time attending them.

If a meeting has been called by someone, then usually that person would control the meeting. Whether or not he is formally designated as the chairperson of the meeting, there is an obligation on them to set the 'rules' for the meeting. The chairperson can opt for a very formal meetings style, making full use of the 'laws' of meetings (e.g. where the chairperson alone controls the discussion), or alternatively, a much more relaxed approach may be deemed more appropriate.

Here are some guidelines for improving the running of meetings.

Plan the meeting   The organizer of the meeting should give careful thought to why the meeting is necessary, who should be in attendance, how long should be allowed for the meeting, where it should be held etc. Most of these points seem obvious, but a little pre-planning can prevent a good deal of wasted effort in the meeting itself.

Inform members thoroughly   Agendas should not only indicate what is to be discussed, they should also explain briefly the reasons for the item being on the agenda, and what is expected from the discussion.

Structure the meeting   The time of the meeting should be managed so as to ensure that the really important items get the full treatment they require. Also, where there are interconnected items on the agenda, they should be arranged logically to avoid the need to jump back to an earlier agenda item. You can even set timed agendas allocating sufficient times to each item.

Manage the discussion   This is probably the most critical task of the chairperson. Handling a meeting well requires great skill. The chairperson must listen carefully to the discussion, encourage the more reticent to express their views and prevent people wandering off the subject by steering them gently but firmly back on to the topic. The chairperson needs to be able to sense when enough time has been spent on an item, and to judge when to bring the meeting to a decision. A key skill is the ability to summarize contributions; this can help bring the meeting to a point where progress can be assessed, and where members can clarify their positions.

Recording decisions and actions   It is a useful discipline to formally record decisions that have been agreed, and to make a note of any follow up actions that are required as a result of the meeting. Most important here is the need to identify the responsibility of particular individuals to take action.

Interaction in meetings

In the same way that we picked up some examples of poor meetings management, we will begin our exploration of interactions in meetings by listing some of the less helpful behaviours people can exhibit.

- *Personal animosity* can be expressed as overt hostility to one or more people in the meeting, or more subtly introduced through attacks on people's ideas and suggestions.
- *Overtalking* is an aspect of unruly meetings where two people (or more) are talking at once. Often used by the person with the loudest voice to get the attention of the meeting.
- *Not listening* either because you are bored, distracted, talking yourself, or you don't respect the speaker.
- *Group climate* can be very charged which can intimidate some members; be 'controlled' by a small number of people; or it may be too relaxed, when little progress is made on the tasks facing the meeting.

There are other instances of poor meetings behaviour to which the reader may relate. For example, have you ever been desperate to make a point in a meeting but no 'gap' in the flow of talk occurs which will enable you to put forward your contribution? Whilst you await the pause in the noise you are phrasing and re-phrasing your point in your head, so that it makes the maximum impact. However, while this is happening you are not really listening to the discussion, so you may end up making a point that someone has already made. As with Rob Hearne's meeting 'hidden agendas' are often lurking under the surface, where, for example, individuals are more concerned with making an impression than in really helping the meeting; or where informal alliances have been arranged in order to attack or ridicule another member of the group.

Where meetings are an important aspect of the organization's functioning, investment should be made in developing skills which contribute to more effective meetings. Staff need to be made aware that there are helpful and unhelpful behaviours in meetings, and techniques like the use of closed circuit TV, could be employed to bring these lessons home. Some helpful behaviours in meetings are:

- Releasing tension.
- Summarizing the discussion.
- Expressing feelings and opinions.
- Raising other people's status.
- Bringing others into the discussion.

Groupthink

In most circumstances cohesive groups can be very effective. However cohesion can also be a problem in decision making groups. This phenomenon has been investigated by Janis, who has coined the term 'Groupthink' to describe it.[16] Cohesion is characterized by friendliness and cooperation within the group, and it is encouraged where the group have similar values and outlooks, and where they perceive themselves to be subject to external hostility.

Cohesion is not a sufficient condition on its own to produce groupthink, it must be coupled with the insulation of the group from outside influences, and with strong leadership. What results is a 'concurrence seeking tendency' where members suppress their critical judgement in an effort to preserve the group's cohesion.

Figure 6.6 summarizes the groupthink model. The symptoms of groupthink are:

1 An illusion of invulnerability, shared by most or all of the members, which creates excessive optimism and encourages taking extreme risks.
2 Collective efforts to rationalize in order to discount warnings which might lead the members to reconsider their assumptions before they recommit themselves to their past policy decisions.
3 An unquestioned belief in the group's inherent morality, inclining the members to ignore the ethical or moral consequences of their decisions.
4 Stereotyped views of rivals and enemies as too evil to warrant genuine attempts to negotiate, or as too weak or stupid to counter whatever risky attempts are made to defeat their purposes.

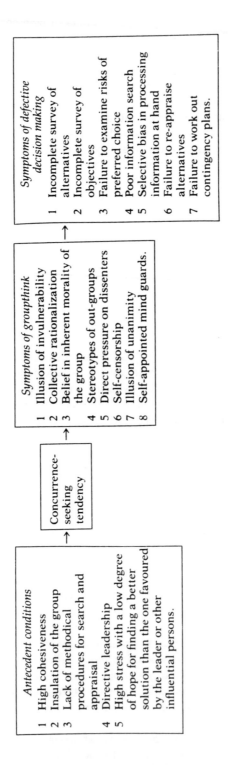

Antecedent conditions

1 High cohesiveness
2 Insulation of the group
3 Lack of methodical procedures for search and appraisal
4 Directive leadership
5 High stress with a low degree of hope for finding a better solution than the one favoured by the leader or other influential persons.

Concurrence-seeking tendency

Symptoms of groupthink

1 Illusion of invulnerability
2 Collective rationalization
3 Belief in inherent morality of the group
4 Stereotypes of out-groups
5 Direct pressure on dissenters
6 Self-censorship
7 Illusion of unanimity
8 Self-appointed mind guards.

Symptoms of defective decision making

1 Incomplete survey of alternatives
2 Incomplete survey of objectives
3 Failure to examine risks of preferred choice
4 Poor information search
5 Selective bias in processing information at hand
6 Failure to re-appraise alternatives
7 Failure to work out contingency plans.

Figure 6.6 *Analysis of groupthink*
Source: Janis and Mann, *Decision Making*, 1979

5 Direct pressure on any member who expresses strong arguments against any of the group's stereotypes, illusions or commitments, making clear that such dissent is contrary to what is expected of all loyal members.

6 Self-censorship of deviations from the apparent group consensus, reflecting each member's inclination to minimize to himself the importance of his doubts and counter arguments.

7 A shared illusion of unanimity, partly resulting from this self-censorship and augmented by the false assumption that silence implies consent.

8 The emergence of self-appointed 'mindguards' – members who protect the group from adverse information that might shatter their shared complacency about the effectiveness and morality of their decisions.

Janis has suggested some ways of overcoming groupthink:

1 The leader of the group assigns the role of critical evaluator to each member, including himself. Doubts and criticisms are positively encouraged within the group. However, this suggestion may be rather hard to implement as nobody relishes criticism. The use of an outside group and organizational consultant can help here.

2 The leader should not bias the group towards a particular decision, wittingly or unwittingly. Therefore the leader has to be careful about the way he gives guidance as to what is to be accomplished and how it is to be accomplished. A group can easily become sensitive to the wishes of the leader, thus producing the 'right' decision.

3 Members of the group should seek advice from trusted colleagues who are outside the group. Fresh perspectives can thus be introduced.

4 A devil's advocate role should be assigned to a group member (or members). The role should have high status in the group and it should preferably be rotated.

5 A 'second chance' meeting should be held to permit members to express any residual doubts they have about the consensus the group has reached.

Teams and team building

It has already been established in this chapter that team work is a vital ingredient in successful flexible and changing organizations. In this section we shall be looking at deliberate attempts to build more effective teams: firstly by considering how an existing group can be developed into a team; and secondly by investigating some evidence about the composition of effective teams.

Team building One of the problems with *management* development is that it is an essentially individual process, and even if the development programme is successful in increasing the manager's learning and competence, these benefits may not be sustainable if the organizational context the manager is operating in has remained static. Consider these examples:

■ The manager returns from an intensive development programme fired with enthusiasm, and wanting to change things. However, his staff are sceptical and reluctant to get involved with his new initiatives as they have not themselves experienced any development process.
■ A middle manager is 'sent' on a development course by his boss. As in the case above, he returns bubbling with new initiatives. His boss, who has never been on any development programme is suspicious of, and maybe just a little threatened by this manager's increasing competence. He therefore discourages or blocks any attempts the manager makes to change things.

In both of these cases, because the focus of development has been on the individual, not on the broader team, the potential for improvement has been limited. Team building is an attempt to broaden the development process to a 'natural' unit or group of people who need to work closely together. The objective of team building is to improve the team's performance by:

(a) Encouraging effective practices.
(b) Reducing difficulties or 'blockages'.

Team building as a deliberate strategy for organizational development is not likely to be effective unless the organization is ready to receive it. This will be the case when:

■ The organization structure relies on a team approach.
■ The senior management recognize and support team building.
■ The teams themselves are prepared to undertake the team building process.
■ The team leaders are aware of the building blocks of effective teamwork.

In other words, 'team building' cannot be pulled off the shelf and rammed into an organization; it is not an instant solution to the organization's problems. Moreover, attempting team building in the wrong organizational circumstances can actually make the situation worse rather than better.

The benefits of team building are:

■ It increases the chances of real improvement in performance because the whole team is involved in the process.
■ Where the process takes place away from the organization it provides a 'breathing space', where the group can step back from the task and look at themselves as a team. As a result, issues will be raised that would not have been confronted at work.

There are a number of techniques that have been used in the team building process to encourage openness and constructive discussion. However, one extreme form of team building leaves the management of the process entirely to the team itself. This can be effective if the team members are very motivated to make the process successful, and where they already have some experience of this type of development activity. More usually, though, some form of structure is provided by the organizer, trainer or group consultant which facilitates the process. Structured team building techniques include:

(a) *Team effectiveness rating* By means of a questionnaire individual team members rate the group on a number of dimensions; such as allocation of responsibility, task clarity, trust, collaboration, conformity, recognition of individual contributions, organization of the team and leadership of the team. The individual ratings are then shared, and the differences and agreements that emerge provide a basis for discussion.

(b) *Personal feedback* Using varying devices and personal question-naires individual members are encouraged to be more frank and honest about other members of the team. One effective technique is for each group member to fill in a form for each other team member listing their strengths, and weaknesses. The comments can be kept confidential, or depending on the feelings of the team, they could be shared.

(c) *Action planning* Here the team identify one or more critical problem areas that inhibit their effective functioning. Together they design an action plan which they are committed to implementing in the future. The involvement in implementation can help to extend the benefits of the team building activity once the group has returned to work.

(d) *'Outward bound' activities* The team are put into situations which are, for most (if not all) members totally unfamiliar, but where they need to rely on each other's efforts to accomplish the task. For example, the team may be required to construct a bridge, hike across moorland, climb a mountain, sail a boat, etc. There are dangers with this technique, however, apart from the obvious physical ones. Some team members (and leaders) who perform perfectly well in the workplace may feel threatened, and have their esteem undermined in these challenging circumstances.

For many teams, though, just the opportunity to get away and socialize together for a time brings enormous benefits, almost regardless of the structured activities organized by the trainer or consultant.

It is not all good news, however. If people are encouraged not to treat problems and issues at 'arms length' but to be more open and honest, some people may not enjoy the outcome. The 'truth' can be painful. It is often the already strong team that can cope best with this requirement for openness because it has the reserves of trust and cohesion required to cope with whatever emerges. The more fragile team may be shattered completely if the team building process is managed insensitively. Teams, like individuals, are unique, and should not, therefore, be expected to respond in the same way to these activities. The use of external help from established institutions can be useful.

The other major problem emerges where team members are sceptical and not prepared to give the process a chance. Because team building is an *active* learning process it requires commitment and involvement for it to work. Without this commitment the exercise is a waste of time and money.

The composition of effective teams

R. Meredith Belbin has undertaken some interesting empirical work on the composition of teams.[17] He was able to construct teams of managers from people attending the Management College at Henley, and set them to work on specially designed management 'games'. Team members were allocated to teams on the basis of personality, intelligence and ability tests. The games were designed to produce winners and losers on a measurable indicator like 'profit'. By analysing the composition of successful and unsuccessful teams, and through extensive research into case studies from industry, Belbin has been able to identify eight types of people that are useful to have in teams. These are described in Table 6.4. He concludes that:

> The useful people to have in teams are those who possess strengths and characteristics which serve a need without duplicating those already there. Teams are a question of balance. What is needed is not well-balanced individuals but individuals who balance well with one another. In that way, human faculties can be underpinned and strengths used to full advantage.

Note that within the eight types are some less than glamorous roles which are, nonetheless vitally necessary. The 'completer–finisher' ensures that projects are followed through; he is concerned about detail. He is a necessary complement to the 'plant' who is good on ideas, but less interested in the practicalities of implementation. On the social functioning of the group, the 'team worker' helps smooth ruffled feathers and promotes a team spirit, and the 'company worker' contributes the necessary organization to the team.

3.5   The individual

The pressures of the flexible structure

The flexible organization places many demands on the individual. In contrast to the large bureaucracy the individual's situation in the flexible organization is often very loosely defined. This can cause stress

Table 6.4   Useful people to have in teams

Type	Symbol	Typical features	Positive qualities	Allowable weaknesses
Company worker	CW	Conservative, dutiful, predictable.	Organizing ability, practical common sense, hard-working, self-discipline.	Lack of flexibility, unresponsiveness to unproven ideas.
Chairman	CH	Calm, self-confident, control.	A capacity for treating and welcoming all potential contributors on their merits and without prejudice. A strong sense of objectives.	No more than ordinary in terms of intellect or creative ability.
Shaper	SH	Highly strung, outgoing, dynamic,	Drive and a readiness to challenge inertia, ineffectiveness, complacency or self-deception.	Proneness to provocation, irritation and impatience.
Plant	PL	Individualistic, serious-minded, unorthodox.	Genius, imagination, intellect, knowledge.	Up in the clouds, inclined to disregard practical details or protocol.
Resource investigator	RI	Extroverted, enthusiastic, curious, communicative.	A capacity for contacting people and exploring anything new. An ability to respond to challenge.	Liable to lose interest once the initial fascination has passed.
Monitor–evaluator	ME	Sober, unemotional, prudent.	Judgement, discretion, hard-headedness.	Lacks inspiration or the ability to motivate others.
Team worker	TW	Socially orientated, rather mild, sensitive.	An ability to respond to people and to situations, and to promote team spirit.	Indecisiveness at moments of crisis.
Completer–finisher	CF	Painstaking, orderly, conscientious, anxious.	A capacity for follow-through, perfectionism.	A tendency to worry about small things. A reluctance to 'let go'.

Source: R. Meredith Belbin, *Management Teams*, Heinemann, 1981

on individuals who are uncomfortable with ambiguity and fluidity. Specifically, flexible organizations cause problems for individuals in the following ways:

(a) *Structural ambiguities cause conflict and tension*   Where individuals have two bosses they can be subjected to inconsistent and contradictory instructions. A lack of clarity in job definitions, and in reporting relationships can increase the pressures on individuals. If individuals try to please both bosses they may be placing impossible demands upon themselves.

(b) *Uncertainty due to short lived projects*   The peaks and troughs in the flow of work can cause anxiety. This will be heightened if the firm has a policy of hiring and firing as a means of matching staff to workload. Where individuals are underutilized for extensive periods, boredom, apathy, and disillusionment often result.

(c) *Career development problems* In flexible structures individuals' careers are usually 'managed' in their 'home' department or function. But, most of the time they are working in teams or on projects away from their functional bosses. How, then, are their bosses able to assess their performance? Individuals have problems in deciding who it is more important to impress: the project manager, who sees their contribution on a daily basis (but who may only have a minor input into decisions about their careers); or their functional boss? This consideration can influence the direction in which individuals jump when functional and project managers place conflicting demands on them.

(d) *Low sense of loyalty* Frequent moves between different working groups can reduce the individual's sense of loyalty and commitment to a department, or to the organization itself.

(e) *Survival of the fittest* Flexible organizations can be highly political working environments. Increased resources, and promotions can often be gained through the exercise of informal power possessed by the individual.

A contingency model of job design Porter, Lawler and Hackman present a model which relates organization design (organic or mechanistic), job design (simple, routine jobs, or enlarged jobs), and employee characteristics (high, or low needs).[18] Figure 6.7 is a summarized version of the model.

These three dimensions generate eight possible combinations of structure, job design and growth needs. If we consider cells 5, 6, 7 and 8 which relate to the flexible structure a number of conclusions can be drawn:

- *Cell 5:* Individuals have high growth needs, but their jobs are routine and restricting. The prediction is that they will try to have their jobs changed, or they will resign.
- *Cell 6:* Here the low growth needs of individuals match their jobs, but the flexibility in the structure causes them unease and anxiety.
- *Cell 7:* Everything matches up in this cell, there is a 'congruence' between the needs of individuals, their jobs and the surrounding organizational context. The model predicts a high quality performance, and satisfied individuals.
- *Cell 8:* Individuals with low growth needs are overwhelmed by organizational and job demands, resulting in 'psychological withdrawal' from the job, or overt hostility and inadequate performance.

This model therefore gives us some useful insights into individual responses to the flexible organization. Before we leave the model it might be worth noting that the other cell where 'congruence' exists is cell 2. Here the low growth needs individual is happy and secure in his routine, undemanding job, in a stable and predictable environment.

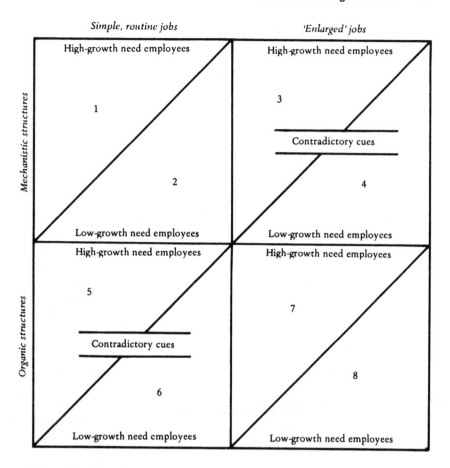

Figure 6.7 *A contingency model of job design*
Adapted from: C. W. Porter, E. E. Lawler and J. R. Hackman, *Behaviour in Organizations*, McGraw Hill, 1975

Where individuals are unable to meet all the demands made on them they can respond in a variety of ways.

- They can try to meet all the demands. This could ultimately debilitate individuals.
- They can simply leave the organization.
- They can 'withdraw' from the organization in different ways: by frequently absenting themselves; by 'hiding' when demands are being made on them; by only responding to the really important demands.
- They can attempt to reduce the demands by negotiating and confronting their bosses.

Further reading

Peters and Waterman's *In Search of Excellence* (reference 2) is a readable and provocative book which proffers some straightforward solutions to managing complexity. Fiedler's work has been developed into a practical approach to management development in *Improving Leadership Effectiveness: the Leader Match Concept* (Wiley 1977). Bowman and Asch's *Strategic Management* (Macmillan 1987) includes chapters on Managing Change and Alternative Models of Strategic Decision Making.

References

1   See case accounts of both Hewlett Packard and Sony in Mintzberg, H. and Quinn, J. B., *The Strategy Process: Concepts, Contexts, Cases*, Prentice Hall, Englewood Cliffs, NJ, 1991
2   Burns, T. and Stalker, G. M., *The Management of Innovation*, Second Edition, Tavistock, 1968
3   Peters, T. J. and Waterman, R. H., *In Search of Excellence*, Harper and Row, 1982
4   Greiner, L. E., 'Evolution and Revolution as Organizations Grow', *Harvard Business Review*, July–August 1972
5   Mintzberg, H., *Structure in Fives*, Prentice Hall Inc., 1983, Chapter 12
6   Toffler, A., *Future Shock*, Bantam Books, 1970
7   Woodward, J., *Industrial Organization: Theory and Practice*, Second Edition, Oxford University Press, 1980
8   Mintzberg *Ibid.* p. 7
9   Trist, E. L. and Bamforth, K. W., 'Some social and psychological consequences of the Longwall method of coal getting', *Human Relations* 4, 1951, reprinted in Pugh, D. S. (ed.), *Organization Theory*, Second Edition, Penguin, 1984 and see Trist, E. and Murray, H. (eds), *The Social Engagement of Social Science: A Transtock Anthology, Vol. 2. The Socio-Technical Perspective*, University of Pennsylvania Press, Philadelphia, PA, 1993
10 *Ibid.* p. 414
11 McGregor, D., *The Human Side of the Enterprise*, McGraw Hill, 1960
12 More detailed accounts of the issues, practice and implementation of management development are covered in (a) Mumford, A., *Management Development: Strategies for Action*, Institute of Personnel Management, 1989; (b) Harrison, R., *Training and Development*, Institute of Personnel Management, 1990; (c) Wood, S. (ed.), *Continuous Development: the Path to Improved Performance*, Institute of Personnel Management, 1990
13 Fiedler, F. E., *A Theory of Leadership Effectiveness*, McGraw Hill, 1967 and Fiedler, F. E., 'How do you make leaders more effective? New Answers to an old puzzle', *Organization Dynamics* I, 1972, pp. 3–18
14 Likert, R., *New Patterns of Management*, McGraw Hill, 1961 and Argyris, C., *Personality and Organization*, Harper and Row, 1957
15 Blake, R. R. and Mouton, J. S., *The New Managerial Grid*, Gulf Publishing Co., 1978
16 Janis, I. L. and Mann, L., *Decision Making*, Free Press, 1979
17 Belbin, R. M., *Management Teams*, Heinemann, 1981
18 Porter, L. W., Lawler, E. E. and Hackman, J. R., *Behaviour in Organizations*, McGraw Hill, 1975

7 The multinational organization

> This chapter looks at the role and influence of large multinational organizations. It makes a distinction between those that have multiple, national markets and those that have truly 'global' markets. We suggest that sometimes the demarcations, as they relate to strategy, structure, political influence and management are less than one might think at first glance.

1 Case study: TRT

Steve Billington slowly replaced the telephone.

Lying on his bed in the Gold Star Executive suite of the Burroni Holiday Inn, he was sweating, even though the air conditioning was almost deafening him. He had just phoned his wife Helen back in Gloucester, England, and like so many other calls home over the past few years, it had been an unsatisfactory exchange. Helen sounded casually off-hand, almost in a hurry to get off the phone, and Lucy couldn't even drag herself from the TV to talk to him.

Still, they had gone over all this time and time again. There was no way he would get the kind of salary and benefits package that TRT were giving him if he moved to a job which kept him in the UK. His job enabled his wife and daughter to live comfortably in a beautiful part of the country. The price they paid for this was his long absences from home. When he did spend time with his family, however, things weren't much better. Helen had her own circle of friends, and was involved in all sorts of activities which seemed to exclude him.

He also felt physically drained. The flight from Nairobi was crowded and the taxi to the hotel took over an hour due to rush hour traffic. The last thing Steve wanted to do was to spend the evening in a formal dinner, but he knew that this was an important part of his trip to the Republic, so he showered, changed and made his way to the Hotel's cocktail lounge.

The point of the dinner was to reassure the Republic's Development Minister about TRT's plans for building a cigarette production facility in the country. Privately, Steve knew that the scale of production envisaged was too small for the factory to be viable, and if TRT could, they would renege on the deal. But this was just one small part of a global marketing strategy conceived at corporate headquarters in Roanoke, Virginia. TRT were prepared to tolerate loss making ventures like the Burroni factory as long as it contributed to the overall objective of gaining a strong share of the rapidly growing African market.

The Minister was aware of the political advantages of the TRT deal. The concerns expressed by the Minister for Public Health about the long term effects of an increase in smoking in the population had to be balanced by the jobs created by the factory, and the foreign currency earnings that would be generated from cigarette sales to neighbouring states.

Once it had been made clear that TRT were to go ahead with the establishment of the factory, the 'business' part of the dinner was over and Steve began to relax.

The following day he was taken on a brief tour of TRT's Central African Headquarters which was located in an impressive modern office block in the business district of Burroni. His guide was John Schaffer, a Canadian, who was in charge of all TRT's interests in the region. Steve and John knew each other quite well. Their paths had crossed on numerous occasions over the years as they had both pursued their careers with TRT. They had spent some time together working in a TRT subsidiary in Eire, and had last met at a senior management seminar held in Roanoke earlier in the year.

John briefed Steve on TRT's battle with its two main competitors for the lucrative, rapidly expanding regional market. Growth in the market as a whole was projected at an average of 11 per cent per annum over the next five years. To date, TRT were the only one of the 'big three' with concrete plans for a production facility, the others were presumably waiting to see whether their market shares would justify such a step. John also explained about this evening's presentation to the sales reps. Steve's role was essentially symbolic, providing a morale boost to the troops. Sales of TRT's premier brand 'Sword' were expanding fast in any event, but the presentation was planned to coincide with a new advertising and promotional campaign which would be launched the following week.

By 7.30 p.m. the sales reps were sitting expectantly in the conference centre waiting for the proceedings to begin. Despite having booked the conference in the name of a different (and non-existent) organization, there were, nevertheless, a group of anti-smoking demonstrators waiting to greet Steve as his limousine pulled up. Steve was getting used to the antics of the anti-smoking lobby by now, and he was almost immune to their chants and jibes. He pushed his way past two women with placards who were blocking his entrance, and proceeded into the conference hall.

Steve's speech was superb. It had just the right amount of humour, corporate anecdotes and references to past triumphs, mixed with positive noises about the new promotional campaign. He wound up his presentation with the following exhortation.

'We know you guys are the best in the business; *you* know there's a market out there waiting to be grabbed, so let's get out there and grab it.'

This was received by a standing ovation, whistles and cheers from the assembled reps.

Issues arising from the case

Environment
1 TRT is operating in a complex, dynamic and global environment. The political issues are at an international level and the ethical issues are vast. How does a company manage and influence such a complex environment?
2 The market in the African region is growing at 11 per cent per year. What will the company need to do to manage its returns?

History and resources
1 The company is US owned and its HQ is also based there. How can it operate effectively across the different cultures? Is there a tinge of old colonialism in the new form?
2 The global resources of the company are presumably vast. Many of the top world companies, e.g. Exxon, have revenues in excess of the GDP of some countries with developing economies. What might be some of the ethical issues involved in how TRT employs its resources.

Task

1 The company sees its overall strategic task in global terms – rather than local. How is it able to retain clarity of focus with potentially so much diversity?

Organizational structure and management
1 How does TRT, a diversified multinational corporation, organize itself? What structural options are there for managing such a large and complex business?
2 To what extent should 'local' businesses be left to manage their own affairs?
3 In what ways does Steve Billington's job differ from the other management positions covered so far in the book?
4 How does a manager like Steve Billington cope with ethical issues arising from his role as a multinational manager?

The informal organization
1 How can the corporate HQ of TRT control businesses across the globe?
2 What relationships between TRT and host governments are hinted at in the case study?
3 What efforts are made by TRT to combat the influence of the anti-smoking lobby?

Individual

1 There is a clear and rewarding career and promotion structure for managers in TRT when compared to some of the other cases in this book. But at what cost is this achieved and how does one evaluate the trade offs?
2 Both John and Steve seemed to be in 'congruence' with the company's philosophy and style. Is this the criteria for those who want to get on in such companies or is there scope for divergence?

Outputs

1 Outputs are seen in terms of global maximization. What other criteria might influence their objectives?
2 Resources in such a company can be mobilized to cross-subsidize lame operations or 'lost leaders' to countries to get a foothold into emergent markets. What issues does such a strategy raise in terms of local efficiency, autonomy and third party interest, e.g. national government? How are these expectations managed? (See Table 7.1.)

Table 7.1 Summary of key issues from case study – TRT

Inputs	
■ Environment	■ Global and world-wide market.
	■ Operating in a highly internationally political context – including countering campaign groups.
	■ Regional markets forecast healthy growth 11% pa.
■ Resources	■ Presumably extensive
■ History	■ USA Parent

Transformation	
■ Task	■ 'Global' maximization over 'local' or regional.
■ Individual	■ Clear career structure.
	■ Job trade offs with family.
■ Organization	■ Centralized HQ generic strategy with regional structures, products and market.
	■ Sub business unit/operating strategies too.
■ Informal	■ Networks.
	■ Company culture strong.

Output	
■ Goal achievement	■ Global
■ Resource utilization	■ Cross subsidies between countries, SDU, operating units, etc.
	■ Use of shadow pricing and maximizing national country tax and excise regulations
■ Group performance	■ Able to rally the troops!
■ Individual behaviour and effect	■ Positive to the company.

2 Context

For the TRT the world is literally their oyster. It is a source of information, development, resources, assets and opportunities. Such companies often have access to vast resources and are able to influence national governments in advanced developed economies as much as in countries with developing economies. Thus, their shear size affords multinational enormous power, both economically and politically.

They can influence, if not set, the rules of the game and are constantly in negotiation (or conflict) with national governments through the promise of direct foreign investment or through the legislature. Here they are often testing national anti-trust laws or anti-competitive legislation in the local nation state.

Multinational organizations can operate as agencies across borders and manage the portfolio of businesses to maximize their total investment and cash flows, but they are different from the global corporation argues Yip.[1] For the more adventurous, they can go for true globalization whereby they have:

- *market penetration* with significant share in major markets
- *a full range of products* – fully standardized world-wide
- *value-added activities* locally so that there is no duplication of effort
- a uniform world-wide *marketing approach*, e.g. Coke
- *competitive strategies* integrated across countries.

What these confer on the company are:

- Cost reductions – through economies of scale, pooling production facilities, exploiting lower factor costs e.g. labour and exploiting flexibility and bargaining power.
- Improved quality of products and programmes as such companies go for a smaller number of products concentrating on both product and process improvement, e.g. Toyota.
- Enhanced customer preference through global availability, service-ability, and recognition which can enhance customer preference through reinforcement. McDonald's is universal!
- Increased competitive leverage as it provides more points to attack and counter attack potential competitors who need to sink costs into development, infrastructure and marketing to compete on like terms.

The disadvantages of globalization strategies include:

- Significant management costs through increased coordination, information management, staff and sheer 'noise' in the communication system.
- Large development costs up front to enter and penetrate new markets to retain a competitive global position, e.g. Motorola struggled to penetrate the Japanese markets.
- Product standardization can mean missing out other customers who are unable to meet the product or do not deserve the standard product specification.

■ Uniform marketing can reduce adaptation to local nationals.
■ Concentration on certain lines of activity can reduce opportunities in international markets.

While these benefits and drawbacks exist the issue for some multinationals of whether to 'globalize' or stay as a conglomerate remains an open question. The multinational company is characterized somewhat differently across the fine features covered for the 'globalized' company.

The multinational organization would have:

■ No global pattern to its *market penetration*, it would more likely be a feature of 'local' circumstances.
■ *Product range* that was more suited or fully customized to each country.
■ *Value added* activities based on a broad rather than narrow coverage so one might expect all activities (e.g. marketing, R&P, production, customer support) in each country.
■ *Market approach* that would be geared to the local country.
■ *Competitive strategy* based on national trends only (or foreign competition as it affects that 'local' market).

It is the latter type of international business organization that will be the focus for the rest of this chapter. None-the-less some of the structural and managerial issues may pertain to global organizations too. Table 7.3 specifically looks at the multinational enterprise and the political and environmental issues as they relate to structure in Section 3.1 of this chapter.

3   Organizational configurations

3.1   Structure

Centralization vs. decentralization

The structure of the multinational organization largely reflects the degree of decentralization that the management of the apex of the organization feel is appropriate. At the heart of this decision is the tension between, on the one hand, the need to be responsive to the various national markets, and on the other, the benefits of integrating activities and strategies across the organization. For example, a multinational chemical company has to balance the benefits of centralizing basic chemical research (which is an extremely expensive activity) with the need to adapt products to the particular requirements of foreign industrial customers.

Decisions about what to control centrally, and what to delegate will be influenced by a number of factors.

(a) *Size of overseas operations:* This can vary from a simple office managing the importing of the company's products, to a large scale manufacturing and marketing unit.
(b) *Breadth of the product line:* The broader the range of products being sold in the overseas market, the greater will be the tendency to delegate more decision making power to the subsidiary. For example, the corporation may choose to centralize decisions about product development, and delegate decisions about the advertising and promotion of the new product to the subsidiary.
(c) *Perceptions about local management:* Corporate management may have a low regard for 'local' management; doubting their professionalism, or even their integrity. In this climate logical reasons for delegating decision making may be overridden by prejudice and mistrust.

This last point has been amplified by Perlmutter, who identifies three different international orientations amongst executives: ethnocentric (home country oriented); polycentric (host country oriented); and geocentric (world oriented).[2] Table 7.2 highlights the implications of these three orientations for the structure and management of the international enterprise. Ethnocentric oriented executives only have faith in domestic employees, and therefore in their view, the strategies, structures and systems used in the domestic business should be applied across all other countries. In contrast, the polycentric oriented executive acknowledges the differences of the foreign operation, and recognizes that there are ways of managing which are appropriate to the overseas operation. He therefore sees the sense in allowing the foreign subsidiary opportunities to develop its own identity. The geocentric executive views all operations as equally important, regardless of their location. Emphasis is placed on integrating activities as far as possible across the globe, where each constituent part of the global organization is expected to maximize its contribution on the basis of its particular strengths. The aim is for a collaborative approach to emerge between headquarters and subsidiaries.

The implications of global strategies The following quotation highlights the increasing prevalence of 'global products':[3]

> Go to large parts of the world and you can fly into the country on a Boeing Jumbo Jet, change the time on your Casio wristwatch, rent a Ford to drive to your standardized 'Western' Hotel, where you can eat hamburgers, drink Coca-Cola or Johnny Walker Black Label Whisky, smoke Peter Stuyvesant cigarettes, watch a Sony television, while wearing Levi jeans. Virtually anywhere in the world, a limited range of calculators are on sale, and the IBM personal computer has become the standard machine against which all other computers are measured around the globe.

Such global product strategies require a highly integrated and centralized operation. Other multinationals have, on the other hand,

Table 7.2   Three types of headquarters orientation towards subsidiaries in an international enterprise

Organization design	Ethnocentric	Polycentric	Geocentric
Complexity of organization	Complex in home country, simple in subsidiaries	Varied and independent	Increasingly complex and interdependent
Authority; decision making	High in headquarters	Relatively low in headquarters	Aim for a collaborative approach between headquarters and subsidiaries
Evaluation and control	Home standards applied for persons and performance	Determined locally	Find standards which are universal and local
Rewards and punishments; incentives	High in headquarters, low in subsidiaries	Wide variation; can be high or low rewards for subsidiary performance	International and local executives rewarded for reaching local and worldwide objectives
Communication; information flow	High volume to subsidiaries' orders, commands, advice	Little to and from headquarters. Little between subsidiaries	Both ways and between subsidiaries. Heads of subsidiaries part of management team
Identification	Nationality of owner	Nationality of host country	Truly international company but identifying with national interests
Perpetuation (recruiting, staffing, development)	Recruit and develop people of home country for key positions everywhere in the world	Develop people of local nationality for key positions in their own country	Develop best people everywhere in the world for key positions everywhere in the world

Source: H. V. Perlmutter, 'The Tortuous Evolution of the Multinational Corporation', *Columbia Journal of World Business*, January–February (1969), p. 12

global strategies for controlling a diverse range of businesses. Some like, for example, ITT and Union Carbide, have expanded through the acquisition of companies in many different industries and markets. In many cases, the customer has no awareness of the existence of the 'parent' company. ITT (which stands for the International Telephone and Telegraph Corporation) has interests in a host of companies outside of its core telecommunications business. These include insurance, hotels, bakeries, timber, fire extinguishers, cosmetics, automotive parts and cellulose. Clearly the structure of ITT is likely to be far more decentralized with regard to product strategies, than say, IBM which, in contrast, offers a much narrower range of products.

Within the centralized–decentralized continuum, there are a number of structural options, which we shall now consider.

Alternative forms of multinational organization

In this section we will look at the advantages and disadvantages of five forms of multinational structure. The fivefold classification is taken from Gilligan and Hird's *International Marketing*.[4]

International subsidiary structure   This is a fairly simple solution to the problem of managing multinational operations. The 'parent company' headquarters contains the production and other functional activities, and the subsidiaries are only responsible for the marketing of the products in the countries concerned. The subsidiary boards report directly to the main board of the company.

Advantages of this structure include the following:

- It is a straightforward and low cost approach to international organization.
- It gives the local board autonomy in the making of marketing decisions, therefore the marketing strategy can be tuned in to local circumstances.
- It provides career opportunities for local management.

Disadvantages include:

- The possible encouragement of parochial thinking in local managers.
- Pressure on HQ staff, as the number of subsidiaries increases.
- The inhibiting effect of the structure on attempts at integrating strategies across the organization.

The international division structure   As firms expand their international operations the marketing and distribution of products is augmented by the establishment of production and possibly research and development activities abroad. Some firms choose to organize with a clearly separated 'international division' to provide a clearer focus for the international strategy. As a result, a group of senior managers in charge of the international division will have a vested interest in seeing that international operations are properly resourced.

Problems emerge, however, with increased growth coupled with greater diversity of products. Coordination across the whole organization of, for example, the development and marketing of a particular product group, becomes extremely difficult. Conflicting strategies emerge along with unnecessary duplication of effort as the international division attempts to establish or retain control of more and more stages of the operation.

Geographic structures   Here the 'international division' has been replaced by a number of regional divisions controlling different parts of the globe (e.g. divisions for Europe, Australasia, Africa and North

America). Day-to-day responsibility rests with the regional management, with broad strategic planning and control being exercised at the headquarters. Within each region, the size and diversity of operations may warrant a further split into product divisions. The great advantage of this form of organization is that it permits close coordination between production and marketing, which improves the multinational's ability to adapt to local demands.

Product structures   A significant problem with geographic structures is that some product lines, and new product developments, may not be enthusiastically promoted in all regions. A possible solution is the product structure, where the major focus is product groups, rather than geographical areas. Each product division (e.g. batteries, agricultural chemicals, resins) may in turn be sub-divided into geographic divisions (e.g. Resins Australasia). Profit responsibility rests with the divisional heads, and they are usually free to make decisions about product additions or deletions. But, with both the geographic structure, and with the product structure, one focus takes priority. Hence, products may be neglected in the geographic structure, and some markets may be neglected in an overly product-oriented structure.

Matrix structures   Our example of a matrix structure introduced in Chapter 6 was that of a relatively straightforward and small nationally based company. Some multinationals have introduced this type of structure as a way of maintaining the balance between geographic imperatives and product promotion and development. Not surprisingly, the multinational matrix will tend to be a more complex manifestation of the form. TRT, the tobacco multinational, has adopted a matrix form. Figure 7.1 shows the part of the structure that relates to Steve Billington. He is in charge of marketing and promotion worldwide for the 'Sword' brand. John Schaffer is in charge of all aspects of the Central African region. As such, John reports to his boss, the General Manager of the African Division, but he also defers to Steve Billington on all matters pertaining to the development of the Sword marketing strategy.

As matrix structures go, this is a relatively straightforward form. Some companies have experimented with a three-dimensional structure where a functional reporting relationship has been added to the product and market foci.

Prahalad and Doz conclude that:[5]

> Managing the multinational matrix demands the use of very complex administrative systems and sophisticated managerial behaviour. A matrix structure by design does not provide a strategic focus to businesses. It must be superimposed by the use of nonstructural mechanisms like relative power.

One last issue, before we leave the consideration of structure, is the problem of government interference in the running of multinationals.

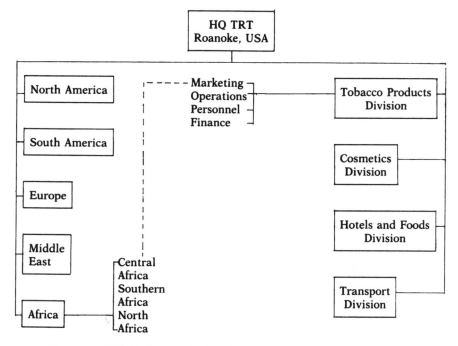

Figure 7.1   *TRT: Partial organization chart*

From the evidence of the case study, TRT engage in direct negotiations with governments. Prahalad and Doz see this aspect of multinational business as a further complication, which cannot necessarily be coped with through structural changes. Table 7.3 on the following page traces the evolution of the multinational organization structure through the interconnections between the environment of the firm, its organizational response, and typical problems that emerge, with host government interference emerging as an important environmental factor in the latter stages of development. The issue of government–multinational relations will be explored further in the following Process section.

3.2   Organizational arrangements

Controlling in the multinational organization

We shall consider two aspects of control that are peculiar to the multinational corporation:

- Internal control systems
- External influencing processes.

Table 7.3 Evolution of multinational corporation organizational form
Adapted from: Prahalad, C. K. and Doz, Y., *Strategic Management of Diversified Multinational Corporations*

MNC	environment	MNC's organizational response	Typical problems
I	Primarily domestic; overseas business not significant	Export department, International Division	Inability to integrate overseas operations with domestic operations
II	Overseas operations and opportunities significant – sales, investment, returns	Global organization – worldwide product groups or area groups	Missed opportunities due to a simple dominant orientation
III	Business environment complex – simultaneous need for sensitivity to diversify in markets and ability to achieve economies	Global matrix structure	Inability to get strategic focus for businesses
		Use of relative power for strategic focus	Need for very sophisticated managerial behaviour and systems
		Use of corporate functional groups for strategic coordination. Use of corporate planning teams	
IV	Host government's interest in containing strategic freedom of salient businesses.	Response contingent upon the relative bargaining strengths of host government and the firm	Judging the relative bargaining strengths
V	Host government's desire to contain the strategic freedom of all MNCs operating within its territory	Opt out or adapt	Businesses that the subsidiary is involved in do not reflect parent's strengths. Tacit host government – subsidiary coalition

Internal control systems are concerned with controlling behaviour and performance inside the corporation, external influencing processes are attempts made by corporations to reduce uncertainty and adverse conditions in their environments.

Internal control systems

Firms that have become multinational face enormous problems in controlling the foreign based operations. Differences in language, customs and laws coupled with the often immense distances involved, add to the problem of control. The yardstick of profitability may not be directly applicable to subsidiary operations as a performance measure, as companies have a range of options in treating investment in, and income from subsidiaries. Moreover, the risks of investing in some countries (due, for example, to the threat of nationalization) may prompt the corporate HQ to require much higher profit performance from more vulnerable subsidiaries. Problems of repatriating profits, and differing taxation systems can encourage firms to manipulate the accounts and indulge in resource transfers to gain an advantage.

The headquarters has the option of adopting a hands-off, holding company approach to the control of its subsidiaries, or it can choose to intervene directly in the decision making processes within each subsidiary.

The problem with the latter system is that it requires the corporate HQ to have the knowledge and expertise to make feasible decisions in all aspects of the multinational's operations. This is possible if an extremely limited product range is offered (e.g. MacDonalds) and the markets for the products can be treated in a similar manner. Where a multinational has not only spread across the world with one group of products, but has also diversified at the same time, specific guidance from HQ becomes increasingly inappropriate. ITT is one such diversified corporation, and it is instructive to see how the man who has steered the company through a period of great global expansion and diversification, Harold Geneen, went about establishing effective control systems:

> From his office on the twelfth floor, Geneen gradually got up the most intricate and rigorous system of financial control that the world had ever seen. Weekly meetings, monthly meetings, annual meetings were summoned to keep check on the managers; a special room with a great horse-shoe table was constructed, where Geneen could inspect and question the managers and their accounts. The head of each company was required to submit to headquarters a monthly report of such complexity that it required a special department to compile it; five year plans were prepared, targets set, profits compared. Each detail was analysed and cross-checked, so that Geneen, poring over his books in Park Avenue, could tell exactly which of his products, in any part of the world, was failing to meet expectations.
>
> From Sampson A., *The Sovereign State*

Geneen clearly opted for active management of ITT's acquisitions. This was achieved through control mechanisms which were built around the one common denominator in all their businesses' profits. So the managers of each subsidiary were free to make decisions about products, research and development, manufacturing and marketing, so long as they achieved the profit targets set by the ITT headquarters.

External influencing processes

All organizations try in some way to influence their environment: the most basic form would be Top Gear Driving School's advertisement to attract customers. The larger the organization, the more efforts are made to influence the environment, and in the multinational corporation we have organizations of giant proportions. These huge enterprises have a vested interest in preserving stability in their operations, and, to this end, they deploy considerable resources to influence and control other people and organizations. Attempts to influence people and groups external to the organization range from public relations and press briefings at the least contentious end of the spectrum to, at the other extreme, bribery and corruption. In between these extremes are organized lobbying, and sponsorship (see Figure 7.2).

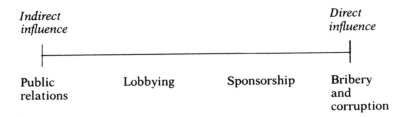

Figure 7.2 *A continuum of external influencing processes*

Public relations   Whereas most advertising is designed to promote particular products, corporate advertising is more of a public relations activity, designed to promote the image of the corporation as a whole. These campaigns can be mounted to counteract specific bad publicity, or, more generally, to promote a positive corporate image (e.g. as a caring organization; a job creating organization; a dynamic and technologically advanced corporation). However, corporate advertising is just one aspect of the public relations activity. Customer relations departments, membership of corporate management on the boards of public bodies and charities, and the efforts of the public relations officers to secure favourable media coverage are just some aspects of image building. The very name of the organization can be an important component in the establishment of the right public image. None of the six giants of the tobacco industry now have the word 'tobacco' in their titles: BAT Industries, Philip Morris Inc., R. J. Reynolds, the Rembrandt Group, American Brands Inc., and Imperial Group Ltd. Consider also the bewildering sequence of name changes at British Leyland (as was!), and the switch of name from 'Windscale' to 'Sellafield' by BNFL.

Nestlé, the confectionery and foods multinational, had to employ a range of public relations devices to counteract an effective boycott of its products. This boycott resulted from the exposure of the impact of baby milk powder sales to 'Third World' countries. Because of problems encountered by mothers who were unable to prepare bottle feeds in the required sterile conditions, babies were suffering illness and even dying. Nestlé counteracted the boycott through various channels in the media, and through the establishment of an office of Corporate Social Responsibility.

Lobbying   Whereas, in general, Public Relations is a broad influencing strategy, lobbying is a much more focused approach, targetting on particular groups or individuals. Multinational companies conduct political lobbying directly themselves, or they may choose to employ specialist consultants. MPs in the UK House of Commons, and members of the House of Lords may be retained by a multinational to represent its interests in parliament. Such interests need to be declared under recent Parliamentary guidelines. Nonetheless the impact of lobbying is still effective.

We can explore the process of political lobbying through a particular case. The threat to multinational corporations of the proposed Unitary Taxation system in the USA provides a good example. This tax proposal would mean that individual US states could cause foreign multinationals to suffer double taxation on group profits. Sixty UK based companies were brought together and a Campaign Committee (organized by Ian Greer Associates) was formed. Meetings were held with the Chancellor of the Exchequer, the Secretary of State for Trade, the Secretary of State for Industry and groups of backbenchers. Visits were made by leading industrialists and MPs, to lobby members of the US senate. The EEC was persuaded to support the campaign and a note was despatched to the US Administration.[6]

Sponsorship   Sponsorship is an attractive influencing strategy, as it not only provides an advertising platform for the corporation, it can also make desirable links in the public's mind between worthy causes, or healthy pursuits, and the company itself. Multinationals have promoted the arts (e.g. concerts and whole orchestras), contributed to charities and appeals, and, particularly in the case of the tobacco companies, have sponsored sporting events. Imperial Group has sponsored motor sport, powerboat racing, cricket, speedway, snooker, darts, bowls, horse racing, tennis, rugby, badminton and show jumping.

Barrie Gill is the Chief Executive of Championship Sports Specialists Ltd., the biggest of the sporting consultancy organizations, that have grown with the expansion of sponsorship. He reflects on why tobacco companies have put so much into motor racing.[7]

> It's the ideal sport for sponsorship. It's got glamour and worldwide television coverage. It's a ten month activity involving sixteen races in fourteen countries. After football, it's the number one multinational sport. It's macho, it's excitement, it's colour.

Bribery and corruption   In some parts of the world, bribery is an unexceptional part of the normal conduct of business. Major payments are made to secure lucrative orders in, for example, the aircraft, construction and communications industries. They often take the form of 'agent's commissions' which reach the politicians and officials who are influential in deciding who gets the contract. In some countries in

Latin America it is standard practice for purchasing agents in the public sector to get 3–7 per cent of any sale for their private account. Payments are also made to labour leaders (to prevent strikes) and to plant inspectors to persuade them to write favourable reports on the company's installations. On a smaller scale, bribes are employed to 'oil the wheels' in the importing of components, in the progressing of planning applications and in the granting of residence permits.

Apart from the ethical issues it raises, bribery causes problems for multinationals. If a company adopts a high moral code and refuses to pay 'commissions', it may lose out to the competition who are less scrupulous in their business conduct. Company employees caught bribing may end up in jail. Harold Williams, the Chairman of the US Securities and Exchange Commission, suggests:[8]

> Corruption results in higher prices, lessened responsiveness to the consumer, and lower quality of goods and services. Business corruption is not only inefficient; it destroys the market place.

On the other hand, in trying to secure a $1 billion contract for military aircraft, paying a few politicians $1 million each does appear to be an easier way to do business than attempting to beat the competition on price, performance, delivery and servicing.

Probably the most sinister and extreme form of interference and unethical practice occurs where multinationals attempt to interfere with the political processes in host nations. This is often difficult to prove (e.g. the alleged sanctions-busting activities of the oil multinationals in Rhodesia). However, in March 1972, Jack Anderson, a US journalist, published articles announcing that secret documents showed that ITT had plotted in 1970 to stop the election of Chile's Marxist President, Salvador Allende and that ITT had dealt regularly with the Central Intelligence Agency to try to create economic chaos in Chile, and to encourage a military coup. ITT engaged in these activities to ward off the threat of nationalization of their telephone business.

3.3 The multinational manager

Steve Billington leads a strangely nomadic existence, moving from hotel to hotel, living for most of the year away from his home. As his various jobs with TRT have taken him to different parts of the world, he has gradually lost touch with people outside the company. TRT has become Steve's community, it offers the only continuing stability in his life. Steve identifies very strongly with TRT, and is unlikely to consider working for another company.

Anthony Sampson was present at an annual ITT barbecue for managers from all over the world held in Brussels. He observed that:[9]

> It was not immediately easy to tell the Europeans from the Americans, except perhaps from the shoes and trousers; for the Europeans, too –

whether Swedish, Greek or even French – had a hail-fellow style and spoke fluent American, joking and reminiscing about old times in Copenhagen and Rio. I soon had a sense of being enveloped by the company, by its rites, customs and arcane organogram, of being swept right away from Brussels, or Europe, or anywhere.

A survey of the readers of the *International Management* journal[10] conducted in November 1986, revealed that:

- Executives are changing their own personal work habits to suit the needs of international competitiveness. They are becoming fluent in at least one foreign language, they travel more and read more foreign publications.
- In an effort to cultivate contacts they are increasingly attending foreign conferences and seminars.
- Over half of the companies are increasing their activities to train managers to function better abroad.

These findings reflect the efforts of companies trying to extend their international business operations, but the evidence of the ITT barbecue suggests the existence of a supernational community, one that is not tied to a particular country, but which transcends nations and cultures. While there are those, like Hofstede[11] who argue cultural differences do matter, the outcome of his research must be treated with caution as its generalization may oversimplify cause–effect relationships and lead to the unhelpful reinforcement of stereotypes.

Perhaps we are witnessing the emergence of 'multinational man', with a life style, culture and value system ideally suited to his environment. Multinational man might need to put the interests of the corporation above his own code of ethics if he is to deal without qualms with governments of all shades of political opinion, and to 'rationalize' awkward by-products of his company's operations. (Like deaths from smoking, pollution and low safety standards.)

Robb Wilmot, who moved from Texas Instruments to become Managing Director of ICL, sums up this aspect of multinational man quite well. In an interview with John Mortimer, he was asked:[12]

> 'Don't you find doing business in South Africa distasteful? What do you think of the politics there?'

> 'South African politics? I'm neutral' replied Mr Wilmot.

Further reading

J. M. Stopford and L. T. Wells *Managing the Multinational Enterprise* (Longman, 1972) provides more depth on the structure of multinationals. Sampson's book, although it has no pretensions to being an academic work, is nevertheless worth reading.[6]

References

1 Yip, G. S., 'Global Strategy in a World of Nations?', *Sloan Management Review*, Fall, 1989
2 Perlmutter, H. V., 'The Tortuous Evolution of the Multinational Corporation', *Columbia Journal of World Business*, Jan–Feb 1969
3 Stopford, J. M. and Turner, L., *Britain and the Multinationals*, Wiley, 1985
4 Gilligan, C. and Hird, M., *International Marketing: Strategy and Management*, Croom Helm, 1986
5 Prahalad, C. K. and Doz, Y., 'Strategic Management of Diversified Multinational Corporations', in *Functioning of the Multinational Corporation*, Edited by Negandhi, A. R., Pergamon, 1980
6 Greer, I., *Right to be Heard*, Ian Greer Associates, 1985
7 Taylor, P., *The Smoke Ring: Tobacco, Money and Multinational Politics*, Sphere Books, 1985
8 Freeman, O. L., *The Multinational Company: Instrument for World Growth*, Praeger, 1981, p. 63
9 *Ibid.* p. 16
10 *International Management*, November 1986
11 Hofstede, G., *Culture's Consequences*, Sage, 1984
12 Mortimer, J., *In Character*, Penguin, 1983, p. 136

8 Managing for change

> This chapter looks at organizational attempts to manage change. It takes the case of a local authority that is about to undergo a culture change and some of the issues it struggles with such as of culture, structure, process and strategy.

1 Gremby County Council: the case study of a local authority

This small district authority was to undergo considerable change in its direction, culture and management style. Central government had reduced their financial balances and had sought to control the authority through various departmental guidelines and regulations. Politically, the local election had seen a large swing in voting patterns from the previous Labour authority to a Tory administration. The new administration had a very different political manifesto and agenda for the council. Politicians saw there being much more involvement of the private sector with the county council taking an 'enabling role' rather than continuing to be the sole or direct provider.

The Chief Executive Officer, John Hoames, was charged with the task of implementing some of the changes and told to do so quickly; within the next year. He had decided to use management consultants to help in the process but was considerably anxious about the nature of the task and often said so when not in the company of his other managers.

The Strategic Management Group (SMG) meeting was about to start. Its members included the top team and their direct lines. The meeting was a regular monthly event and its declared aim was to be the body of the organization to implement strategic decisions. The group numbered fifteen in total.

John: Well, the next item on the agenda concerns our change management directive. This item has been on the table before. Various members of this group were involved in the brief and the final selection of the consultants, who are here to today to go through their proposal.

Jane (the Consultant): Thank you John. We are very pleased to be working with you on this proposal and I'd like to go through the key phases of the work.

Jane and her other two male colleagues go on to describe the main phases of the work. This included process consultation, workshops and an intergroup event of the top team and their managers. After a formal presentation of overhead slides the group is invited to ask questions.

Jerry (Assistant Director of Social Services): I thought the main idea of the consultancy was to provide us with information on management style. I did not think it was going to look at the whole organization.
There are murmurs of agreement.

Griff (Assistant Director of Human Resources): Yes I saw it as a training and skills workshop so that we could improve our inter-personal communication.

Harry (Head of Finance and Corporate Services): I still do not see exactly what we hope this will do. We will need to justify what we are doing to elected members and staff, especially given the cuts in other areas of our work.

Gary (Assistant Director – Contract Services): I don't see why there is so much concern. We already have undergone competitive tendering in the manual areas of our services such as leisure and refuse collection. And now we need to think about 'white collar' services and this programme will enable us to do it.

Jennifer (Director: Planning and Environmental Services): Well, I think it's really about how we work as a team. We never seem to make decisions, we're rarely sure about the agenda, our communication is something to be desired and I feel we're re-creating the same cycles that we go through in every meeting.

John: I really do not understand! We all saw the brief, agreed the selection of the consultants and now we seem to be backing off.

Jennifer: Well, it's typical of the way we work. And again it shows that we thought we'd made a decision when we didn't. The meeting is unwieldy, our role as a group is ambiguous to say the least and people are getting their bit in and not really listening to other suggestions or ideas. How can a group of fifteen make effective decisions anyway!

Jerry: Yes, I think we should look at the brief again. There clearly is some confusion here. We're really sorry about this (looking at the consultants)
There is a pause.

Jane: It seems there is a lot to consider. Perhaps we should look at the brief again and consider what has just taken place.
After the meeting, Jane and John undertake a short post-mortem. They walk across the car park.

John: Well, what did you think of that? That's just typical of what we're dealing with. The pressure from the top demands change and the group has not really come to terms with it.

Jane: Their reactions were not surprising given the speed and magnitude of the proposed changes. It's one thing seeing it all on paper but when we actually turned up, the reality must have hit them hard.

John: They will all go off to their little groups, chew it over and get ready for the next meeting. I know things are not what they should be but no one ever says so. You've certainly got your work cut out.

Jane: Yes, we have but that's our role. I suspect that what they are feeling and articulating holds true for others in the organization as well. Thus, the meeting was not what we expected but it did give us a lot of information about how we might arrange the next meeting.
   The two parties bid farewell.

Issues arising from the case

Environment

1 The county council is facing a complex and dynamic environment. There are both economic and political pressures to change. How will it meet the expectations of its multiple stakeholders?
2 Central government edicts and guidelines appear to cause concern and reduce the capacity of local politicians and managers using their discretion. How might one manage these imposed contraints?

History and resources

1 The organization had a bureacractic and authoritarian culture in the past. It needs to move to a commercial and enterprising culture where managers will have to influence and negotiate with others, often without role authority. How might such a process begin?
2 The level of resources has been reduced and is likely to continue to do so over the forthcoming years. How does one maintain an acceptable standard of service and retain staff goodwill with a declining resource base and the threat of redundancy?

Task

1 The organization needed to change its strategic task from 'regulation' and 'service provision' to 'enabler' and 'competitive player'. This was the result of a complex and dynamic environment with new rules being established for the role and mission of local

government. The ability to do so will also be a function of the organization's informal processes. How will these be managed?

2 The complementary or 'dual' task is to manage the change itself. Resistance to change is inevitable and at some level is positive as it gets concerns into the open. But what is the right balance to strike between airing legitimate concerns and pandering to people's whinges?

Organizational structure and management

1 As an authority going through change it experienced the problems of any large organization (see Chapter 5), It had bureaucracy built into its veins through the systems and structures. This can be partly explained from local government traditionally working in a relatively steady and protected environment. But some of it is also due to organizational inertia. Will the pressures of change be enough without being debilitating?

2 There was also the tension of moving from a mechanistic to a more organic and decentralized decision-making approach which was difficult to manage. Could the change be made?

3 The Strategic Management Group was a key strategic co-ordinating mechanism but remained an unsatisfactory compromise: with poor role and task definition.

4 Such temporary structures do get set as a way of managing structural changes (see Chapter 6 on the flexible organization). However, the role of SMG was not used in that way. It was also used to fulfil too many tasks and thus it was swamped by insufficient mechanisms and resources to do a range of disparate tasks. How far was there congruence between the demands and resources of the group?

5 John seemed to have difficulty in maintaining his role authority, preferring a more democratic style of management. How far do you think that such a style was appropriate?

Informal structures

1 The 'old' culture seemed forever prevalent. What service did it provide for the group?

2 The group 'climate' was characterized by mistrust, little listening of each others ideas and attacks. How might this be explained in the context of the organizational changes more generally?

3 Cliques and subgroupings were evident and they helped the process of change to be discussed. However, they could also be a source of power and resistance against the change.

Individuals

Group members were driven by their own agenda as shows in the account of the meeting. Their own needs and interests were in conflict with the organization's more generally and we saw departmental or political motivations having more sway over the needs of the authority more corporately. How can these people be turned around? What strategies need to be employed?

Outputs

1 The organization continued to survive but was likely to be experiencing 'strategic drift': an incongruence between the task environment and the actual configuration of the organization.
2 Resources were locally optimized instead of corporately and the intergroup relations and general culture was one of distrust, blaming, competitiveness and generally unsupportive. The internal Darwinian principle of the survival of the fittest was incongruent with the organization's espoused public service ethic and orientation. How could these contradictions be reconciled?
3 The group's ability to adapt to change was clearly articulated. Should the consultants quit now!?

Table 8.1 gives a summary of key issues from the case of Gremby County Council.

Table 8.1 Summary of key issues from case study

Inputs	
■ Environment	■ Increasing level of central government 'control'.
	■ Political swing locally.
	■ Dynamic and complex environmental changes generating enormous pressures for change.
■ Resources	■ Level of resources declining and expected to do so over the next few years to come.
■ History	■ Authoritarian management style and bureaucratic culture in the context of local government politics.
Transformation	
■ Task	■ Generally complex and demanding – two areas:
	■ contents: become an 'enabler'
	■ process: manage the change itself
■ Individual	■ Generally skilled but 'wedded' to 'the past'.
■ Organization	■ SMG – main managerial coordination group – but ineffective due to poor decision making, structure and unclear role.
■ Informal	■ Coalitions and cliques form to compensate the inadequacies in the managerial organizational arrangement.
Output	
■ Goal achievement	■ Uncertain.
■ Resource utilization	■ Competitive with local dept needs seen as greater than corporate needs.
■ Adaptation	■ Poor with resistance to change.
■ Group performance	■ Inadequate to the tasks.
■ Individual behaviour and effect	■ Generally ego-centric.

2 Context

The world is a rapidly changing place: becoming 'smaller' through telecommunications, travel and the media. It has a range of divergent and competing values; the East–West conflict has been changed for North–South; and a range of innovations in products, services and processes means that customers have more choices, option and capacity to make more demands on the organization. Many countries across the world are experiencing deregulation of protected industries and monopolies and the role of the State is moving from 'sole provider' to 'market enabler'.

Some of the old values and assumptions about organizational life have already come to an end. No longer will people have a job from cradle to grave. This was something that the then giant of the computer industry, IBM, had to come to terms with by the early 1990s. The notion of a career will also be questionable. Professor Shaun Tyson of Cranfield University, School of Management argues that people will have a bundle of tasks that will make a 'job' and this may be a contractor or 'consultant' to a number of organizations.

Large institutions will no longer be seen as the custodians of industry. Examples are plentiful: from the crash of international banks through to the demise of large airlines.

The future holds the need to respond flexibly and quickly to a diversity of 'customer' demands. It suggests that the role of niche firms, network organizations and firms with strategic partnerships will be among the new organizational configurations.

New technology will also be among the main drivers of change for managers and organizations into the 21st century. The virtual organization, cyberspace and the everyday and ever increasing application of personal computers, with the various links between different types of telecommunication devices will make 'Star Trek' seem even closer.

Thus, it means that the management agenda needs to include the ability to manage effectively across multiple boundaries: both inside and outside the organization.

It means that:

- Managers will need to be able to work with process and interpersonal and intergroup dynamics within the workplace.
- Managers will need to work with influence and task expertise over line or role authority as they manage internal and external clients on projects and contract work
- Managers will need to work with the rational and emotional elements of the task in order to maintain team and organizational effectiveness.
- Managers will need to be able to manage uncertainty, risk, their own and others' anxiety as organizations go through change, enter new domains and seek to survive in a new environment within each of the contexts described in the earlier chapters.

In Gremby County Council we have seen an example of these sea changes in the public sector: where organizations are now required to 'market test' their services, become more competitive, contract out to third parties, meet the specifications of internal customers and prioritize services. These are the sources of the pressures for change; the implications and processes are discussed in the next section.

3 Organizational change

What do we learn in relationship to managing change in this case study? The first thing that the case shows is that there is usually a level of resistance. Furthermore, people will weigh up the costs and advantages to change and ask: 'Will I be any better once the change is implemented?' or 'What's in it for me?'. Some people will even welcome the changes. These are perfectly normal responses and should be considered by those leading the change be they the Chief Executive, managers or change agents who have a staff function.

Assessing the system's willingness or ability to change is a tricky business. Kurt Lewin's[1] work in group dynamics and 'field theory' provides the key frameworks that have become popularized in the management and consultancy world. There are three main frameworks: the change equation, the 'unfreeze'–change–'refreeze' model of change and Force Field Analysis. These three models underpin modern change theories and each are briefly desribed.

The change equation

This simply states that the benefits of the change must exceed the costs. It is often expressed:

$$C = (A + B + D) > X,$$

where C is the nature of the change to be undertaken. Gremby County Council had to change from a traditional bureaucracy to a more responsive and enabling agency – akin to the administrative adhocracy described in Chapter 6 on flexible organizations. A is the level of dissatifaction with the status quo. This was clearly expressed by the politicians but was not shared by the senior staff in the group. B is the desirability of the proposed change. Again while some aspects were necessary, the changes were generally seen as undesirable by the senior managers. D is the practicality and risk of disruption of the change. Both Harry, the finance director, and Griff, head of Human Resources, questioned the relevance of the changes in the context of current demands. X is the cost of changing: the tangible costs of using external consultants, any investment costs, relocations costs, emotional energy and of course, opportunity cost, where people could spend their time more 'usefully'.

When applying this model to Gremby, what would you say were their chances for change?

The three stage model of change

Lewin's work was based on a wide range of experiments and observations of groups. He used mathematical equations and notation based on topological principles used in geographical mapping of land, which he called 'field theory'. It is because of his dedication to precision and conceptual thinking that the complexity of his work is able to be reduced to simple rules: sometimes oversimplified!

In his model of change Lewin suggests three key stages in the change process:

(i) *Unfreezing:* this is the first step in the change process which requires reappraising and giving up inappropriate old messages. It means being open to consider a different point of view of disconfirming data. The aim being to 'break open the shell of complacency and self righteousness . . .' (Lewin,[1] p. 35).
(ii) *The Move:* this involves putting into place the new structure, procedure or behaviour.
(iii) *Freezing:* this is to give the change 'permanency' at the new level.

Thus for Gremby, the overwhelming weight of the politicians, central government and reduced resources might put the lever to 'unfreezing'. The message being that past is gone and we need to face reality! The group would appear to need more help in the next phase of undertaking the move.

The model is sometimes criticized for being too simple or for reinforcing a new point of complacency with another. However, these views reflect a reductionism that arises from the model's considerable simplification and thus some misunderstanding about the nature of Lewin's contribution. For example, the notion of 'permanency' does not mean ossification: it means a new point of equilibrium, which can change if new forces are brought to bear. Other variations of Lewin's model can be found and generally they continue to validate its use.

This leads us to consider force field analysis.

Force field analysis

Force field analysis is based on field theory which suggests that points of equilibrium will be maintained if the status quo remains and everything remains the same. To reach a new point of equilibrium requires us to start the ball rolling. In practical terms it may mean holding a meeting to discuss how the organization is doing in terms of meeting its strategic goals, politicians' demands, or simply comparing with other companies or local authorities in the published tables of indicators.

Once there is a force developed to consider a change – to keep to the needs of politicians, to do as good as the local authority in the neighbouring county or whatever – the laws of physics will come into force. The principle borrowed from physics was that where there was an action, there would be an opposite and equal reaction. Thus, to move to a new point of permanency so that the changes stayed and things did not return to the old ways, required the changes to be managed.

Force field analysis suggests that we need to be able to identify all of the forces that are operating in favour of and against the change. These hold the status quo. To move on requires increasing the levers and factors that 'promote' change and reducing the impact of the 'resistors' to change. So what are the 'helping' and 'hindering' factors? It may be difficult to act on all of them together so focusing and prioritizing on the key 'promoter' and 'resistors' to change should assist the process.

In the case of Gremby County Council, clarity about what the changes may look like (promoter) and developing better managerial structures (resistor) may be an initial start.

Figure 8.1 *Example of force field analysis for Gremby County Council*

These models are used as principles for change and form a backcloth for what follows.

Resistance to change

Given our models, it is a mistake to assume that everyone resists change. Managers that make this assumption may adopt change strategies that actually provoke resistance (e.g. power strategies). The range of individual responses to change can be depicted on two continuums, one referring to the employees' *attitudes* to change, the other indicating the range of *behavioural* responses to change. These are displayed in Table 8.2.

Normally, the attitudinal response to change matches up with the behavioural response. So, for example, an enthusiastic attitude is likely to lead to compliance. However, this congruence is not always present.

Table 8.2   Responses to change

Attitudinal response		
Enthusiasm	Neutrality	Hostility
←		→
The employee feels positive towards the change	The employee has no strong feelings about the change	The employee feels negative towards the change
Behavioural response		
Compliance		Resistance
←		→
The employee implements the change		The employee attempts to prevent the change taking place

An individual's attitude to the change may be hostile, but he nevertheless complies as he perceives that he has no alternative. Naturally, his lack of enthusiasm is liable to influence the effectiveness of his contribution. It is therefore important to establish the reasons for particular responses to change if we hope to understand why people react as they do.

Factors influencing responses to change

Individual factors influencing perceptions of, and responses to change, can be grouped into factors peculiar to the change itself, and personal factors.

Change factors

The nature of the change itself, and the strategy employed to implement it, affect individual responses. If people think they will lose out as a result of a change they are likely to resist. Changes which affect social relationships and status appear to cause more resistance than changes in the 'technical' aspects of the work (e.g. the work itself, conditions of service). Change which is imposed without consultation may be resisted just because staff have not been able to discuss it.

Changes which require new skills, or new ways of working may cause anxiety amongst some who feel they are unable to cope with change. The individual may not agree with the change proposed for other reasons. They may see it as a bad move for the organization, or they may believe that the change is unworkable. Also, changes suggested from superiors, or external consultants may be resisted as they imply that there is a problem with the existing situation. This may cause resentment in individuals who have invested time and effort in bringing about the existing state of affairs.

Personal factors

It is wrong to overgeneralize personal responses to change, but perceptions can be greatly influenced by the more stable characteristics of the individual like age and personality. Lack of self-confidence and a low tolerance of uncertainty will lead to cautious reactions to any type of change. On the other hand, positive experiences of past changes may produce an optimistic attitude to future changes. Intuitively, one might anticipate that older people in general would have a lower tolerance to change.

It is not just individuals that resist. The organization will also do so. They will do this partly through the actions, behaviours and affects of the individuals and groups but also through the systems, structures, procedures and organizational culture they create. These can take a number of forms:

- *Organizational inertia:* The organization does not recognize the need for change or if it does, there isn't the capacity to change. The organizational culture or its structure may hinder any changes by the organization being very introspective or the systems and structures being unresponsive or bureaucratic, i.e. incongruent with its organizational environment.
- *Power plays:* Eric Miller[2] suggests in his lecture on organization change that: 'change is not possible unless there has been shift or change in power relations'. The power blocks and coalitions will not want to lose their status, power or resource leverage. Such groups can sometimes be a department that is critical to the core activity, a small group of chief officers, or even the top team itself!
- *Defensive routines:* Chris Argyris'[3] work and his book with Donald Schon[4] implies that organizations have difficulty in learning how to manage change because they have a range of 'defensive routines' that stop them learning so they repeat the same mistakes or simply keep things the same. Examples of defensive routines include:
  - Ignoring the signs of changes and being very insular and closed.
  - Shooting the messenger of bad news.
  - 'By-passing' or not confronting difficult strategic issues – for example the budget fixing process.
  - Not sharing information, and innovative practices.
  - Not owning up to mistakes – a source of potential learning – but covering them up for someone else to do the same on another project, in another department, sometimes a year later!

■ Not taking any action – either because of criteria or paralysis by analysis
■ Not effectively monitoring the outcomes of strategies and action – excessive or insufficient feedback in reporting procedures is often the case but its impact is significant.

Are any of these resistors to change familiar to you?

So what can we do about them?

Strategies for making change

In managing change there have been a number of strategies used by companies that are based on the three models presented above. They aim to facilitate the transition of change. Each has its advantages and disadvantages. The strategies include: information and communication, education and training; counselling; projects and new initiatives; process involvement/participation; and the use of power and authority.

Information and communication

Here the assumption is that, by presenting people with the facts about the change, they will see the need for it, and therefore accept it. Advantages would be:

■ It is a straightforward and easily implemented change strategy.
■ If resistance is based upon inadequate or inaccurate information (e.g. from the grapevine) a clear presentation of the facts can prevent opposition to the changes.

There are some disadvantages, however:

■ Like the participation strategy, education and communication can be a time consuming and expensive process.
■ For it to be effective, the management must be trusted and believed.
■ There are dangers if the management presume there is only one 'rational' solution, or one true version of the 'facts'. If there is a clash of interests, a change which may be seen to be perfectly rational by the management, may be viewed otherwise by other employees.

Education and training

Much of the customer service initiatives to meet the customer with a smile were led by customer training to mainly front line staff. British Airways was among the first to successfully launch this model of change through its 'Putting the Customer First' Programme. Companies that emulated such training aimed only at one part of the organizational system: the task–individual interface. Fortunately, this was not the case for BA. However, using the approach on its own often led to most of the pressure to serve the customer focused on the front-line staff with other parts of the organization remaining unchanged. Jerry, the Human Resource member saw the change initiative in a limited way, very much in the realms of managerial skill enhancement.

The main advantages are:

■ It provides competencies and skills for people to manage new tasks.
■ It provides consistency across the organization.
■ It can reduce the fear and anxiety that arises out of change.

While some of the disadvantages include:

■ Organizations can use training as a substitute for change and a defence against change.
■ The training can be provided for the wrong group in the organization – either because of misdiagnosis or because it does not address the change directly.
■ There can be training without support from other parts of the organization or the managers so the benefits are limited.
■ The cost of training may be high.

Counselling

Counselling staff through the difficult times of change is generally valuable. Managers need to have skills in these areas or use referral services. Some organizations go through 'grieving processes' about the loss of the organization as they knew it but present the need as team development or some other management training event. These tend to be more socially acceptable and are more likely to be supported by senior staff and money. However, counselling can also be seen to be negative either as a sign of weakness or it may be for redundancy or exit counselling.

In terms of the model framework it aims to address the individual–task and individual–organization links but it will also pick up informal elements of the individual, which may be outside the workplace, but impact upon performance and task. This was an area that was around in the organization but it was not spoken of explicitly. People would act out their anxieties, fears and anger through other dysfunctional ways and then blame someone else.

The advantages of this approach are:

■ It aims to treat people with respect and recognize the personal impact change may have upon them.
■ For some staff it's just the right type and support they need to allay anxieties, manage in their role and flourish from the change process.

Some of the disadvantages include:

- Over indulgence in personal issues.
- Managers being inappropriately used in a counselling role either because of insuffient skill, experience or sensitivity; issues of confidentiality and trust; the subject matter inappropriate; roles and boundaries not being respected.
- It can be costly – especially if offered on an open basis.

Projects and initiatives

The quality movement led by Denning and Duran saw a wave of project initiatives as vehicles of change within many corporations and institutions. Total Quality Management, BS 5750, ISO 9000 and other initiatives were taken up during the late 1980s to improve customer retention and satisfaction. They also aimed to reduce defects, wastage and costs in the manufacturing process or early stages of the service chain. Some organizations did follow through TQM in spirit and letter thus addressing many of the difficulties and problems of cultural change, strategy, leadership and structural changes that were needed to gain success. Other companies followed the rule books and manuals and focused their attention on the formal organizational structure and ignored the informal, task or individual needs of the staff and company.

In the case of the local authority, some group members in later meetings began to see project based initiatives as a way forward. But at the beginning it was the furthest thing from their minds. Too many were still in a state of 'denial'. The top team and leadership group had failed to give the vision and strategic imperatives that the group needed to realistically tackle the task and the group thus floundered in the early stages of its work.

Advantages:

- The ability to gain results from the project that help the process.
- It makes change manageable: bit sized, clear targets and expected outcomes.
- It increases skills, experience and competence as the system goes up the learning curve.
- It provides people with authority and involvement in the process.

Disadvantages may include:

- Fear of failure and the self-fulfilling prophecy.
- Projects being scoped too widely or without clear guidelines.
- Projects being used for political or other agenda.
- People in the group not getting on (remember Rob's experience at Pearson, Merriman in Chapter 6).

Process involvement

Process involvement has come mainly from Japanese management practices. These include manufacturing and logistic processes such as Just-in-Time, the introduction of process improvements in retooling machinery in minutes rather than days and the development of team work through 'Kaizan'. Nissan (UK) in Sunderland, North East England, provides an excellent example of these principles being developed at a 'greenfield' site. Business Process Re-engineering has taken hold in North America and in Europe where whole organizational processes can be radically changed or a key process such as customer orders or complaints can be changed to reduce staff and paperwork but keep or even improve performance by taking a fresh look at old problems. Such an approach has many of the features of a 'flexible organization' (Chapter 6). The financial services sector, some of the international airlines and car manufacturing plants have provided examples of such changes. The smaller firms have offered more customer-based, flexible services such as the mobile doctor surgery, or the virtual office where the client is served on their own site. The larger BPR initiatives, or a radical change for the smaller practice or firm requires an examination of the six components of the model framework all at the same time to ensure holistic change.

The case study of the local authority showed that it was difficult for them to accept and consider the need for change. To undertake holistic change was perceived as too great a risk and thus incremental changes were more likely to take place in the first instance.

Participation

This strategy actively and genuinely involves those who will be affected by the change in the design and implementation of it. The main advantages of such a strategy are:

- It is likely to improve the quality of the decisions being taken, as more expertise and information can be brought into the decision making process.
- Involvement usually increases commitment to the change. This is especially important where the change will be difficult and where some resistance is anticipated.

But there are some disadvantages with a participation strategy:

- The process can be very time consuming.
- The success of the strategy depends to a great extent on the organizational context. An atmosphere of mistrust and suspicion may result in the exercise being seen as a cynical attempt at manipulation.
- Participation must be seen to be worthwhile, it cannot be 'forced' on to people.

- It can be very threatening to managers, who may perceive the process as restricting their freedom of action, or as one which undermines their authority.

Power and authority

It has to be accepted that in hard times, redundancies and massive change that some companies take have staff screaming and shouting through the process of change. A study of Australian service organizations suggested that performance was the greatest where the company had experienced a 'turnaround' strategy with the CEO pushing them through radical changes.[6]

The politics of change means that implicit and overt coercion will be used in some instances. However, some words of caution. A forceful action generates an opposite and equal reaction; and this holds for human systems as well.

Pushing through changes needs to be nurtured after the fallout otherwise resentments and feelings can lead to informal coalitions that undermine the changes. It can miss out individual and informal elements of the fit in the model framework (Chapter 2) and become a greater problem of resistance later on.

John, the Chief Executive did not have the taste, personality or authority to use coercion as a management style. Instead he used reason and rational argument, which much to his surprise did not yield the outcomes expected. The emotional, political and various interests defied rational argument and common ground. Thus, his managerial style probably needed a greater range of responses for the range of different situations that the task of change required.

How could John have engaged with his authority? The use of power, manipulation and negotiation are briefly discussed as the last part of this section.

Power

A manager could decide to simply impose change. The power to do so can derive from his formal authority (which can be bolstered by powers to reward or punish staff) or his 'personal authority' (whereby he relies more on loyalty, friendship or charisma). Advantages of power strategies include the following:

- They can be useful where a change needs to be implemented quickly.
- If few resources are available for programmes of education the exercise of power may be a feasible alternative strategy.
- If the proposed changes do not require much commitment and if little resistance is anticipated from those affected then power strategies may be successful.

However, where commitment is required, and where resistance may be provoked by a power approach, then such strategies may well cause problems for the management. In particular, if resistance is crushed, then, in the long term, serious difficulties can emerge.

Manipulation

Manipulation strategies involve the changing of a person's situation, or his *perception* of the situation in such a way that he complies with the manipulator's wishes.[2a] Manipulation can be *positive*, where the person feels better off as a result of the manipulation, or *negative* where he feels worse off.

The offer of inducements to the person would be an attempt at positive manipulation; threats of punishment if the individual does not comply would, on the other hand, be negative manipulation. Persuasion can be used, not to materially change the situation, but to change the individual's perception of the situation. Through persuasion the individual can be made to feel good about the change or alternatively he could merely feel obliged to go along with the management's wishes.

Manipulation strategies can have advantages in that they are cheap and easy strategies to implement. However, if negative manipulation is used, resentment may be increased which could cause problems for the manager later.

Negotiation

Negotiation is the process whereby people whose interests conflict come to some agreement. Usually, neither party gets everything they want. In order for a deal to be struck there must be a 'contract zone' where the two parties can potentially reach some agreement. If the minimum acceptable position of one group is above the maximum that the other group will concede, there is little likelihood of a negotiated deal.

Negotiation is an important strategy where it is clear that there will be losers as a result of a change, and where those losers are likely to resist. But overuse of the strategy can lead to expectations that *every* change needs to be negotiated.

So, there is a wide range of strategies potentially available to the management. However, in considering each of these strategies it should be clear that in a given situation some strategies will be more effective than others. The organizational context in which change takes place should influence the choice of strategy, as should the particular aspects of the change itself. The following 'task factors' need to be considered:

(a) *The location of expertise:* If the expertise and information required to plan and implement the change is spread amongst a group of people, a participative change strategy is indicated. If the manager does not need others in designing the change he can choose to use non-participative strategies.

(b) *Speed of introduction:* If the change needs to be implemented quickly, power or manipulative strategies may be appropriate as participation, negotiation and education strategies can be very time consuming.

(c) *Amount of commitment required:* In some cases, all that is required from the employees is compliance with the change the management wish to implement. Where genuine commitment is required for the change to be a success, participative strategies are likely to be more effective.

Figure 8.2 brings together the factors involved in the selection of change strategies.

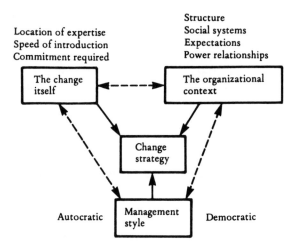

Figure 8.2 *The selection of a change strategy*

However in practice, like John, some managers may be unaware of alternative ways of managing change. Furthermore, even when a manager is aware of alternatives, in any given situation the different factors might point to different strategies. For example, the manager may be more comfortable with an autocratic style, but the particular change requires the involvement of subordinates if it is to be properly designed and implemented.

The model in Figure 6.6 poses more questions than it gives answers, but in trying to come to terms with the complexity of change indicated by the diagram, the manager would, hopefully, avoid making simplistic assumptions about managing change.

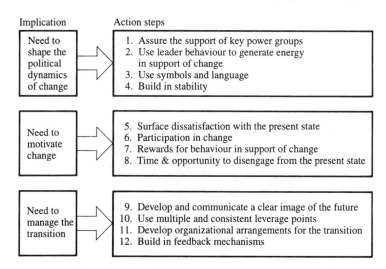

Implication   Action steps

Need to shape the political dynamics of change
1. Assure the support of key power groups
2. Use leader behaviour to generate energy in support of change
3. Use symbols and language
4. Build in stability

Need to motivate change
5. Surface dissatisfaction with the present state
6. Participation in change
7. Rewards for behaviour in support of change
8. Time & opportunity to disengage from the present state

Need to manage the transition
9. Develop and communicate a clear image of the future
10. Use multiple and consistent leverage points
11. Develop organizational arrangements for the transition
12. Build in feedback mechanisms

Figure 8.3 *Implications for change management and related action steps.*
(Reproduced with permission from Nadler, D. A. (1993) Concepts for the management of organisational change. In M. L. Tushman, W. L. Moore (eds) *Readings in the Management of Innovation*. Copyright © 1982 by Michael L. Tucker and William L. Moore. HarperCollins Publishers Inc., New York)

Implications for managers

There are several implications of such a case scenario for managers. Not only do managers have to possess new competencies but they also need to take into account the emotional roller coaster of change and transition.

The task of implementing change means that managers also need:

■ to manage power relationships and shape the political dynamics of change;
■ to address the issues of resistance to change by motivating individuals and 'enrolling' staff, or getting them on-board;
■ to ensure that the change is not too disruptive to the organizational life and create some boundaries and security by actually managing the transition.

However, for organizations to be able to fully regenerate, managers need to be able to use other lenses and paradigms to make sense of their experience and new roles during periods of major change.

Further reading

An excellent overall book of readings has been edited by Christoper Mabey and Bill Mayon-White, *Managing Change*, Paul Chapman Publishing and The Open University, 1993. The Addison-Wesley series in Organizational Development is particulary useful of which the following three books are taken. Richard Beckard and Reuben T. Harris, *Organizational Transitions: Managing Complex Change*, 1987; Warner Burke, *Organizational Development: A Normative View*, 1987; and Edgar Schein, *Process Consultation: Lessons for Managers and Consultants*, Vol. 2, 1987, all published by Addison-Wesley.

References

1 Lewin, K., 'Frontiers of Group Dynamics: Concept, Method and Reality in Social Equilibrium and Social Change', *Human Relations*, Vol. 1, No. 1, 1947
2 Miller, E., *Lecture on Managing Change*, Advanced Organisational Consultation Programme, Tavistock Institute, London, 1995
3 Argyris, C., *Strategic Change and Defensive Routines*, Pitman, London, 1985
4 Argyris, C., and Schon, D. A., *Organisational Learning: A Theory of Action Perspective*, Addison-Wesley, Reading, MA, 1978
5 Dunphy, D. and Stace, D., 'The Strategic Management of Corporate Change', *Human Relations*, No. 8, 1993, pp. 905–20
6 See MacMillan, I. C., *Strategy Formulation: Political Concepts*, West Publishing Company, 1978, pp. 10–15.

9 Managing for the future

This final chapter looks at the key characteristics that a manager will need to have to manage in complex and dynamic environments. It explores four additional competencies and approaches for managers and four dimensions for organizations that build on the systems model throughout the previous chapters of this book.

Managing for the future needs managers:

■ to be able to assess and manage risk,
■ to work at the emotional level,
■ to work within new organizational structures,
■ to have new frameworks and models to cope with a rapidly changing environment,
■ to manage oneself and one's career.

Managing risk

Task, uncertainty and managing in a complex and dynamic environment generate risk and anxiety. Some of the risk is real and some of it is fuelled by fear and the subjective risk of failure, rejection and isolation.

For task and environmental risk managers will need more sophisticated and relevant techniques of identifying, assessing, making decisions and implementing those decisions without being paralysed by the negative consequences. Or even being able to stand up for themselves and say this is an inappropriate level of risk and we should stop the project now. The Challenger Disaster was certainly a case where 'group think', 'irrationality' and peer pressure led to the known risks to be underestimated and ignored with grave consequences.

A full discussion on risk assessment is another book in itself. The fields of investment appraisal, project management and other disciplines will have much to say about risk. However, from a systemic and organizational view, it is useful to draw upon the work of Cyert and March.[1] Their work falls within the systems framework and is often described as the 'decision-making approach'. . . . They argue that under circumstances of uncertainty and risk it is impossible for individuals and organizational systems to be perfectly rational because those involved have limited information processing capabilities.

They suggest that people:

■ usually act on the basis of incomplete information about possible courses of action and their consequences;

- are only able to consider a limited range of alternatives as they relate to the decisions under review;
- search for information to support them in their decision-making, which is limited by the nature of the problem, how it is defined, and the cost of searching;
- are unable to attach accurate values to the possible outcomes.

Thus, decisions are not totally rational and are said to be made under the conditions of 'bounded rationality': commonly expressed as 'rule of thumb' or 'established practice'. These routines make the anxiety and information processing of making decisions manageable. They also form institutionalized and defensive routines that inhibit organizational learning and change. These defences may take the form of reducing the complexity of information inputs or managing it better through new technology. Thus, the so-called rational element of risk assessment is already less than perfect. This is then complicated by the subjective and emotional side of risk, transition and change.

The emotional element of change

Even when change is intentional, planned and desired it still brings with it stress and a range of unfamiliar feelings. The joyous acts of marriage, moving house, having a baby and taking up a new job are all among the top six major activities that induce high levels of stress.

On the other hand, the need for change has not always been recognized and people inevitably experience a series of emotions as they manage the unintended transition. In managing change there is a period of transition which brings uncertainty, loss, risk and anxiety, which make the *transition* difficult and complex. However, there are some generally agreed stages that people and organizations experience. These move from denial and shock, to grief, acceptance and finally new beginnings.

The *transition curve* (Figure 9.1) comes from the field of bereavement counselling and addresses the themes of loss and change.[2-4] There are four main classic phases:

- 'psychic crisis', compromising shock – including confusion, denial and irrationality;
- 'emotional reaction' – expressing anger, rage, sorrow, grief, feelings of failure, depression;
- 'adaptation' – letting go, acceptance, gaining a realistic appraisal of the situation;
- 're-orientation' – beginning to organize, seek help and develop and plan for the future.

Each stage can be actively supported and managed to smooth the multiple transitions that will occur for individuals and the organization as they go through change.[5,6]

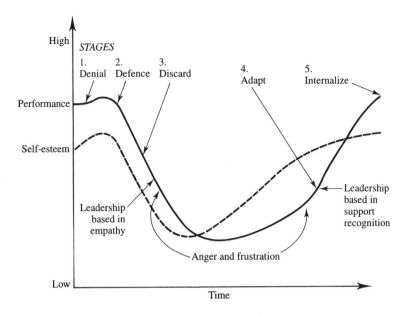

Figure 9.1 *The transition curve.* (Reprinted from *Long Range Planning*, 19 (6), Carnell C. A., Managing strategic change: an integrated approach, pp. 105–15 (1986), with kind permission from Elsevier Science Ltd, The Boulevard, Langford Lane, Kidlington OX5 1GB, UK.)

The first stage of shock can be supported through information, incontestable data, education, honesty and a vision of what things will look like at the end. Typical statements might include: 'Yes, its true . . . , I'd like to put a stop to these rumours and tell you the latest news. There will be changes in roles but I can tell you where you stand: or I am not in a position to tell you where you stand right now!'.

Stage two needs support and a listening ear. The role of the manager may be to validate how people may be feeling and to be the steady rock of certainty and security. Thus, managers need to keep cool, manage their own anxiety and that of others and the team.

It is here that the manager may also need to work with the problems and difficulties that arise from the depression and anxiety that can be associated with change. The discussion on the role and limits of counselling that were covered in Chapter 8 certainly apply here. It may be difficult as a line manager to strike the right balance between listening and trying to motivate staff into action.

Typical statements might include: 'I understand from what you've said that you feel let down by the company and the team . . . . You're quite angry with the way the process is being handled . . .'. 'I really feel that you do have the skills in . . .' or even 'we need to move from here and consider the next step . . .'.

Stage three should involve people letting go of the past and considering changes. Here training and support is valuable in that it provides people with confidence, new skills and competencies to meet the external task and environmental demands of the change. Not everybody will feel comfortable. Those that welcome the changes, it will be hard to hold back; while others will have a range of coping strategies and skills.

Stage four should mean the establishment of new norms, practices, routines and systems. These should reflect the new culture and regime. Structures and custodians of change need to be established through organizational structures, 'buy-in' or exportation of the informal leaders, clear rewards systems and symbols that reinforce the corporate goals and reorientation. Matching of organizational and individual goals can take place through recruitment practices, training and education, role modelling and organizational rituals and changes in culture.

These steps do not guarantee change. Also many change curves exist for the organization and for individuals with different people's range depending on the changes. An office move for some may be more significant than the strategic goal or the structure. Changes typically take from four to as long as ten years and hopefully individuals, groups and organizations are learning along the way. Changes can be managed through projects to establish and manage processes of continuous development.

Being aware of these stages will reduce some unnecessary and harmful dynamics within the organization irrespective of the context.

Managing within new organizational forms

As organizations attempt to respond to their environments we will see new organizational forms. A phenomenon of the 1990s was delayering and downsizing. While such a strategy met the cost imperative, it has reaped disadvantages as well. Some companies are finding it difficult to 'recover' and are suffering from downsizing anorexia. Concomitant with that has been the potential loss of staff loyalty as a major company asset.[7] Such trends will have to change to maintain the organizational sustainability and flexibility that will be required in the future.

The other effect is that organizations are taking on new forms: partnerships (e.g. IBM, Motorola and Apple), network organizations (inter-organizational projects in the pharmaceutical industry) and virtual organizations such as associates of independent consultants. The application and use of new technology and telecommunication networks will be another key driver to this change. The use of the Internet will be the norm rather than the exception. Managing interfaces will be the key issue in such systems.

Thus, players in these new forms have to manage complex and temporary, possibly unstable, organizational systems. Thus, they will need to be able:

■ to define boundaries – be clear about the task, who is involved, in or out, timescales and deliverables;

- to define, negotiate and agree roles, i.e. authority relations will need to be clear, e.g. project manager, liaison officer, provider – and informal power basis negotiated;
- to specify, negotiate and monitor contractual relationship and take action when things are going off plan;
- to manage without line authority and be aware of multiple stakeholder interests;
- to manage the issue of organizational and group identity;
- to manage and contain their own anxieties and those of the 'group' and its stakeholders.

These share many of the issues and dilemmas of managing a flexible organization.

A brighter future: new dawnings

Radical times require radical changes: a paradigm shift. Some argue that what you see is what you look for; and what you look for and your interpretation of what you see is a product of your theory about the world. The same argument holds for organizations. The organizational model you hold will influence how you see it and what you do in a managerial role. It might mean a time for change if the business you are in is to survive.

Managers in organizations of the future will need to be more holistic. They will need to take in the whole picture of the person or the organization and not to see things in isolation or from a partial perspective. They will need to consider the multiple level and elements of the organization and see how they fit together.

Such a perspective needs one to take a transformational approach and see things outside their existing paradigms or mindsets. Systems will need to be learning organizations that question their assumptions and mindsets and gain new and deeper insights from their collective experience.[8-10]

Gouillart and Kelly[11] suggest that the rational, emotional, spiritual and ecological aspects of business should form the transformation of tomorrow's organization. They suggest that organizations need to take up the four Rs of renewing, reframing, revitalizing and restructuring (see Figure 9.2).

A business transformation is defined as: 'the orchestrated redesign of the genetic architecture of the corporation, achieved by working simultaneously – although at different speeds – along the four dimensions of Reframing, Restructuring, Revitalization and Renewal'.

Reframing is a shift in the organization's mindset about its capability and mental models. Reframing means a paradigm shift and an openness to the corporation or business being a learning organization of the highest level. Thus, reframing also addresses strategy, culture and leadership, all key factors in the equation.

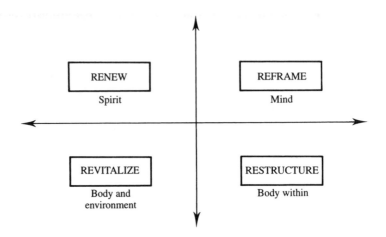

Figure 9.2 *The four Rs of transformation.* (Reproduced with permission from Gouillart, F. J. and Kelly, J. N. (1995) *Transforming an Organisation*. McGraw-Hill, New York.)

Restructuring deals with the body of the organization and aims to gear the company for better performance. Here is where the scope is to reduce the organizational slack, reduce costs and achieve some early performance gains. However, it is also the area that often means trauma from 'downsizing' or redundancies. If the wounds of radical change are not dealt with or healed through revitalization then the gains will remain short term. Thus, the individual in relationship to the organizational structure and task must be addressed in restructuring.

Revitalization is linking the corporate body with the environment. It is the difference between simply layoffs and transformational change. The pains of loss are replaced and by innovation, the creation of new business opportunities and the re-engineering of the organization through new technology.[12] Research[13] on the role of 'reengineering' within the context of organizational change suggests that the factors that facilitated change included: clear corporate goal, cross-functional teams and training. Issues included the need to be flexible, manage the process and be able to change the informal aspects or culture of the organization. Thus, the task environment, strategy and new organizational arrangements also form the basis of this part of change.

Renewal addresses the people side of change explicitly. It means developing staff for new competencies, self confidence and a willingness to engage in risk and uncertainty. Gouillart and Kelly argue that the human side is probably the greatest and most powerful source of transformation.

These four dimensions share many of the themes of the model framework of Chapter 2. However, they go further in that they are 'generative' and aspire to work outside of established routines, assumptions and mindsets. They also include the spiritual and human side much more in the analysis and predict that these will be central to successful organizations moving in a context of rapid and technological change in the future. The opportunity to be a truly learning organization, that is able to transcend its present framework and *modus operandi* as well as systemically take in, share and learn lessons from its environment, is a high goal. Thus, while many organizations large and small will aspire to the goals it will not be appropriate or relevant for all organizations.

Managing one's career

The flexible individual – the 'core skills' concept

The days when a school leaver could join a firm, train for a job and could expect to stick to that job for life are gone. Now, even when individuals work as accountants, electricians or teachers for their whole careers, they cannot expect to spend all their time in the same organization. Increasingly, however, the concept of a career is taking on a new meaning. The pace of change is such that no one can rely on one set of job skills providing him or her with employment for all of their working life. Mid-career job shifts are becoming quite common; adult training and retraining are on the increase.

R. Bolles has specialized in the problems of career management, and he introduces the concept of 'core skills' to help the individual identify what career moves and opportunities are likely to be successful.[13] People possess three groups of skills:

- *Specialist knowledge:* e.g. about nursing, engineering, computer applications.
- *Self-management skills:* like perseverance, diligence, personal organization.
- *Functional skills:* these are skills that are transferable to other fields of work when they are married to specialist knowledge.

It is this last group, the functional skills, that are of most interest in the career management process. Bolles breaks the functional skills down into three categories, skills with things, with information and with people.

- *Skills with things:* e.g. being able to manipulate a keyboard, drive a car.
- *Skills with information:* handling information in a logical way; observation; analysis; evaluation; planning; comparing.
- *Skills with people:* serving, helping, training, counselling, monitoring.

He has derived a skills checklist that can be administered by the individual to provide an audit of his capabilities. The checklist requires the individual to recall problems that they overcame in the past, and the skills that they drew on in overcoming those problems.

On the basis of a thorough insight into their capabilities, people using this approach will be better able to identify jobs which draw on their particular skills profile. Similarly, employers can use the technique in making selection and promotion decisions.

■ Balanced learning habits and skills. Managers who took responsibility for their own learning, were able to engage in abstract thinking and apply it and use a range of learning processes were more successful in reaching senior posts in their area of work, were usually 'fast trackers' or whose work was recognized as above average in terms of effectiveness.

■ Self-knowledge – successful managers had a realistic assessment of their strengths and weaknesses and a host of other personal factors.

These 'personal' qualities, especially the last two of balanced learning habits and self-knowledge are likely to be critically vital for managers creating and managing their careers in an uncertain and changing working environment.

In addition to core skills, two further ranges of skills are required. Drawing on Pedler *et al.*[14] these are: 'skills and attributes' for success and 'personal qualities' too.

Summarizing their case based on research of successful managers they suggest that such people have three broad ranges of qualities.

(i)   The core skills, as explained by Bolles.
(ii)   'Social' skills and attributes which include:
       ■ Political sensitivity and awareness of events both inside and particularly outside your organization.
       ■ Analytical and problem solving skills and good judgement in making decisions.
       ■ Social and interpersonal skills were seen as important.
(iii) Personal qualities. These included:
       ■ Emotional reliance, the degree to which the individual is able to manage uncertainty, anxiety, emotional stress, interpersonal conflict and ambiguity.
       ■ Being proactive and respond purposefully and strategically to the events of change, rather than merely responding to the demands of the immediate crisis or avoiding the changes through defensive routines.
       ■ Creativity – being creative is essential so that new ways of thinking and insight can be gleaned as well as recognizing a good idea when it hits you in the face.
       ■ Mental agility – the ability to grasp concepts, see the whole picture, group problems quickly and to work through multiple tasks (without overloading) is key. 'Thinking on your feet' is

a useful expression to capture the essence of this personal quality.

Conclusion

From small business, to large and complex, to networks of complexity, we have turned full circle. Back to the future and returned. What do we conclude?

We have covered a lot of material in our journey from Stan Gordon's driving school to the giant multinational corporation TRT and the difficulties of managing change. The tiny informal organization that Top Gear Driving School represents, differs in so many respects from the multinational organization or the network organization of the future. The multinational is clearly much bigger, more complex, and more sophisticated than the driving school. And the organization of the future is both small, large and complex.

But, there are nevertheless fundamental similarities which run across all the organizations we have explored. They all have clear authority and role relations either in the form of hierarchies or through negotiated roles. They all have specialization which requires some degree of coordination across the organization. They all employ people, and sack people.

So, although our device of dealing with management theory within particular organizational contexts has been useful, we should be wary of overplaying this approach. Moreover, these types of organization do not represent all the variations that can be seen around us. Some structures will not fit easily into any of these five categories. Others will have some departments that look like a bureaucracy, and others that feel much more like an adhocracy.

Similarly, we should avoid making rigid connections between the size of the organization and the processes of coordination, communication and control that are employed. Top Gear Driving School was a fairly informal organization with a very limited amount of bureaucracy. But we can envisage a similarly sized organization that has been established for over 200 years (e.g. a bespoke tailors) having much more rigid and formal processes. And although a management position in the middle of a large bureaucracy is likely to constrain the individual manager's freedom of action; it would be a mistake to assume that *all* managers are content to work within such restrictions. An individual with a more entrepreneurial, maverick style may well prove to be an effective catalyst for much needed change in a stuffy bureaucracy. During the 1980s such characters were a welcomed source of innovation and were called internal entrepreneurs or 'intrapreneurs'.

Through description to prescription

If there are so many variations within and between organizations are we able to make any sensible suggestions for improving the way organizations are managed? One point that should be crystal clear from this book is that there are no prescriptions about managing or organizing that can be universally applied. A management style that may be very effective in one situation could be a disaster in another. Detailed job descriptions may be extremely useful in a stable bureaucracy; they would be rapidly redundant in a flexible adhocracy or network system. Corporate planning may be very helpful in guiding the strategy of one company; it may impose unnecessary rigidity if employed in another firm. And at the individual level, additional responsibility might be just the thing to motivate one person; it may well overwhelm someone else who can barely cope with the job's existing demands.

A little knowledge can be dangerous in the area of management and organization. Unless managers are sensitive to the complexities and realities of the particular circumstances facing them, they may well introduce inappropriate 'solutions' into the organization. And, as very few managers have had the benefit of any formal study of organizations, the chances of making wrong decisions in this area would appear to be quite high.

If there are no universally applicable 'right answers' does this mean that there are no 'answers' at all? The response to this question must be no, but in searching for solutions that fit the situation the manager is faced with a much more difficult task than if he simply operated a limited number of 'rules of thumb' gleaned from experience, or if he picked universal panaceas 'off the shelf' and forced them into the organization. So the *contingency approach* requires considerably more analysis, and draws on more theoretical perspectives than either relying solely upon experience, or using the classical principles of organization and management. But, hopefully, more sophisticated insights into the realities of organizations should lead to more appropriate, and sustainable prescriptions for improved performance.

In short there is no 'blue-print' or single way of doing things. There is no substitute for careful thought and a contingency approach probably facilitates you asking some of the right questions.

Further reading

For different perpectives on the future of organizations, the nature of change and management, the following respectively are recommended: Charles Handy, *The Age of Unreason*, Business Books, 1991; Eric Miller, who takes a systems and psychological view of the development of organizations in his book *From Dependency to Autonomy: Studies in Organisation and Change*, Free Association Books, 1993; a book to help managers develop their systems thinking is Nano McCaughan and Barry Palmer's, *Systems Thinking for Harassed Managers*, Karnac Books, 1994 and a multiple of perspectives is in Gareth Morgan's book *Images of Organisation*, 1986.

References

1 Cyert, R. M. and March, J. G., *A Behavioural Theory of the Firm*, Prentice Hall, Englewood Cliffs, NJ, 1963
2 See Bowlby, J., *Attachment and Loss*, Hogart Press, 1969
3 See Marris, P., *Loss and Change*, 1974
4 Kubler-Ross, E., *On Death and Dying*, 1970
5 Carnell, C. A., *Managing Change in Organisations*, Prentice Hall, Englewood Cliffs, NJ, 1990
6 Scott, C. D. and Jaffe, C. T., *Managing Organisational Change*, Kogan Page, 1989
7 *Economist*, January, 1996
8 A classic text on the theory and implications of the organization learning, see Arygris, C. and Schon, D. A., *Organisational learning: A Theory of Action Perspective*, Addison-Wesley, Reading, MA, 1978
9 A popular examination of the learning organization is presented in Senge, P., *The Fifth Discipline: the Art and Practice of the Learning Organisation*, Doubleday, 1990
10 A review of material and practical examples can be found in Garvin, D. A., 'Building a Learning Organisation', *Harvard Business Review*, July–August, 1993, pp. 78–91
11 Gouillart, F. J. and Kelly, J. N., *Transforming the Organisation*, McGraw-Hill, New York, 1995
12 See Hammer, M. and Champy, J., *Re-engineering the Corporation: A Manifesto for Business Revolution*, Harper Business, 1993
13 For a comparative study on the success factors and challenges of reeginering using case study material of large corporations see Ascari, A., Rock, M. and Dutta, S., 'Reengineering and Organisational Change: Lessons from a comparative analysis of company experience', *European Management Journal*, Vol. 13, No. 1, 1995, pp. 1–30
13 Bolles, R. N. *What Colour is your Parachute*, Ten Spreed Press, 1986
14 Pedler, M., Burgoyne, J. and Boydell, T., *A Manager's Guide to Self-Development*, McGraw-Hill, New York, 1986. The book also has a self development questionnaire for readers and activities to work on each of the qualities briefly described above

Index